# The Public Ivies

ALSO BY HOWARD GREENE AND MATTHEW GREENE

*Greenes' Guides to Educational Planning: The Hidden Ivies*

*Greenes' Guides to Educational Planning: Inside the Top Colleges*

*Greenes' Guides to Educational Planning: Making It into a Top College*

*Greenes' Guides to Educational Planning: Presenting Yourself Successfully to Colleges*

*Greenes' Guides to Educational Planning: Making It into a Top Graduate School*

# THE
# PUBLIC IVIES

## AMERICA'S FLAGSHIP
## PUBLIC UNIVERSITIES

Howard R. Greene, M.A., M.Ed.,
and Matthew W. Greene, Ph.D.

Cliff Street Books
*An Imprint of HarperCollinsPublishers*

HarperCollins books may be purchased for educational, business, or sales promotional use. For information please write: Special Markets Department, HarperCollins Publishers, Inc., 10 East 53rd Street, New York, NY 10022.

FIRST EDITION

*Designed by Stratford Publishing Services*

Library of Congress Cataloging-in-Publication Data

Greene, Howard, 1937–
    The public ivies: America's flagship public universities / Howard R. Greene and Matthew Greene.—1st ed.
      p. cm.
    ISBN 0-06-093459-X
    1. College choice—United States. 2. Public universities and colleges—United States—Admission. 3. College students orientation—United States. I. Title: At head of title on cover: Greenes' guide to educational planning. II. Greene, Matthew W., 1968– III. Title.

LB2350.5 .G75 2001
378'.05'0973—dc21                         2001028712

01  02  03  04  05  RRD  10  9  8  7  6  5  4  3  2  1

# [Contents

## Part Four: Advice If You Are Going Public                          175

# Introduction

"Well, first of all, I'm not staying at home! Tell THEM," she asserts, gesturing toward her hapless parents, "that they can FORGET about the state university. There's NO WAY I'm going to the state university!" We see many students voicing this preference as they begin the college admissions process.

"I don't know why they want me to look out of state," he protests, with evident exasperation toward his concerned parents. "I'm staying close to home and going to the state university, with all my friends!" We see many students who look forward to the end of high school and the transition to their state's public university, with its football team, recognizable fight song, and mascot.

"I'm not sure," another student wonders. "I'd like to expand the list of colleges I'm applying to, but I want something different, not those same old small colleges where the kids are just like the ones in my high school. What about some public universities out of state?" The college search process for other students includes this possibility.

Public universities have long been a dominant option in the world of higher education. They remain so today, attracting students from in state and out of state and challenging even the most prestigious and selective of the private colleges and universities in their efforts to attract the strongest applicants. Eighty percent of students in college today attend public two- and four-year colleges and universities. Two-thirds of all students enrolled in four-year institutions are in public colleges and universities. With their large endowments, support from the state legislatures, and impressive facilities, the public universities are able to provide an excellent education at a lower price for state residents and out-of-state applicants. Although tuitions have risen dramatically at public universities, they remain significantly lower than those at private colleges and universities. In addition to lower costs for students and parents, America's best public universities offer major research facilities, many curricular options, top faculty, and exciting environments.

Do these benefits come at a cost? Of course. Larger class sizes, a less accessible institutional system, inexperienced or unqualified graduate teaching assistants, off-campus living, and a fragmented campus setting can be seen as liabilities on the large university campuses. As we discussed in *The Hidden Ivies*, the small classes, contact with full-time faculty, access to the campus administration, and sense of community that accompany a smaller residential college environment can offer substantial benefits to a student's learning experience. Yet for many students, the sacrifice of such "college" elements at a public university is worth the trade-off. These students are willing to tolerate some of the negatives of the big system to reap its rewards. Many of the best public universities attract top students by balancing the negative attributes often associated with a campus of 20,000 or more students with selective honors programs and merit-based scholarships.

We have written *The Public Ivies* to present students, parents, and counselors a rationale for "going public." We explore the benefits of attending a top public university and the positive attributes of the nation's flagship public institutions. We profile the most outstanding public universities and who should attend them. We outline what you will need to do to succeed at these schools. *The Public Ivies* will give you a grounding in the basics of choosing public higher education. You will learn the key criteria by which these schools are evaluated and will benefit from our counseling experience with students who have been happy and unhappy at public institutions. You will take what you learn in this book to visit and evaluate particular colleges and universities to determine whether going public is the right choice for you.

What do we mean by "public ivies"? More than 15 years ago, Richard Moll used the term in his book *The Public Ivys* to refer to public colleges and universities that offered an education comparable to the eight private Ivy League schools. We use "public ivies" here to connect with our book *The Hidden Ivies*, in which we discussed private colleges and universities that offer students an Ivy-quality education and experience and the criteria that make an Ivy an Ivy. These criteria serve as a basis for the evaluation of any school, and in this book we judge 30 of the flagship public institutions, the top research universities and leading academic centers in a state, on these criteria, focusing particularly on these institutions' liberal arts or arts and sciences schools. We do not rank these schools and, in fact, want to stress right now that students should consider public institutions other than those discussed in this book to see how they measure up for different needs.

Top private college admissions officers and administrators already point out that public colleges and universities now provide some of the stiffest competition for attracting and educating the best students in the country. It is time that more students and parents became aware of what so many others know: for the right student, public universities offer an exciting, affordable, and flexible educational experience.

## GOALS OF THIS BOOK

We hope that *The Public Ivies* will make readers more aware of the options available at flagship public colleges and universities. We write primarily for students but at times address parents directly. Surveys continue to show that parental advice is one of the biggest factors influencing a student's choice of college. Families reading this book together can discuss the key points and answer some of the questions posed in it to decide whether or not public schools should be part of their college search. We believe the student, and not the parents, should decide which school he or she will attend, but it should be an informed and reasoned decision. *The Public Ivies* provides information and tools to help students make such a decision.

By discussing important criteria for evaluating colleges and universities, we hope to enable students to recognize the differences among institutions, and by focusing on 30 top public universities, we inform students about the best choices available. We hope to help students determine whether they are up to and excited by the challenges posed by these very large schools. They'll be able to say, "Yes, I see myself in that kind of school," or "Wow, I didn't realize what I'd have to do to make it there. That's not for me." Parents will be able to help their student imagine the reality of life at a public ivy. Though a student can survive anywhere, our goal is for readers to find the most preferable and appropriate school for them, the place in which they can thrive.

Many graduates of large public colleges and universities complain about having had to take, say, Psychology 101 with 500 students, 3 multiple-choice tests, 2 lectures a week, and a poorly trained teaching assistant leading a 40-person "discussion section." They may even reflect fondly on the trials and tribulations of confronting the administration during registration time or trying to obtain on-campus housing. Although things have not improved in these areas, the research and study opportunities at a public university can be impressive and astounding enough to outweigh a student's or parent's concerns. If you are headed to a public university, *The Public Ivies* will prepare you to meet the challenges from day one, and not only survive but succeed.

## GOALS OF THE FLAGSHIP PUBLIC UNIVERSITIES

Students and parents must understand from the start that the public ivies, unlike smaller, private liberal arts colleges, have missions that go beyond educating the undergraduate. Teaching is important at the publics, but they place equal or greater emphasis on the research function and on the education of graduate students. The universities we discuss are almost entirely categorized as the highest level research and doctorate-granting institutions in the Carnegie Classification of Institutions of Higher Education (see the box at the end of this Introduction), as are the Ivy League schools. Many of the hidden ivies, the smaller private liberal arts colleges and universities, are not. In a doctorate-granting research institution, faculty not only teach their undergraduates as they advance toward the bachelor of arts (B.A.), bachelor of science (B.S.), or other first degree, but also teach and mentor graduate students working for master's (M.A., M.S., M.Ed., M.Eng., etc.) or doctoral (Ph.D., Psy.D., Ed.D., etc.) degrees. These professors are expected to produce original and revenue-generating research as they compete for *tenure* in their department and to bring private and public research dollars into the university's coffers.

Officially, faculty at both private and public colleges and universities are expected to teach, to research and publish, and to engage in service to their department, institution, and academic discipline, but the smaller private colleges and larger public universities differ in the emphasis they place on each of these three functions. Faculty at the big flagship public universities have lighter teaching loads, especially in connection with the undergraduates and introductory courses, and stronger research and writing expectations. They have more demands placed on them to justify their positions and their work to state legislatures, which control the purse strings of their institutions. These schools were chartered to serve the citizenry of the state, a point to which we will return in our discussion of in-state versus out-of-state student admission and tuition.

The overarching mission of the flagship public universities is to educate a broad range of students at different levels and in many disciplines, as well as to achieve important discoveries and advances in knowledge that will bring prestige and compensation to the university and the state.

## TRENDS IN HIGHER EDUCATION AND PUBLIC EDUCATION

In the twentieth century, America experienced a clear trend toward more citizens earning not only their high school degree, but also their associate (two-year) and/or bachelor's (four-year) degree. At the start of the twenty-first century, a bachelor's degree (typically a B.A. or B.S.) is a fundamental calling card for those desiring long-term success, flexibility, and security in an ever changing job market. Today, about 70 percent of high school graduates in the United States go on to some kind of higher education. In the population as a whole, fewer than 50 percent of people actually hold college degrees. About 45 percent of high school graduates ages 18 to 24 are enrolled in college. Of those in college today, 80 percent are in two- and four-year public colleges and universities. In 1998, according to the U.S. Department of Education, more than 14.6 million students were enrolled in some type of college. By 2009, more than 16.3 million students are expected to be pursuing a college degree. Of those, 6.7 million are expected to be enrolled in four-year public institutions, compared to 3.3 million in four-year private colleges

### Rise in the Total Number of Advanced Degrees Conferred in the Next Decade

| Degree type | Degrees conferred | |
| --- | --- | --- |
| | 2001 | 2009 |
| Associate degree | 581,000 | 628,000 |
| Bachelor's degree | 1,150,000 | 1,257,000 |
| Master's degree | 383,000 | 400,000 |
| Doctoral degree | 43,800 | 44,300 |
| First professional degree (law, medicine, business, etc.) | 73,100 | 74,300 |

and universities. Out of the almost 9.3 million students estimated to be enrolled in four-year institutions in 2001, some 6.2 million are enrolled in public four-year colleges and universities. That's 66 percent of the total! Including both two- and four-year institutions, 10.6 million undergraduates are estimated to be enrolled in public colleges and universities—about five times as many as in private schools. Clearly, public colleges and universities have been and will continue to be a major provider of higher education in the United States.

The total number of high school graduates in the United States is expected to grow from some 2.9 million in 2001 to about 3.2 million in 2009. Even more of these high school graduates than today's high school grads are expected to pursue college and even graduate degrees.

In *Making It into a Top Graduate School,* we claim that a graduate degree will increasingly become the means by which talented and ambitious students prepare themselves for particular careers and professions and distinguish themselves from the larger number of peers holding bachelor's degrees. More than half of all graduate and professional education takes place at the public universities. Of the approximately 2 million students in graduate and professional programs in 2001, about 1.2 million were enrolled in public universities.

Another interesting trend to note is the increasing imbalance between women's and men's enrollment in college today. More women than men are graduating from high school in America. More are earning their bachelor's degrees (645,000 bachelor's degrees were awarded to women and 505,000 were awarded to men in 2001), and more women are expected to do so in the future (it's predicted that 725,000 women, compared to 531,000 men, will earn bachelor's degrees in 2009). Surprised? So are many educators. In the not so distant past, many lamented

## Numbers of Colleges and Universities in the United States

There are 3,278 two- and four-year nonprofit institutions in the United States:
    2,067 institutions are four-year nonprofit institutions:
        608 are public
        1,459 are private

- 700 of the private institutions enroll fewer than 1,000 students

- 715 of the private institutions enroll between 1,000 and 10,000 students

- 351 of the public institutions enroll between 1,000 and 10,000 students

- 212 of the public institutions enroll between 10,000 and 30,000+ students

- Thus there are fewer public institutions, but on average they enroll more students each

- There are 72 public institutions that have student enrollments of more than 20,000 students in the United States. Nearly all of the public ivies have student enrollments of more than 20,000.

Data are from the U.S. Department of Education for 1996 (www.nces.ed.gov/Ipeds/ic97981). All numbers include graduate and undergraduate students, although the very large majority are undergraduates.

---

### NOTABLE TRENDS IN HIGHER EDUCATION

- Distance learning is evolving and becoming more popular.
- New technology is used more and more in and out of the classroom.
- Tuition costs are rising.
- Tuition prepayment and savings plans are proliferating.
- Merit-based financial awards for students are increasing.
- Honors programs are offered to talented students.
- Affirmative action is being challenged, and alternatives are being developed.
- The tenure-based hiring and teaching system is weakening.
- Graduate students are forming unions.
- Standardized tests continue to be used in admission.
- Rankings guides have an impact on universities' attempts for positive public relations.

---

the underenrollment and high noncompletion rates of women in college. Today researchers are trying to encourage men to emulate women's success in education. Many of the public ivies reveal just this pattern of enrollment; for example, at North Carolina University 60 percent of the students are women.

We discuss many trends in higher education throughout this book. The public ivies, and public universities overall, have been at the forefront of many of these trends, some of them quite controversial. The campuses of the public ivies—from Berkeley, California, to Madison, Wisconsin, from Boulder, Colorado, to Ann Arbor, Michigan—have long been sites of protest and challenges to established rules and authority, as anyone who lived through the 1960s can attest. Today, some of the debates have changed, as have the means of organization and expression of dissent. Since some of the most talented students in the country enroll in publicly financed institutions organized to educate the many populations of the various states, the public ivies will remain at the center of these important trends. These universities will often act as lightning rods and innovators in moving the trends forward.

## WHY THE INTEREST IN PUBLIC HIGHER EDUCATION TODAY?

More than 15 years ago, Richard Moll predicted that interest and enrollment in the public universities would continue to increase, because of the quality of education as well as the economic, academic, and admissions context of the mid-1980s. Since then, the percentage of students enrolled in public universities has remained fairly constant, even though overall enrollment numbers are up significantly. Interest in the public universities has continued to rise. Applications at the prestigious private colleges and universities—the ivies and what we call the hidden ivies—are at record numbers, even though tuitions have reached new heights. The context for students today is very different from what it was 15 years ago. More students than ever before in America are graduating from high school and going on to college. We have seen a record economic expansion, allowing more families to pay for college. The top private institutions expanded their endowments by intensifying their fundraising efforts and investing those funds in a booming investment market. Columbia University recently announced that it had raised $2.7 billion (yes, billion!) in its decade-long fundraising campaign. With numbers like those, the wealthiest and most selective private institutions will not be losing their attractiveness anytime soon.

Yet the cost of education is high, and families that are not wealthy enough to ignore the tuition and room-and-board costs at the top private colleges and not poor enough to qualify for significant need-based financial aid often find themselves squeezed out in the middle. Many private colleges and universities are offering significant amounts of need- and merit-based financial aid. Yet, the students graduating from college today hold record amounts of debt, even before they attempt to earn a graduate degree, and in this context, the comparatively low cost of the public colleges and universities looks ever more attractive. Though tuition and fees have also increased dramatically in the last 15 years at the public ivies, they are still significantly lower than at the private ivies. Parents and students who wish to save money while pursuing a topflight education often focus on the lower price tag and substantial amount of need- and merit-based aid available at the public universities. Many top public colleges and universities offer good students major financial incentives to lure them away from private schools. Take Georgia, for example, where under the HOPE Scholarship program, the state covers the full tuition at any public university in Georgia for any state resident with a GPA of 3.0 or higher. Students who earn HOPE Scholarships may also receive housing, research, and study-abroad benefits. More than a dozen states have implemented similar programs for their students, and other states are considering efforts in this direction. The states aim to retain their own top students and attract strong out-of-state students by increasing the overall talent pool and programs in the university system.

Price and the availability of special merit scholarships are not the only reasons why more and more top students are interested in the public ivies. There are more flagship public universities that compare favorably to the top private institutions. More have implemented honors colleges and programs to cater to the student interested in a smaller, more challenging, more personal liberal arts–based education. More have expanded their research and residential facilities. More have attempted to raise standards across the board.

One of the major reasons students look at public universities is the extraordinary breadth of resources they offer. For example, their library holdings are immense, and they continue to spend significant resources on their library systems to keep them up to date in terms of volumes and technology. A glance at the holdings and expenditures of the top 25 research libraries as indexed by the Association of Research Libraries reveals that 14 of them are at public universities, all of which we categorize as public ivies. In fact, a majority of the top 100 research libraries are at public institutions.

## Holdings and Expenditures of the Top 25 University Research Libraries in the United States and Canada, 1998–99

| University | Volumes in Library | Total Expenditures | Rank* 1998–99 | Rank* 1993–94 |
|---|---|---|---|---|
| Harvard University | 14,190,704 | $77,021,323 | 1 | 1 |
| Yale University | 10,294,792 | $42,791,000 | 2 | 3 |
| Stanford University | 7,151,546 | $52,772,788 | 3 | 8 |
| University of Toronto (Canada) | 8,668,036 | $35,697,404 | 4 | 9 |
| **University of California, Berkeley | 8,946,754 | $37,959,895 | 5 | 2 |
| **University of California, Los Angeles | 7,401,780 | $37,984,020 | 6 | 5 |
| **University of Michigan | 7,195,097 | $39,310,808 | 7 | 6 |
| **University of Illinois at Urbana-Champaign | 9,302,203 | $26,700,017 | 8 | 4 |
| Columbia University | 7,144,703 | $32,302,233 | 9 | 7 |
| Cornell University | 6,448,496 | $32,262,079 | 10 | 11 |
| **University of Texas | 7,783,847 | $28,695,585 | 11 | 10 |
| **University of Washington | 5,937,690 | $30,143,019 | 12 | 12 |
| **Pennsylvania State University | 4,391,055 | $34,167,912 | 13 | 16 |
| **University of Minnesota | 5,747,805 | $29,715,493 | 14 | 15 |
| **Indiana University | 6,177,219 | $24,541,261 | 15 | 14 |
| **University of Wisconsin | 5,962,889 | $29,681,576 | 16 | 13 |
| Princeton University | 5,751,978 | $29,785,800 | 17 | 18 |
| **University of North Carolina | 5,024,221 | $25,580,957 | 18 | 19 |
| University of Pennsylvania | 4,791,947 | $29,740,103 | 19 | 21 |
| University of Chicago | 6,419,936 | $21,967,696 | 20 | 17 |
| **Ohio State University | 5,285,344 | $25,711,099 | 21 | 22 |
| **University of Virginia | 4,588,606 | $24,386,384 | 22 | 20 |
| New York University | 3,835,540 | $28,412,910 | 23 | 26 |
| Duke University | 4,865,471 | $23,807,735 | 24 | 23 |
| **Rutgers University | 3,777,538 | $26,034,808 | 25 | 24 |

*Rank is based on a combination of factors, including total expenditures and volumes.
**Public university.

Source: Adapted from Association of Research Libraries, "Holdings of University Research Libraries in U.S. and Canada, 1998–99," Chronicle of Higher Education, May 19, 2000, p. A23.

Where do the public universities get the money to support such library systems? Traditionally, they have relied on publicly financed budgets granted by the state legislatures. Now, they increasingly rely on private fundraising and endowments to supplement their public dollars. Mimicking their private counterparts, the public universities have been emphasizing planned giving, participation in annual alumni fund drives, and major gifts from foundations and individual benefactors. Want to name a law school after yourself? Make a whopping gift to the public university of your choice, and you just might be able to. New research programs in genetics, state-of-the-art science and technology facilities, modern libraries, new dormitory suites, football stadiums, performing arts centers—all are costly. Just like private colleges and universities that rely totally on their endowments, tuition dollars, and foundation grants, the public institutions of higher education have realized that if they are to keep up with changes in the ways in which education is provided and the rising expectations of top students and faculty, they need to raise private money. And they have done so exceptionally well.

Faculty at the public ivies are expected to do their part to bring in money to the university. They are among the top recipients of public and private grants and research awards. If you are interested in studying the human genome, it would be smart to go where some of the leaders in research in this area may be found, at some of the major public research universities, supported by federal and private research grants and publicly supported academic research facilities. Although the research potential and focus of the public ivies are a mixed blessing for the undergraduate student, the facilities, faculty, and research programs at the public institutions remain a major draw for many top students.

## EXAMPLES OF STUDENTS WHO WENT PUBLIC

### Steve: Socially Active Sports Fan, Honors Student at Michigan

Steve knew himself and what he wanted in a college early in the admissions process. He indicated to us that he wanted a very large, challenging, urban university. In our questionnaire, he wrote, "I am a very easy-going guy. I find that I can be shy in the company of others. I am not very vocal. I like to listen to what others say. I am a huge sports fan. I could watch or play sports for the rest of my life and be content, but I do have other goals in life. I spend a lot of time with my youth group and have become more active in Jewish Youth since my trip to Israel." Steve attended a competitive, urban, public high school, and was interested in economics, medicine, sciences, and math. He saw himself in a big, spirited university that would provide him with challenging but not cutthroat academics, and lots of social and athletic outlets.

Steve hit the road with his parents, seeing some of the very competitive private and public universities. His GPA, in a curriculum that included some advanced placement (AP) and honors courses, was in the low 90s, good for his school, and he was working on his SAT scores, which were around 1300. He chose to attend the University of Michigan's summer program for high school students, to explore some academic areas of interest and see what life was like on a big university campus. He loved it. His eventual college list included Michigan, Wisconsin, Penn, Dartmouth, UCLA, Duke, and Vanderbilt. Steve brought his SAT scores up over 1300, and wrote seriously about his intellectual interests across the liberal arts, from the biological sciences to economics to European history. Steve was reaching for some of the more competitive private colleges, but he knew he would be very happy at Michigan. He was accepted by Vanderbilt and Wisconsin, and offered admission to the honors program at Michigan. After careful consideration, he chose Michigan, where he would find not only all the academic programs he wanted, and all the sports he cared to go crazy for, but also the attention and challenge of the honors program. He felt he had found it all: a small liberal arts college environment in the midst of one of the largest universities in the country.

## Arthur: Expatriate, Military Historian, AP Scholar at Virginia

Arthur was an American student living abroad with his family in Asia at the time he contacted us. An exceptionally bright young man, Arthur had a learning style that occasionally required some extra time on tests at school. Yet Arthur excelled at a demanding international school in Asia, taking a challenging curriculum, captaining the cross-country and track teams, participating in drama productions, and lecturing to his high school classes on military history, his particular intellectual passion. Initially, Arthur was looking for a college or university at which he could get some learning support, possibly run track or cross-country, and study military history, government, and advanced Chinese. Given his serious interest in military history and the fact that a number of his elder family members were graduates of West Point, Arthur was focused on West Point and a career in the U.S. Army.

Arthur's parents had attended the University of Virginia. The entire family had concerns about the size of UVA and the possibility that contact with faculty would be limited. Arthur was seeking a balanced environment, in which he could find challenging courses in his areas of interest without feeling overly pressured. He was not doing well on standardized tests, with scores in the 1200s on the SAT I and 600s on the SAT II, but he was excelling in AP history classes, other honors-level courses, and advanced Mandarin Chinese.

For a number of reasons, we were hesitant to recommend West Point to Arthur, and his parents shared some of our concerns. We talked about the demanding nature of the military academy's program, including an academic curriculum that still strongly included the sciences, as well as the military science courses and practice, which would take up much of Arthur's time. The program would not be flexible enough to accommodate Arthur's diverse interests and particular learning style. If Arthur wanted a career in the military, or a career that involved teaching, research, or consulting in military history, West Point was not an essential first step. A liberal arts education with a focus in history and government could serve him just as well. He could also consider Reserve Officer Training Corps (ROTC) programs on college campuses or Officer Training School in the future. We continued to emphasize that not going to West Point did not mean that Arthur had to give up his intellectual interests or dreams of a career involving the military.

A next major issue was whether UVA would potentially be an appropriate school for Arthur. As a legacy candidate, he would be treated as a Virginia resident during the application process, which would make this competitive university a more realistic admissions prospect, given his lower test scores relative to out-of-state UVA applicants. Arthur discovered from his research that UVA had all the programs he was looking for: military history, Chinese, ROTC, competitive running. He had initially wanted a smaller school, but this cosmopolitan and mature student began to feel that he would not grow enough at a small college. He had lived abroad for a number of years and had friends all over the world. UVA seemed to offer a richness of programs, resources, and students that he desired. Arthur continued to explore a few of the more competitive smaller colleges that had programs in which he was interested, but he began to lean more and more toward UVA. Eventually, after visiting the university again and addressing his concerns about size, faculty contact, academic support, Arthur chose to apply Early Decision to UVA (for an explanation of Early Decision, see "The Rolling Safety"). With extended time, his SAT scores had risen to 1400, and his GPA was in the 3.3 range. Here is an excerpt from one of Arthur's essays:

> "Because I have grown up interacting with different types of people, many of whom associate themselves with different communities, I find it hard to identify myself within one certain group. I would not hesitate to say that I am a member of at least three separate communities, each of which represents something important in my life. Although I have grown up in Hong Kong, I have a strong sense of my American identity and Virginian heritage. After college, I plan to serve my country in the United States Army. However, I also view myself as partly Asian, and feel a loyalty to Hong Kong, my home of eighteen years. I enjoy losing myself in the city and speaking Chinese to people on the street. Because I have lived in an international community for many years and have traveled extensively, I feel that I understand and work well with people from other cultures. Finally, I identify myself with athletes, those who enjoy all sports. The most important aspect of my life is running. Running has helped me prioritize my time and achieve better grades. It has made me more self-confident and mentally tough. There is a certain mystique associated with running which I find attractive. I am a member of all three communities, something not uncommon. I feel that identifying myself solely with one community is unnecessarily limiting."

Arthur was accepted to UVA Early Decision, and would enter the university knowing that he would be able to take advantage of all the opportunities this larger institution offered. He could find the balance he wanted among academics, athletics, and multiple communities and take advantage of whatever academic and organizational support he would need through college. He had been helped in his application by his legacy status, his running (even though he was not a heavily recruited athlete), his interesting international experiences, and his determination and intellectual passion, which came through clearly in his writing.

## Total Enrollments at the Large U.S. Public University Campuses, Fall 1999

| Campus | Total Enrollment |
| --- | --- |
| University of Texas, Austin | 49,034 |
| Ohio State University, Columbus | 48,003 |
| University of Minnesota, Twin Cities | 44,361 |
| University of Florida, Gainesville | 44,276 |
| Arizona State University, Tempe | 44,215 |
| Texas A&M University, College Station | 43,500 |
| Pennsylvania State University, University Park | 40,658 |
| University of Wisconsin, Madison | 40,045 |
| University of Michigan, Ann Arbor | 37,846 |

*Source:* Adapted from the Ohio State University website, www.osu.edu.

### A Diverse Array of Students Who Fit

We will talk about a number of students throughout this book. Although we may make some generalizations, there is not one perfect type of student who does best at a public college or university. Diverse types of students share the campuses at the public ivies. Each fits the institution in his or her own way and is more or less happy, depending on the fit with the particular program and the institution as a whole. The students we discuss as case studies sought their niche, and some were happier than others. In the following chapters, we will discuss some qualities we think help a student succeed at the public ivies, institutions that are larger and less personal than most private colleges. We will discuss what defines the public ivies and what differentiates them from the private colleges and universities. You may or may not see yourself in our presentation, which we hope will assist you in making your decision on where to attend college.

## THE MYTHS ABOUT PUBLIC EDUCATION

There are many false assumptions about public universities and colleges. Here are some:

- A public university is always a last resort or, at best, a second choice.

- No one from my high school voluntarily goes to our state university.

- Public universities have second-rate faculty and departments.

- The libraries at public universities are understocked and impossible to use.

- Only jocks and computer nerds go to public universities.

- I don't like football, so a big state university is not for me.

- Since they're cheaper, public universities attract mostly poor kids.

- Public universities aren't very diverse, since they enroll mostly their own state's students.

- It's really hard to transfer to or from a public university.

- All the classes at public universities are huge, with hundreds of students in them.

- Full-time faculty don't do any of the teaching anymore.

- The social scene is all about fraternities and sororities.

- There's a lot of animosity between in-state and out-of-state residents.

- It's impossible for an out-of-state student to gain in-state residency.

- Students study only the sciences at the public universities, and I'm interested in the liberal arts.

- None of the graduate student teachers know what they're doing.

- Public universities are mainly graduate research schools and don't care about the undergraduates.

- It's nearly impossible to get into the flagship university in my state.

- If I can't get into a flagship public university when I graduate from high school, I'll never be able to get into one.

We could go on.

Though there is a grain of truth in each of these statements, they are gross generalizations that mask the true character of and opportunities available at the better public colleges and universities, and especially the public ivies. We will address each of these myths in this book. Very often, the public ivies are a first choice for talented, motivated applicants. Many students from public and private high schools in your state and other states actively seek out your flagship state school. The public ivies have some of the top faculty and most highly rated departments in disciplines across the liberal arts. These universities have huge investments in their libraries and use advanced technology to deliver online catalogs, interlibrary loan access, and distance education courses. Of course, some of the public ivies are football powerhouses, but only a tiny percentage of students there play on the football team or compete in other intercollegiate sports. Nor is the rest of the student body locked away in computer labs. The public ivies have thriving social scenes and strong academic and extracurricular activities, where most students find themselves through their college years. Remember: attendance at the football games is not mandatory!

## Myth: "A Public University Is Always a Last Resort or at Best a Second Choice"

Take a look at the National Merit Scholarship list, and see how many National Merit students, some of the most talented students in the country, decided to attend public universities. Most of those who chose the public universities on this list were sponsored by the institution. The university underwrote the student's educational scholarship in order to attract that student to the campus, reflecting a trend to use merit-based aid to attract top students to public universities. Merit-based aid is based on talent. In addition to those highly publicized athletic scholarships, the public ivies award academic scholarships to deserving students, rich or poor.

### Colleges with the Most Freshman National Merit Scholars, 1999

| Institution | Total number of National Merit Scholarship winners | Number of winners whose scholarships were paid for by the institution* |
|---|---|---|
| Harvard University | 394 | 0 |
| ** University of Texas at Austin | 244 | 186 |
| ** University of California, Berkeley | 235 | 167 |
| Stanford University | 229 | 0 |
| Rice University | 183 | 104 |
| ** Texas A&M University | 181 | 143 |
| ** University of Florida | 176 | 145 |
| Yale University | 170 | 0 |
| University of Chicago | 139 | 93 |
| ** University of Oklahoma at Norman | 136 | 115 |
| Massachusetts Institute of Technology | 133 | 0 |
| ** Arizona State University | 132 | 114 |
| Washington University in St. Louis | 131 | 96 |
| Brigham Young University | 130 | 97 |
| Northwestern University | 128 | 71 |
| New York University | 125 | 103 |
| University of Southern California | 122 | 102 |
| ** Iowa State University | 116 | 94 |
| Princeton University | 111 | 0 |
| ** Ohio State University | 109 | 91 |
| ** University of Kansas | 101 | 84 |
| ** Georgia Institute of Technology | 100 | 71 |
| Vanderbilt University | 98 | 61 |
| ** University of California, Los Angeles | 97 | 82 |
| ** Florida State University | 94 | 89 |
| ** University of North Carolina at Chapel Hill | 92 | 61 |
| Carleton College | 85 | 71 |
| Duke University | 76 | 0 |

## Colleges with the Most Freshman National Merit Scholars, 1999 (continued)

| Institution | Total number of National Merit Scholarship winners | Number of winners whose scholarships were paid for by the institution* |
|---|---|---|
| Johns Hopkins University | 74 | 49 |
| University of Pennsylvania | 68 | 0 |
| Case Western Reserve University | 67 | 37 |
| ** University of Kentucky | 65 | 52 |
| Wheaton College | 61 | 46 |
| Boston University | 58 | 37 |
| Harvey Mudd College | 58 | 39 |
| Dartmouth College | 54 | 0 |
| ** University of Alabama at Tuscaloosa | 54 | 42 |
| Brown University | 52 | 0 |
| California Institute of Technology | 52 | 0 |
| ** Purdue University | 52 | 36 |
| Baylor University | 51 | 40 |
| ** University of California, San Diego | 51 | 41 |
| Tulane University | 50 | 35 |
| ** University of Arizona | 49 | 34 |
| ** University of Georgia | 49 | 33 |
| ** Michigan State University | 48 | 36 |
| Emory University | 47 | 34 |
| ** University of Maryland College Park | 47 | 37 |
| Tufts University | 45 | 34 |
| Cornell University | 42 | 0 |
| ** University of Washington at Seattle | 42 | 26 |
| Macalester College | 41 | 33 |
| ** University of Minnesota, Twin Cities | 41 | 31 |
| Furman University | 40 | 30 |
| Oberlin College | 40 | 34 |
| ** University of Michigan, Ann Arbor | 40 | 0 |
| ** Miami University (Oxford, Ohio) | 37 | 31 |
| ** University of South Carolina (Columbia) | 37 | 32 |
| Columbia University | 35 | 0 |

*The number of Merit Scholarship winners whose scholarships were paid for by the institution, not by the National Merit Scholarship Corporation or other corporate sponsors.
**Public university.

Note: The figures were determined by the Chronicle of Higher Education from a list in the 1998–99 annual report of the National Merit Scholarship Corporation.

Source: Adapted from National Merit Scholarship Corporation, "2000 Freshman Merit Scholars," Chronicle of Higher Education, February 16, 2001, p. A48. Available at www.chronicle.com/weekly/v47/i23/23a04801.htm.

## Racial, Ethnic, and International Diversity at U.S. Universities, 1997

**All students enrolled**

| | | |
|---|---|---|
| Total | 14,502,300 | |
| Men | 6,396,000 | |
| Women | 8,106,300 | |
| Public | | |
| Four-year | 5,835,400 | 40% of all students |
| Two-year | 5,360,700 | |
| Private | | |
| Four-year | 3,061,300 | 21% of all students |
| Two-year | 244,900 | |
| Undergraduate | 12,450,600 | |

**American Indian students**

| | | |
|---|---|---|
| All | 142,500 | |
| Men | 59,000 | |
| Women | 83,400 | |
| Public | | |
| Four-year | 55,700 | 39% of all American Indian students; 1% of total public four-year enrollment |
| Two-year | 67,900 | |
| Private | | |
| Four-year | 15,800 | 11% of all American Indian students; 1% of total private four-year enrollment |
| Two-year | 3,000 | |
| Undergraduate | 130,800 | |

**Asian students**

| | | |
|---|---|---|
| All | 859,200 | |
| Men | 417,700 | |
| Women | 441,500 | |
| Public | | |
| Four-year | 349,300 | 41% of all Asian students; 6% of total public four-year enrollment |
| Two-year | 331,100 | |
| Private | | |
| Four-year | 169,200 | 20% of all Asian students; 6% of total private four-year enrollment |
| Two-year | 9,600 | |
| Undergraduate | 743,700 | |

**Black students**

| | |
|---|---|
| All | 1,551,000 |

## Racial, Ethnic, and International Diversity at U.S. Universities, 1997 (continued)

| | | |
|---|---:|---|
| Men | 579,800 | |
| Women | 971,300 | |
| Public | | |
|   Four-year | 589,000 | 38% of all Black students;<br>10% of total public four-year enrollment |
|   Two-year | 616,200 | |
| Private | | |
|   Four-year | 307,400 | 20% of all Black students;<br>10% of total private four-year enrollment |
|   Two-year | 38,400 | |
| Undergraduate | 1,398,100 | |
| **Hispanic students** | | |
| All | 1,218,500 | |
| Men | 525,800 | |
| Women | 692,700 | |
| Public | | |
|   Four-year | 371,400 | 31% of all Hispanic students;<br>6% of total public four-year enrollment |
|   Two-year | 660,200 | |
| Private | | |
|   Four-year | 158,600 | 13% of all Hispanic students;<br>5% of total private four-year enrollment |
|   Two-year | 28,300 | |
| Undergraduate | 1,125,900 | |
| **White students** | | |
| All | 10,266,100 | |
| Men | 4,548,800 | |
| Women | 5,717,400 | |
| Public | | |
|   Four-year | 4,249,600 | 41% of all White students;<br>73% of total public four-year enrollment |
|   Two-year | 3,608,300 | |
| Private | | |
|   Four-year | 2,246,500 | 22% of all White students;<br>73% of total private four-year enrollment |
|   Two-year | 161,800 | |
| Undergraduate | 8,783,900 | |

*Source:* Adapted from U.S. Department of Education, "College Enrollment by Racial and Ethnic Group, Selected Years," *Chronicle of Higher Education Almanac,* www.chronicle.com/weekly/almanac/2000/facts/2402stu.htm.

## Myth: "Public Universities Aren't Very Diverse, Since They Enroll Mostly Their Own State's Students"

From the broad figures on the ethnic and racial makeup of various college populations in the preceding table, you can see that there is not a huge difference in the proportions of American Indian, Asian, Black, Hispanic, or White students at four-year public versus four-year private colleges and universities. Of course, figures vary from school to school, and are one of the important considerations for students looking at any particular institution. In terms of overall ethnic or racial diversity, public universities are not less diverse than their private counterparts. It is a well-established fact in research on education that non-White ethnic/racial groups are underrepresented at the four-year colleges and universities overall. As the preceding table shows, 41 percent and 22 percent of all White students attend public and private four-year institutions, respectively, figures just over the totals for all students of 40 percent and 21 percent, respectively. Similarly, 41 percent attend public and 20 percent of all Asian students and private four-year institutions, respectively. A slightly smaller proportion of Black students, 38 percent, attend public four-year colleges and universities, while 20 percent of Black students are at private four-year schools. Thirty-nine percent of American Indian students, close to the number for all students, attend public four-year schools, but only 11 percent of American Indian students attend private four-year institutions. The Hispanic student population goes to public and private four-year schools at a much lower rate: Only 31 percent and 13 percent of Hispanic students attend public and private four-year institutions, respectively.

Public universities are diverse in different ways, and, of course, some are more diverse than others. If we understand diversity to include geographical, international, socioeconomic, academic, and extracurricular interest, we see that these universities are much more diverse than we might think, given an in-state student population of 60 to 95 percent.

## Myth: "It's Really Hard to Transfer to or from a Public University"

Students do transfer to and from public universities. These schools are big and flexible. Large proportions of the student populations at the flagship schools have transferred there from junior or community colleges, other state schools, and smaller private colleges. State universities have rules to give special consideration, including preference in transfer admissions and the awarding of academic credit, to graduates or attendees of their own two- and four-year colleges and universities. Alternatively, many students start their college life at their state university and then transfer to a more competitive private or public university, a smaller college, or an engineering, business, music, or other specialized degree program. Students also transfer internally within the bigger state schools, from liberal arts to business, from engineering to liberal arts, from music to education, and so forth. That is one of the benefits of the public ivies: the vast resources and numbers of programs and students allow for many choices.

## Debunking Some More Myths

The myths about public education do not accurately capture the reality of life at a public ivy. There are some enormous lecture classes, but they are usually limited to introductory courses that students take during the first year or two. Well-prepared students may be able to earn AP course credits or course placement through SAT II Subject Tests, for example, and leapfrog Chemistry 101, Introduction to American Politics, or Introductory Psychology. Others grin and bear it, recognizing what it takes to make it through a five-hundred-person lecture class taught twice a week by a professor and a third time in a recitation or discussion section of forty students taught by a graduate instructor. With the proliferation of honors programs, critical thinking curricula, special college programs for top students, guaranteed graduation plans, and other means of making a big school small, students will find that, particularly in their junior and senior years, they can take challenging, smaller scale seminars and discussion-oriented classes with full-time professors. Perhaps they can even take advantage of a master's-level class in their area of expertise.

There has been a trend in the United States toward more part-time faculty employment at both public and private colleges and universities, but particularly at public institutions. At the public ivies, undergraduates vie for the attention of faculty with graduate students, who are often teaching or research assistants for these full-time faculty mentors. Some graduate students are better teachers than others, just as some faculty are more or less effective than others in the classroom. Students can be wise in the ways in which they choose courses and professors and negotiate the leading public university systems. Generalization does not capture the true picture.

Finally, the social scene at a public ivy is as diverse as the student body. There are academic clubs and intellectual opportunities in abundance, as well as thriving Greek (fraternity and sorority) systems in some cases. We tend to believe that at these large schools, the Greek systems, which may attract 10 to 30 percent of students, play a less dominant role than they do at smaller, isolated campuses. Students say take it or leave it; fraternities and sororities are there if you want them. Other social avenues are available at the public ivies, including social clubs, athletic teams, campuswide events, and on-campus and off-campus residential environments.

The key to debunking these myths will be your own research, visits to some campuses, and conversations with current students and graduates. You may find that one or more of the criteria we discuss, or which these myths address, may be very important to you. Perhaps the Greek system is too large, or the classes too big, or the faculty too distant. As with any college, the dictum *buyer beware* remains the order of the day. This book should help you to learn about the public ivies, about public universities in general, and about the differences between public and private higher education. Our aim is for you to ask the right questions in your college search to learn what you need to know to make your own best choice.

# WHAT IS A PUBLIC COLLEGE OR UNIVERSITY?

This seems an obvious and simple question, but a sophisticated explanation is required. Public institutions of higher education are supported directly by the taxpayers of the states in which they're located. Since they are chartered to serve primarily the citizens of that state, they charge lower tuition to and have lower admission standards for state residents. Almost all selective colleges and universities, public and private, receive various types of funding from the federal government, be it through financial aid support, research grants, or particular academic or enrichment programs. Some states provide support and incentives for the private colleges and universities in the state as well. The public colleges and universities are specifically public entities governed by the state. The governing board that makes decisions about the budget, policies, and planning of the public higher educational system is either publicly elected or appointed by publicly elected officials (for example, the regents in the University of California system). The governing board is accountable to the general public in the state, whereas the boards of trustees for private colleges and universities are not.

With public control and support come certain expectations and strings. The budgetary process for public institutions is managed by the state government's budget stream. Many public institutions are engaging in more and more private fundraising to supplement their state budget allocations. In addition, they try to secure research grants from the federal government (the Department of Defense, the National Science Foundation, the National Endowment for the Humanities, NASA, the U.S. Department of Education, and so forth) and corporate sources (pharmaceutical companies, mining companies, computer hardware and software manufacturers, athletic shoe and apparel companies, agribusinesses, and so forth). The simple answer is, public colleges and universities are state controlled and supported.

# TWO-YEAR VERSUS FOUR-YEAR INSTITUTIONS

All of the public ivies are referred to as four-year institutions, even though at all college-level schools more students are taking more than four years to graduate. Graduation statistics are often reported now as five-year or six-year graduation rates. As we often tell students, the notion of college as a four-year endeavor is outdated. Some students have so many credits from high school advanced course work that they can graduate in three years. Others want to travel abroad, double-major, transfer from one college to another, or take time out. It may take them five or more years to earn a degree. And that's fine! It is quality, not pace, that matters in the long run. Four-year institutions are places where students go to earn their bachelor's (baccalaureate) degree—the bachelor of arts (B.A.) or bachelor of science (B.S.) in most cases. This is what most students think of as "college."

Two-year institutions are places where students go to earn their associate (A.A. or A.S.) degree. Often, they then transfer to a four-year school to finish out two or three years of course work to earn their B.A. or B.S. Sometimes, students begin college at a two-year school, attending part- or full-time, and then transfer to a four-year college or university. This helps them solidify their high school record, get a taste for college course work, and save some money.

The Carnegie Foundation for the Advancement of Teaching recently reclassified all the institutions of higher education in the United States into new categories (see following box). These help educators, researchers, and students identify where different institutions fit for comparison and evaluation purposes. All of the public ivies are four-year institutions in the category Doctoral/Research Universities—Extensive, except for the College of William and Mary and Miami University, which are in the category Doctoral/Research Universities—Intensive.

## THE LIBERAL ARTS VERSUS PARTICULAR PROGRAMS

In this book, we focus on the liberal arts programs at the public ivies. We are most concerned with the ability of students to gain a broad-based education in one or more of the liberal arts fields listed in the Carnegie classifications: English language and literature/letters; foreign language and literatures; biological sciences/life sciences; mathematics; philosophy and religion; physical sciences; psychology; social sciences and history; visual and performing arts; area, ethnic, and cultural studies; liberal arts and sciences, general studies, and humanities; and multidisciplinary and interdisciplinary studies. We are interested in an education that exposes students to one or more academic disciplines as well as methods of critical inquiry essential to success in and out of the university. The skills in critical thinking, analysis, problem solving, close reading, revised writing, and discursive writing that students develop with a liberal arts education become their ingrained talents for the rest of their lives. By mastering at least one academic subject and being introduced to many others by core or distribution requirements in college, you will gain an appreciation for a broader spectrum of knowledge. You might even unexpectedly find your true passion as a result of this exposure.

Although we recognize the value of the many other academic programs available at the public ivies and the importance of having these other disciplines at hand, we concentrate on the student who is liberal arts bound. Students with such specific major interests as music, education, business, engineering, veterinary and agricultural sciences, journalism and communications, art, architecture and design, or drama will find what they want in the public ivies. These universities offer some of the country's top undergraduate programs in these disciplines. Students in a college of business or engineering at a Michigan or Texas or Colorado, for example, can still take advantage of the liberal arts offerings on campus. This provides a wider range of course options than is available at a freestanding technical college, business school, or music conservatory. At the public ivies, the university as a whole is an umbrella encompassing a number of different schools or colleges, each with its own requirements, offerings, and admission standards. While you are researching the liberal arts or arts and sciences schools at these universities, take some time to look through the other colleges on campus. You might decide that one of them suits you better.

## CARNEGIE CLASSIFICATION OF INSTITUTIONS OF HIGHER EDUCATION

The following are the new Carnegie classifications for most of the institutions granting at least the baccalaureate (bachelor's) degree.

**DOCTORAL/RESEARCH UNIVERSITIES—EXTENSIVE:** "These institutions offer a wide range of baccalaureate programs and are committed to graduate education through the doctorate. They award 50 or more doctoral degrees per year across at least 15 disciplines." 3.8 percent of all higher educational institutions.

**DOCTORAL/RESEARCH UNIVERSITIES—INTENSIVE:** "These institutions offer a wide range of baccalaureate programs and are committed to graduate education through the doctorate. They award at least 10 doctoral degrees per year across three or more disciplines, or at least 20 doctoral degrees per year overall." 2.9 percent of all institutions.

**MASTER'S (COMPREHENSIVE) COLLEGES AND UNIVERSITIES I:** "These institutions offer a wide range of baccalaureate programs and are committed to graduate education through the master's degree. They award 40 or more master's degrees annually across three or more disciplines." 12.7 percent of all institutions.

**MASTER'S (COMPREHENSIVE) COLLEGES AND UNIVERSITIES II:** "These institutions offer a wide range of baccalaureate programs and are committed to graduate education through the master's degree. They award 20 or more master's degrees annually in one or more disciplines." 3.3 percent of all instititutions.

**BACCALAUREATE COLLEGES—LIBERAL ARTS:** "These institutions are primarily undergraduate colleges with major emphasis on baccalaureate degree programs. They award at least half of their baccalaureate degrees in the liberal arts." 5.5 percent of all institutions.

**BACCALAUREATE COLLEGES—GENERAL:** "These institutions are primarily undergraduate colleges with major emphasis on baccalaureate programs. They award fewer than half of their baccalaureate degrees in liberal-arts fields." 8.0 percent of all institutions.

**BACCALAUREATE/ASSOCIATE'S COLLEGES:** "These institutions are undergraduate colleges with significant baccalaureate programs; however, the majority of conferrals are at the sub-baccalaureate level (associate degrees and certificates)." 1.3 percent of all institutions.

*Source:* Carnegie Foundation for the Advancement of Teaching, "Carnegie Classification of 3,941 Institutions of higher Education," *Chronicle of Higher Education,* August 11, 2000, www.chronicle.com/stats/carnegie/.

## PLAN OF THIS BOOK

*The Public Ivies* is designed to educate readers about trends in public higher education and what it means to choose a public university. In Part One, we provide parents, students, and counselors with an overview on choosing to attend a public university. Why might different students choose to add public universities to their college list? How do the public universities make their admissions decisions, and what does this mean for potential applicants? We look at important aspects of the public ivies, including athletic and learning support programs, scientific research opportunities, undergraduate relationships with graduate students, honors programs, and financial support.

In Part Two, we develop the key criteria to consider when examining and comparing public universities. From class size to endowment, in-state student percentages to full-time enrollment rates, a number of important measures are available to evaluate any particular school. We discuss the importance of searching for special programs of interest to a student and of recognizing the value of honors colleges, teaching, research facilities, and fellow students. We focus on the flagship campuses as being of primary interest to strong students looking to attend public universities in their own state or across state lines.

In Part Three, we present data on each of the thirty public ivies. Our goal is to offer a picture of these schools based on factors we believe are important to consider. Building on our discussion of the criteria in Part Two, we present information on endowment and enrollment, special programs of note, admissions statistics, and so forth. We do not spend time trying to capture the individual personalities of these larger universities, a task we think is unrealistic. Almost without exception, these are large, eclectic places that are similar to each other. In other words, big state schools have a lot of things in common. The discerning student, parent, and counselor can focus on a smaller group of these institutions and compare them according to the criteria and programs most important to them. We expect readers to visit and learn about some of the places of interest to which we introduce them. We believe in the value of the public ivies in American higher education and encourage potential applicants to take them seriously.

Finally, in Part Four, we offer words of wisdom for parents and students as they undergo the transition to college. We mention some of the most relevant aspects of college life students should consider as they prepare to enroll in the great state schools. What should students know about life on campus? What words of advice do graduates of these schools have? What survival skills will students need to negotiate the corridors of a larger state university? How does one manage an A in a five-hundred-person lecture class? How does one avoid those classes in the first place? For parents, we hope to alleviate some concerns they might have about watching their son or daughter board a plane for the Midwest, South, East, or West to enroll in State U. and to advise them on their important role for the next four years. *In loco parentis* (schools serving in the role of the parent in the absence of the parent) may be the rule of the day in education, but this concept means different things at a small, rural secondary school and at a large state university. Although these universities may treat parents as out of the loop, parents have some important duties, beyond writing tuition checks, during their children's college years.

# ONE
# Choosing to Attend a Public College or University

## REED: A COMMITTED RELIGIOUS STUDENT AND ATHLETE AT THE UNIVERSITY OF VIRGINIA

When he first met with us, Reed was fairly clear about his intentions for college. "I am a strong Christian and a very competitive athlete. My life is very busy because of school, Church, sports, and friends. My goals are to be either a sports surgeon or physical therapist receiving under-graduate and graduate degrees from UVA. I also want to play soccer in college on the highest level I can at UVA." Reed knew UVA because one of his parents had earned a graduate degree there. This would give him some preferential treatment in the admissions process, even as an out-of-state student. Reed lived in the South, though not in Virginia, and saw the university as a good combination of what he wanted in a school. He perceived UVA as traditional, balanced academically and socially, athletically competitive, and, though large, small enough to provide the classroom interaction and connections to faculty he hoped for. Reed attended a strong private day school, and then a private boarding school, and did well in a curriculum that included honors and advanced placement (AP) courses. We encouraged Reed to look at a number of different colleges, especially some smaller private schools, to challenge and potentially confirm his interest in UVA. Vanderbilt, the University of Richmond, Wake Forest, and Davidson became other strong choices for Reed, and he began to talk about going into the ministry. Furman and Stetson were added to his list. After a lengthy discussion, Reed chose to apply Early Decision to UVA, where he was accepted. He wrote earnestly about his religious commitment, his ability to relate to people of many backgrounds, and his learning about himself through his transition to boarding school.

# WHO SHOULD CONSIDER PUBLIC COLLEGES AND UNIVERSITIES?

Many students like Reed consider public colleges and universities, ruling them in or out as they go through the college research, admissions, and selection processes. The first words of advice you will hear at any public university admissions office are that there is no one *type* of student who does best at a public college or university. Among the more than 6 million students enrolled today in public four-year colleges and universities, there certainly are many more individuals and types of students than can be listed here or anywhere. That said, there are some classifications that may help to define the kinds of students we see applying to the public ivies. Often, seeing examples can help you move beyond general statistics to see yourself, potentially, at a large university.

Reed fit several categories of public-bound students. He knew himself and what he wanted out of his education. He was a committed athlete interested in his own sport and a larger, spirited athletic program on campus. He was an advanced student in a private school who would be able to gain course credits through AP and SAT II Subject Tests, enabling him to skip some larger introductory courses. He was a legacy, which gave him an advantage in the admissions process. By approaching UVA as an Early Decision applicant, he let the university know that it was his first choice. He was a southerner, a traditional and religious young man who wanted to remain in a culture similar to that of his home. Reed did not relinquish responsibility for carefully evaluating all of his options and comparing and contrasting different colleges and universities. He knew UVA and suspected it was right for him, but he still did the legwork of visiting and researching not only UVA, but also a number of other private and public schools that could challenge his assumptions about himself and Virginia. In the end, Reed targeted his first-choice school correctly and realized that he had circled back to his original instincts about which school was right for him.

Our counsel is that many different types of students should consider public universities, and the public ivies in particular, though most likely for different and sometimes contradictory reasons. The following are descriptions of other types of students who might find their niche at a public ivy. Individual students usually fit into more than one category. You may be a local hero who is an athlete, or a legacy applicant who has a learning disability.

## The Local Hero

Are you a top student in your high school? Have you excelled in one important area of your life? In science? In writing? In sports? In drama? Your public university may want you! Whether you want it remains to be seen, but you should be aware that many states, from California to Florida to Texas to Georgia, have instituted programs to attract the best and brightest students in the state to their flagship institutions. Merit Scholars, for example, often receive excellent and attractive merit-based packages to convince them to remain in state. Some states have offered admission guarantees to students in the top 4 percent, for example, of their high school class, in response to challenges to prior affirmative action plans. Whatever the reason for the policy or program, you should be interested in the special offers your state, or perhaps another state, may make to you, which campus you would be admitted to, and whether you could continue to shine in your area of expertise, academic or otherwise, at the state school. The local hero shines in his or her high school, public or private, and fits a particular niche that has been created at a public university. This star student becomes a Morehead Scholar at the University of North Carolina, or an Echols Scholar at the University of Virginia. This student has excelled academically and usually in another area as well. The local hero is just the kind of student a public ivy loves to keep on the farm, someone who might merit an article in the local paper or the university's alumni magazine.

### *Peter: a top student in a small Texas town applying to an in-state honors program*

Peter was a student in a small town in Texas. He was interested in exploring college options outside the state, unlike almost all the students in his class at a large public high school. Peter's parents had each attended college in Texas, one at a private college and the other at the University of Texas, but they encouraged Peter to think about some of the more selective public and private colleges around the country to learn about other options. He was a very strong student, with seven AP courses on his curriculum by senior year and twice that number of honors-level classes. He described himself as "hardworking, dedicated, competitive, and serious-minded. I think that I have a good sense of humor and I can get along with just about anybody. Having been away from home a lot in the summer, I do not have a lot of anxiety about going off to college. I am very interested in sports, especially spectator sports. I also like computers." The summer before his junior year, Peter attended a college prep and academic discovery program on a small college campus in New England. He loved it, discovering a major interest in computers and website design, as well as a taste for a nice campus and small class environment. The following summer, Peter took a more advanced web design class in London. As a senior, he continued his service work, designing a website for a nonprofit organization, volunteering locally, and working with the National Honor Society.

As Peter began to explore colleges out of state, he decided that a small college would be too limiting for him. He was at a large high school, and felt he needed more space, activities, and types of students. He became quite interested in the University of Pennsylvania, Duke, and Vanderbilt, but did not feel ready to commit early to any of them. Peter was going to shine in his high school class. He was confident and excited about a bigger, more challenging school. He and his parents felt that it was worth going farther away from home, but only for a smaller group of competitive schools. We began to talk about a safer school for Peter's list—one that Peter was sure he could get into—and about Peter's prospects at the University of Texas. It was obvious that Peter would be accepted under Texas's plan to admit all students in the top 10 percent of their class and that he would almost certainly make it to the Austin flagship campus.

Given UT's size, Peter was a bit uncomfortable about that prospect. Then he began to look into UT's special programs for highly talented students.

He visited the university and sat in on a class in the Plan II honors program, a selective program that creates a small liberal arts–style environment within the larger university. The Plan II program immediately appealed to Peter. He would be just the kind of local high school academic star the program was looking for, and he decided to apply there, not only as a backup, but also as an exciting possibility. As he wrote in his application,

> "Earlier this fall, I visited a Plan II World Literature class. I knew that the difference between this and my high school World Literature class would be most noticeable, since at UT it would be a much smaller class and a more knowledgeable and experienced professor. But what I did not take into account beforehand was the unique style of interaction between teacher and students that resulted. In a short forty-five minute discussion of *The Iliad*, each student had ample opportunity to submit his or her opinion or ask a question. From my visit, I know Plan II is the ideal place for me to be in an intellectually challenging and interesting environment. This is the atmosphere that I long to participate in. A Plan II Liberal Arts education will allow me the flexibility to take an assorted collection of classes and to pursue a dual degree in business. The opportunity to participate in the Plan II program is exciting because it combines the small environment of a great liberal arts college embedded in one of the most celebrated universities in the country. The goals that I have set for myself, based upon my website design class and my high school academic experiences, can best be fulfilled in Plan II. I truly believe that a Plan II education at the University of Texas at Austin will open more doors and avenues of profound development for me than any other program in the United States."

## The Honors Student

As a strong student, Peter fit another category of applicants: those eligible for the competitive honors colleges, honors programs, residential colleges, special scholars, and other selective "school-within-a-school" options at the public ivies and other public universities. In an effort to attract more students like Peter, the public universities have set up merit-based financial award systems, special honors divisions, and other means of creating a more intimate, challenging, advanced, and highly focused or broader liberal arts education. Some, like the Morehead Scholars program at UNC, have been around for several decades. Others, like UT's Plan II or Michigan's Residential College, are more recent innovations. The talented honors student finds a unique educational path within a larger state school. He or she seeks to take advantage of special advising systems; seminar-style classes; critical thinking courses with top faculty; preferred dormitories, which sometimes include advising or faculty-in-residence options; and other benefits of additional resources and selectivity. The honors student can have the advantages of a small liberal arts college education in the context of a big university environment, with all the resources that entails. Or if the student has a particular interest, say, in journalism, international relations, or community service, he or she can take advantage of a special program at a public ivy that focuses on that area. Perhaps the honors student receives a research grant or foreign travel stipend for the summer. Perhaps faculty are available to mentor the student during the year while he or she pursues advanced course work on topics of interest. The honors student wisely compares the financial, educational, and social attractions of special programs while researching and visiting colleges.

We offer a very broad definition of honors programs. By "honors programs" we mean not only programs the universities refer to specifically as "honors programs," which exist across individual college lines in the university, and the "honors colleges" that are at a few universities, but also special scholar designations and awards, residential living arrangements, and different plans within the university curricula. As students research universities, they should be aware of the multiple options available at each and keep in mind that many paths are open to them at the public ivies.

### Diane: a future veterinarian in the honors program at the University of Connecticut

Diane was a serious equestrienne who loved all animals and worked in a veterinary center in the summer. A quiet, shy girl who attended a small, academically demanding private school, Diane dreamed, like so many young people who love animals, of becoming a veterinarian.

Diane's writing and foreign-language skills were not particularly strong. She studied honors math and sciences, played varsity soccer, and worked for her honors-level grades. Though not an obvious candidate for a large, public university, Diane could find the specialization, honors curriculum, and preveterinary courses she wanted at a state school, if she could handle the size and social demands placed on her. We reviewed some of the smaller liberal arts colleges, as well as a few highly competitive larger private universities with her. Initially, her interest centered on Cornell, with its highly regarded animal sciences programs. She worked with a local vet, attended a two-week preveterinary program, and did well in her science classes in school. As she visited a number of schools, she began to lean toward the larger universities, including, besides Cornell, Tufts, the University of Vermont, and surprisingly to her, her own state's flagship school, the University of Connecticut.

In her senior year, Diane's interests were solidifying, as was her résumé. Her SAT I scores were over 1400, with a 760 math score, and she had SAT II scores of 710 on the Chemistry test and 720 on the Math IIC. She would be able to reach for Cornell, Tufts, and a few other highly competitive private colleges and universities and would be an excellent candidate for UConn's honors program. We talked with Diane and her parents about academic focus and workload at college, and the demanding nature of Cornell's program. We did not want Diane to be overwhelmed at college and lose the vital balance she had managed to preserve in her academic, social, and extracurricular life in high school. We discussed the need to prepare strongly for graduate school in the veterinary sciences. Excelling at the undergraduate level in the right curriculum would be her best preparation—not struggling, potentially, at a more competitive or prestigious college. Keeping this in mind, Diane chose to apply Early Decision to Cornell's agriculture school to show the university her real commitment to the program. She wrote,

> "Animals have always formed a large part of my life. Some of my first memories are of our bearded collie dragging me around while I held onto her tail. My family now has two dogs, a Dalmatian and a chocolate lab, and both sleep on my bed. I have always dreamed of becoming a veterinarian. I took the first steps toward this dream already. I have worked at the local veterinarian's office since I was thirteen. I would do mainly office work and observe the doctors whenever I had free time. Last summer, I did a program at Tufts Veterinary School called Adventures in Veterinary Medicine. . . . This two-week program made me realize how much I really wanted to be a veterinarian."

Diane also described her admiration for the vet with whom she had worked for four years.

> "Beyond the khaki shorts, brightly printed shirt, and wild tie, is a man who has saved the lives of thousands of dogs and cats around the country. He is a homeopathic veterinary oncologist. Homeopathy is the skill of treating the whole body as opposed to just the sick part. Oncology is the study of tumors. He has developed a method of treating and often curing cancer without the use of radiation or antibiotics. Instead, he uses such alternative approaches as injecting ozone into a tumor, building up the animal's immune system so it can fight the disease on its own, and doing a test to see the activity of the cancer-fighting enzymes. . . . My experience working for him not only confirmed my thoughts about becoming a veterinarian, but also increased my admiration for him. It was always amazing seeing an animal that had cancer come back after a month of treatment and look like a new animal. For these reasons he has influenced me and compelled me to follow him into the practice of veterinary medicine."

Diane had done everything right to show that her interest in animals was more than a childhood fancy. She had worked a long time with her local vet, had pursued a summer program to develop her understanding of the field, and had excelled in science and math classes and on standardized tests. She wrote about her experiences, about her goals for the future, and about her horseback riding competitions and work with animals. She scored two 4s and a 5 on the AP biology, chemistry, and calculus tests.

Diane did well in the admissions process overall. She was eventually accepted to Cornell, but for the January rather than the fall semester. She was also accepted at Colorado State University, UVM, Vanderbilt, and UConn's honors program. She was faced with a bit of a decision. Should she wait for January to head off to Cornell and in the meantime do something exciting, something educational? Should she go to Vanderbilt, a well-known private university? UConn's offer was tempting, and she examined the honors program closely. The cost would be next to nothing, and she would be catered to with advising, smaller classes, and research opportunities in the university's honors and preveterinary programs. If she came out on top of that program, we advised her, she would have many choices for graduate veterinary programs, including UConn's, in a few years. Considering the appropriateness of the public university's offerings for her, and the potential to be overly stressed at Cornell, Diane chose Connecticut, where she is thriving.

## The Top Athlete

The public ivies are NCAA Division I schools. Though they are in different conferences and subdivisions and vary in their level of athletic commitment, they all compete at the highest level of college sports. Some are perennially in the running for national titles in the high-profile sports football and basketball. Less visibly, they also tend to dominate swimming, track and field, baseball, soccer, and other sports, to which they make major commitments of resources, facilities, and recruiting. The top athlete says, "This is my niche." He or she is nationally competitive in a particular sport and wishes to continue to excel at the highest level in college. This student begins the athletic recruiting process (see Part Four and also our discussion in *Making It into a Top College*) early in the admissions process and has many direct contacts with coaches and athletic administrators. Often, especially in a major sport, he or she will commit quite early in the process, in February of senior year, to a first-choice school. Coaches at the public ivies generally have a great deal of discretion in recruiting their desired prospects, and they shepherd these students' applications through the admissions process, assessing them and obtaining assurances from the admissions office about which "slots" they will be able to fill and with whom.

Without going into the ethics, desirability, faults, legitimacy, or fairness of athletic recruiting, let us say that this is a process that is well entrenched in many public universities and benefits the top athlete in admissions and financial aid. This student is able to take advantage not only of preferred admission standards as a recruited athlete, but also of the benefits of an education at a public ivy and a competitive athletic program in his or her specialty.

Who gets recruited? Few high school athletes. One in a hundred? Perhaps. Most high school athletes, even most very good ones, will not play their sport at the intercollegiate athletic level, and even fewer will compete in Division I. How do you know if you are a top athlete? Usually, you have competed at least at the state level in your sport, and possibly at the regional, national, or even Olympic or Junior Olympic level. If you are a runner or a swimmer, it is pretty easy to get a sense of how your times compare to those of the athletes at any other university. If you are a linebacker on the football team or a goalie on the lacrosse team, immediate comparison becomes more difficult. You will be attending competitive summer camps and travel programs and meeting coaches during the summer before your senior year, if not before. If you are a tennis player, you will be climbing the tennis ladder in your state, competing in national tournaments and getting a ranking.

How will you know if you are being recruited? It is hard to describe, but you'll know it if and when you see it. The top athlete receives phone calls from coaches, and even living room visits (following NCAA requirements), which become more frequent in the fall and winter of senior year. Early on, the top athlete gets letters from colleges acknowledging his or her potential and encouraging an application. The wise scholar-athlete uses his or her sport to access a public ivy education and looks beyond the athletic program to make sure he or she is choosing the right environment overall. The top athlete at a public ivy may receive an athletic scholarship, which is often tied to continued athletic participation. The top athlete weighs the pros and cons of playing at a Division I public ivy versus Division I Ivy League versus Division III school, in terms of financial assistance, athletic goals, academic interests, and overall educational balance.

### Charlie: a recruited football player and scholar-athlete at the Division I level

Charlie was a top athlete. A serious football player at a medium-sized high school in the South, he maintained a B+ average in a traditional curriculum while working with the Campus Ministry, community service activities, basketball, and journalism. "I have a laid-back personality," Charlie said, "and I value family, honesty and good friendships. My interests now are in training weights and aerobics, playing football, fishing, and scuba diving. My aspiration now is to be a great student athlete."

Charlie was on the honor roll and in the top 25 percent of his class, but he had trouble with standardized tests. He was not receiving much specific academic support at school, but he had benefited from smaller to middle-sized classes throughout his lower school and secondary education. Charlie's parents noted on our questionnaire that "although academic reputation or institutional prestige is important to us, more important is his success in the institution; therefore, with his desire to play football in college being a factor, as well as his learning difficulty, we want to choose a college where he will realize his gifts, strengths, and potential as well as one that will work with him on his weaknesses, including his learning difficulty." Charlie and his family, like Peter, were fairly sure that their state university would accept him. Yet they wanted to explore out-of-state options, including public and private colleges and universities, to follow through with the athletic recruiting process and learn how different programs would suit Charlie's needs and interests.

We spent time talking with Charlie about the different styles of education in smaller private colleges and larger state schools, as well as the kind of learning support he would need and the type of environment in which he wanted to play football. In his junior year, Charlie was already getting signals that he would be a prospect at such powerhouses as Texas, Boston College, Notre Dame, and Florida State. He attended football camps at Notre Dame, Duke, Boston College, and Michigan State the summer before senior year, which helped him to place himself in the national pool of potential recruits and to see these four different campus environments. Charlie began to feel that he wanted to be close to home, in the South, and at a Division I school. His GPA rose to 3.8 as a senior, and a number of Ivy League schools became interested in him. It was becoming clear to Charlie and his parents that the workload and academic demands of Princeton or Dartmouth, Notre Dame or Duke, could potentially overwhelm him and jeopardize his involvement in sports. Charlie wanted more balance, some business courses, and good learning support. The key question was, were these things available at a Florida State or Texas?

Charlie and his parents did the legwork. They contacted the academic support programs at the several universities that were heavily recruiting Charlie and in which he was becoming more interested. They were all satisfied that the academic resources were more than sufficient to meet Charlie's needs. He could arrange for tutors, reduced course loads, and other support mechanisms to make sure he did not fall through the cracks. The family felt that a university's commitment of financial support to a top athlete would also help ensure that the university would not let Charlie down. After official visits to major football programs, including two private universities out of state, Charlie chose to sign his official letter of intent in February at a public university whose football team ranked near the top in the country.

## The Student with a Learning Disability or Special Needs

Charlie was clearly a top athlete, yet he also had some special academic needs. The student with a learning disability or other special need requires additional resources in his or her educational program to help promote long-term success. For Charlie, this meant tutors who would sit down with him to help him organize his lecture notes, plans for homework, exam schedule, and course planning. It included an extended time accommodation on exams if he needed it, and possibly a quiet room outside the big lecture hall in which to take the exam. He could use a laptop computer to take essay tests and use a spellcheck program to correct errors he made because of his dyslexia. As a student officially "identified" as learning disabled, and who had shared his professional learning evaluation with the university (and with his high school), Charlie would be guaranteed a trained learning specialist who would serve as his additional advisor at the university. This person could work with Charlie not only on specific course material, but also on reading, writing, organizational, and study skills and strategies overall. The advisor could help Charlie communicate with faculty to obtain his academic accommodations through telephone calls or letters to Charlie's professors at the beginning of each semester. If Charlie's parents had questions about his progress or concerns about information he was sending home, they would have a point person they could call to check in with on Charlie's classes, grades, and work.

Since the Americans with Disabilities Act was passed a decade ago, support for persons with recognized disabilities—learning, physical, or otherwise—has increased dramatically for students on college campuses. This includes, perhaps most strongly and surprisingly, large state schools. Students with learning disabilities or special needs are increasingly recognized as a particular category of applicant. If you are such a student, you should carefully consider your needs, your rights, and your expectations as to what type of college program will work best for you. It may come as a surprise, but some of the best academic support programs exist at the large state schools. Many learning-disabled students like Charlie believe smaller or middle-sized colleges to be better environments for them, because of their smaller classes, more intimate contact with faculty, easier systems, and so on, but it is precisely because of their size and resources that the public ivies and other big state schools can offer comprehensive learning support programs and facilities.

Students who have been identified as having special needs add a particular criterion to their college search. They want to find a place where they will be recognized and supported. This means asking the right questions and talking to the right people (see Part Four), as well as comparing the services offered at various environments. These students often submit supporting materials with their application, including an essay on their particular needs and the challenges they have overcome, a learning evaluation from a high school or independent learning or medical specialist, and a recommendation from a special needs tutor. "Special needs" is a broad category. It includes those with impaired hearing, who want to make sure they can have sign language translators in all their classes; students with impaired vision, who need access to Braille books, books on tape, and taped lectures; students with physical disabilities, who may need particular dormitory accommodations and accessible classroom buildings; and students with special dietary or other health needs. What we recommend to all of these students is that they bring their story forward and discuss the challenges they have dealt with and overcome, and why they feel they will be successful in the program to which they are applying. Remember: if you tell it like it is, and they don't want you, you wouldn't want to be there, anyway!

### Laura: a future elementary school teacher with a learning disability

Laura wanted to be a teacher. She knew that from the start. The question for her was, where she should go to college to take courses in child development and elementary education, as well as a balanced curriculum in the liberal arts? She wanted to graduate as a certified teacher with a major in one of the humanities. A very caring person, Laura taught gymnastics and Sunday school and was involved in concert choir, field hockey, and lacrosse at school. She was an A and B+ student in a moderately strong curriculum in a middle-sized public high school. She was qualified for untimed testing and a few other accommodations as a student with a learning disability. She was comfortable with her learning style and had developed excellent coping skills in her academic work. She carried a full set of core classes, including German, physics, and honors English. Her scores on the SAT I were approaching 1100. Laura was looking for an active, spirited, fun environment for college. She explained to us,

66Even though I live in a small town, I have found many different activities to do in my free time. I have participated in all kinds of sports activities, church activities, and also I have worked and played with the children of the community. Sports have always been an important part of my life. I have been playing all different kinds of sports, from individual to team sports. When I was growing up, I participated in soccer, baseball, softball, lacrosse, skating, field hockey, track, and tennis. Now that I am in high school, the number of sports I can play is limited. I had to narrow them down to one sport per season. I am also an active member of the Varsity Club. I think my personal qualities make it easy for me to work with children. I have been a Sunday school teacher for the past four years. I am loving it and learning a lot about how children think and react. Last summer, I was a gymnastic instructor for children in grades pre-K through eighth grade. I enjoy being around children of all ages. I have set many goals for myself with the start of the new year. They are: to continue my strong academic performance, complete another year of Sunday school teaching, and play hard on all my sport teams. I am thinking of interning at the hospital this year, which might help me decide if I want to study medicine or stay with education. I am also looking forward to continuing my college search. "

Laura took a broad approach to her college search. She liked very much a few of the smaller to middle-sized private colleges and universities, including Bucknell, Richmond, and Villanova. However, she began to be drawn to a few of the not-so-large public institutions, including James Madison. Education did indeed become Laura's main focus, and she also tried to find a "nicer, safer, prettier, socially warmer" campus environment where she could potentially continue her field hockey. This helped us to help her focus and expand her list. We suggested she look at a few of the Ohio schools, primarily Miami University, a public ivy, and also Denison and Ohio Wesleyan. Miami began to seem more and more attractive. After a visit, Laura felt it might have everything she wanted, including good learning resources to support her academic needs. They had a wealth of resources in elementary education, and she would be able to get the degree she wanted in the context of a larger liberal arts university. She applied to a broad list of colleges, including smaller schools like Gettysburg, Ohio Wesleyan, and Bucknell. We encouraged Laura to write a supplemental essay about her learning challenges. This gave a clear picture of her strengths and her motivation for going into teaching.

"In first grade, I was diagnosed with a learning disability, and was held back to repeat first grade. In my early years of elementary school, I was pulled out of my mainstream class to attend the reading and math center. I also went to a speech therapist. With hard work and dedication, I graduated from speech therapy in third grade. In middle school, I spent most of my time in mainstream classes, except for English, where I went to a resource center. In the resource center, we would read books at a slower pace and discuss them in more detail. After finishing sixth grade, I went to the junior high school, where I took all mainstream courses, but had a tutorial class. My tutorial teacher was there to explain or help me with my homework or class work. By eighth grade, my tutorial teacher was using my notes to make study guides for the other students. During the tutorial, I was usually working independently on my homework or going over something that I did not understand with my teacher. I feared that I would never be on my own and that I would always be in a 'special' class. This fear motivated me to work even harder in preparation for high school. In my freshman year of high school, I surprised myself by succeeding in mainstream classes, taking level two (intermediate level) classes instead of level one or modified classes. Freshman year was a big step for me. I was in a new school and was expected to take care of myself. I learned to meet with teachers for extra help if I did not understand something. I learned that I had to be proactive about seeing teachers if I had any concerns or problems, because they would not come to me. I also learned that the teachers wanted me to excel and were willing to help me at any cost. During my high school years, I have found out what my weaknesses and my strengths are. The knowledge of my abilities and intelligence has helped me to earn good grades and earn the honor roll status for the past three years. I have learned to use my strengths to improve my weaknesses and therefore overcome them. I am confident that I will do well in college, since I know how to use my strengths and can advocate for myself. With this knowledge, I feel the experience at Miami will help me continue to succeed at college and beyond. Miami offers challenging academic classes where, if needed, I can get personal attention from faculty who are eager to teach. Since the classes are small I will be able to excel and work to my fullest potential. In addition, the close-knit community will allow me to meet faculty and other students on campus, and this will make my college experience an outstanding one."

Clearly this was a student who knew herself, her talents, and her needs. Given her long history of coping with some learning difficulties, Laura could be that assertive, proactive person able to handle the workload and personal demands of a university like Miami. Laura was accepted at Miami, Ohio Wesleyan, Gettysburg, the University of Massachusetts at Amherst, American University, and Denison. After making visits that included overnight stays at Gettysburg and Miami, Laura was able to discern the differences between her two most desirable options. We had a long talk, and she went in the direction she had been leaning. She would attend Miami's education program and find the courses, spirit, community, and support she had been looking for.

## The Financially Needy Student

"Needy" is a relative term. Some students require a financial aid package combining loans, grants, and scholarships covering the total cost of their college education, public or private, and also take a part-time job. Other students have significant wealth in their family, and costs of any kind are of no concern to them in their college search process. Most families and students today fall somewhere in between these two poles. Most prefer to have at least some assistance in paying for their college education and to have that assistance be in the form of grants and scholarships, which do not need to be repaid, rather than loans, which do. We do not believe the cost of any college's tuition, public or private, should deter talented students from applying.

Usually, if the fit is right and the offer of admission is made, a suitable financial aid package can be assembled to make attendance possible. The student with some financial need, who is at least cost aware and does not necessarily expect significant need-based financial aid, should have a particular interest in public universities.

More and more families are asking us about building their college list to include schools that might cost less in the first place. Sometimes, such educational bargains come from private colleges and universities able to offer merit-based awards to top applicants, thereby *discounting* the sticker price of tuition, fees, and room and board. Often such bargains can be found at the public ivies, in and out of state. As you can see from the following box, the average cost of tuition and fees is significantly less at the public universities, for both state residents and those out of state, than at the private institutions.

Financially needy students see the advantage in securing a topflight education at a significantly reduced price. They weigh the educational benefits of private and public options with the savings for themselves and their family. The average student loan debt has skyrocketed in the past decade in the United States. As we noted in *Making It Into a Top College,* public university students graduate, on average, owing about $12,000, while private university graduates owe more than $14,000. Both figures are quite high, and they *exclude* privately held debt in the form of credit card or car loans, for example. These debts influence graduates' job choices and their ability to plan and provide for a family. Savvy students with financial need or the expectation that college costs will put an undue burden on them or their family encounter the public universities as a major relief. With the rising amounts of financial aid, savings, and merit scholarship programs available at the public institutions, these students can often secure excellent tuition packages throughout their college career.

## Average Annual Costs of Four-Year Colleges, 2000–01

| Cost | Public colleges (in state) | | Private colleges | |
| --- | --- | --- | --- | --- |
| | Resident | Commuter | Resident | Commuter |
| Tuition and fees | $3,510* | $3,510 | $16,332 | $16,332 |
| Books and supplies | $704 | $704 | $730 | $730 |
| Room and board | $4,960 | $2,444 | $6,209 | $2,495 |
| Transportation | $643 | $1,014 | $573 | $926 |
| Other | $1,521 | $1,557 | $1,102 | $1,221 |
| Total | $11,338 | $9,229 | $24,946 | $21,704 |

*The average surcharge added to the tuitions of nonstate residents at public four-year colleges was $9,020, making the average tuition and fees figure for out-of-state students $12,530.

*Source:* The College Board, "Tuition and Fees," www.chronicle.com/stats/tuition.htm; Andrew Brownstein, "Tuition Rises Faster Than Inflation," *Chronicle of Higher Education,* October 27, 2000, p. A50.

## The Social Butterfly

Some students are extroverts. The more people they are around, the more fulfilled and excited they feel. These social butterflies thrive on the size, social opportunities, and spirit of the public ivies. They feel that bigger is better when it comes to numbers of people, places to go, social outlets, and stadium size. They do not feel threatened by large lecture halls or high-rise dormitories. They would feel stifled in a rural campus of two thousand students and energized by a university that feels like its own small city. The comments of these students indicate that they realize they are "people people," outgoing, friendly, social, independent, and eager to meet new and different kinds of folks and try new things. These are some of the predispositions and a few of the skills to be cultivated that will help the public ivy student thrive.

### *Blaire: cheerleader and honors student with attentional difficulties*

We saw Blaire early on in her college search process. After noting her parents' and her own complaints about her poor organizational, copying, and standardized test skills and meeting with Blaire to talk about her schoolwork, we recommended that she undergo a learning evaluation to understand why she was earning As and Bs in a good curriculum at school but struggled with PSATs, exams, and the length of time it took her to complete her homework. We also talked about the kind of college experience Blaire wanted. She was a cheerleading captain, a people person, who wanted a bigger, social school with "a different kind of atmosphere." She saw herself working hard but having some balance, joining a sorority, and getting involved in campus leadership and activities. Blaire attended a large, suburban public high school. She was taking AP U.S. history and honors English, had a 3.5 GPA, and was signed up for AP English and precalculus as a senior, but she had scored a 42 on the PSAT verbal and a 38 on the math. She was in the top 15 percent of her class.

We talked with Blaire about Syracuse, where she was a legacy, Wisconsin, Colorado, the University of Miami, Tulane, Michigan, American University, Boston University, and Maryland. Blaire focused on her grades and obtained some tutoring for the SATs, and her parents set up an appointment for her with a clinical psychologist, who would assess her intellectual functioning, the differences between her classroom work and her performance on timed standardized tests, any current evidence of learning or attentional problems, possible school or testing accommodations for her, and the potential key components of a right educational match. The test results were a revelation for Blaire. She was clearly a bright, capable young woman, but she had a learning style strongly favoring verbal over nonverbal problem-solving skills and had difficulties with visual attention. She was diagnosed with attention deficit–hyperactivity disorder (ADHD) and was recommended for extended time on classroom and standardized tests, as well as on in-class writing assignments as necessary. Through the evaluation process, Blaire recognized her learning style, her strengths and weaknesses, and what she needed to be successful throughout college. She wrote a wonderful essay for her applications that showcased her determination, enthusiasm, self-knowledge, and confidence. Her essay and applications were accompanied by a summary letter from the learning evaluator, which detailed the findings for the learning support programs at the universities to which she applied. Here is the essay Blaire wrote to her college choices:

> ❝Wile E. Coyote, a fictional cartoon character who never caught the elusive roadrunner but kept trying despite all of his failed attempts could easily be compared to me, given many of the obstacles I have had to face as a child, a friend, a daughter, and now as a student. His persistence can compare to mine and can serve as a good thesis statement for my life thus far. Although I am the captain of outstanding football and basketball cheerleading squads, and cheer my heart out for teammates, for friends, and at sports events, unfortunately at times I find it difficult to cheer for myself. I have been in school for a period of nearly thirteen years, and although I have had the urge many times, I have never once said 'I quit.' My academic life has never been easy, and now with the latest findings of my ADHD, it seems to have gotten more challenging. I have always been at the top of my class, striving to reach all my goals and to compete in the same league as my friends in honors classes and Advanced Placement courses. I have never received less than a B in any of them, thanks to all my hard work and dedication. I have gone through all my schooling with not an ounce of help from resource teachers. I have taken it upon myself to stay after school with teachers and I have stayed up endless hours of the night perfecting my term papers and studying for immeasurable numbers of tests. At times I feel as if I have to quit, but I know if I did I would be selling myself short. Despite my learning difficulties, I have managed to succeed in school and surpass many expectations. My learning style allows me to explore many different aspects of education, where many of my peers are unable to succeed. I find many positives in learning about my ADHD because it has given me a reason to understand and delve into all the different learning styles, and it showed me that learning in a new way can be interesting as well as fun. Through my schooling, I have received superb grades, in part because of my willingness to ask for help. I never hesitated to ask a teacher for his opinion as well as his expertise. By asking for help, I have improved my schoolwork and succeeded through many projects with which I had struggled at the beginning. I find that a great accomplishment, because it shows how dedicated I am to my schoolwork, and how nothing can hold me back from reaching my goals. During my four years in high school, I have enjoyed taking many classes. I have a great love for English and writing and the field of retail. I have taken a wonderful course by the name of Design and Publication that has enabled me to help design and learn all about the publishing of a yearbook. I was given the opportunity to be an editor of the Student Life section of our book, which has been awarded first and second place by the Columbia Press Association for a number of years. In college, I would love to focus on the field of advertising and retail marketing.
>
> I have great confidence that I will be able to succeed, and will strive to do my best in the four years that I will be attending college. I am willing to take the challenges of

college life and academics here on with a smile and work very hard to achieve my goals in whichever major I choose. The idea of college life is exciting for me, knowing that this big transition will be part of my life forever. I am looking forward to meeting many new people and making friendships that will last a lifetime. Of course, in college, I'll be pursuing my courses, and not the roadrunner."

Blaire focused on the bigger universities—Wisconsin, Syracuse, Colorado, Maryland, and Arizona—as major interests. She was excited to learn that these universities had some of the best academic learning support programs in the country. Precisely because they were so big, they had the resources to devote to a comprehensive learning program, with highly developed facilities, instructors, tutors, classes, and resources. She would be in some big lecture classes at these schools, but she would have access to personalized learning support, a coordinator who would help her outline her course choices and assignments regularly, a quiet place to take her exams, sophisticated technology to help her with her writing and communications skills, and so forth. Wisconsin gradually became Blaire's first choice, especially after she visited the campus. She was excited about the spirit and community of Madison, the diversity of course offerings in her areas of interest, and the attention she felt she was getting through the admissions process. In fact, the representatives of the learning support program made several personal calls to Blaire's learning evaluator to ask for additional information, clarify key points, and aid in their recommendation of Blaire to the admissions committee. Blaire was accepted at Wisconsin, Syracuse, Miami, Arizona, and Indiana, and she chose Wisconsin. She felt rewarded, validated, and overjoyed.

## The Academic Specialist

As we mentioned earlier, our focus in this book is on the liberal arts curriculum at these major research universities. One type of student who often pursues the public university track is the academic specialist. We often talk to such students about the public ivies as a third option, something between a classic liberal arts college and a technical school, conservatory, or business college, all of which can stand on their own and provide in their own way a more limited set of options. At a liberal arts college, the engineering specialist may feel he or she has too few science and technical courses and too many requirements in foreign language, English, and history. At a music conservatory, the cellist may feel he or she is losing out on the educational enrichment and excitement of studying philosophy or physics. At a business college, the future financier may find that he or she misses the history and art that were once so enjoyable and has trouble maintaining the pragmatic approach emphasized in the business curriculum and world. Such academic specialists see the public ivies as places where they can have the best of both worlds. They can begin to specialize but continue to gain exposure to other areas of interest. The business student at Michigan's college of business, since it is housed within a larger university, is well versed in European history as well as in finance, management, and accounting. Our cellist at Indiana's music school learns music theory, performs with major talent, reads Kant, and researches quantum theory. The mechanical engineer at UCLA can avoid some humanities requirements but will have access to those that are most appealing. He or she will also have all the science and math courses one could want and the technical training to go on to graduate study or a career in engineering.

Some conservatories, business schools, and liberal arts colleges have instituted interesting cooperative agreements that allow students to pursue the liberal arts as well as some design, arts, or music courses at two different institutions simultaneously. These are 3/2 programs in which students study the liberal arts at a liberal arts college and then go on to study engineering, for example, at a university, or exchange opportunities in order to broaden their offerings. They are, in many ways, emulating the public ivies. At our bigger research universities, academic specialists may focus and expand, concentrate and diverge. If they find that their original specialization is no longer of interest, they may transfer *within* the same university to another school or program quite easily, as long as they are in good academic standing. Academic specialists look for a niche, be it music, art and design, science, or business, to exploit their talents and pursue their passions.

### Tyler: sailor and computer scientist

Tyler was an experienced sailing instructor with strong grades and test scores, and a serious interest in computer science. "I think my greatest asset is my mind," he said to us. "I take pride in being able to use logic properly and reason well. This is why I enjoy mathematics and science, especially physics, and computers." Tyler was looking for an academically demanding university that was large enough to offer a wide range of majors. His father had attended a large state university, and we talked about the differences between that type of environment and some of the technical schools to which Tyler had been attracted early on. Tyler began exploring engineering as an interest but decided he wanted to pursue computer science in a liberal arts program rather than engineering in a tech school or an engineering college within a university. This way, he could more easily continue to study history and economics, two other serious interests. He would also have access to all the scientific and technical resources available at a major research university. Tyler ended up reaching for a few ivies, some other competitive private universities, and some strong public universities. Among a number of admissions, Tyler was torn between Tufts and the University of Texas. He visited UT, looking into their honors program and Plan II program (which creates a small liberal arts college environment within the university) as well as their substantial computer science resources. He loved the university, but seemed surprised that he was finding this big, out-of-state public university preferable to a nearby, well-regarded private school that many students from his town attended and had a good sailing program. It became clearer and clearer to him from our discussions that UT had everything he was looking for, and he went on to become a Longhorn in the fall.

*Doug: an independent student with a future in the music business*

"I would like to grow up with a family living in an urban area working in the music industry," Doug explained to us. "I grew up in Greenwich Village in New York City. I enjoyed it thoroughly. I still go into the city with friends on a regular basis. I enjoy the independence. That's one major reason I am looking forward to college." Doug saw himself in a larger, diverse college environment where he could meet lots of people, be independent, and pursue music, business, and other academic interests. Yet he also wanted a campus environment. He was a highly verbal person, earned honors at school, pursued independent studies in music, and had a band with friends. We suggested that he consider, among other larger schools, the Universities of Wisconsin and Colorado, both of which fit his interests closely. Doug wrote about growing up with a passion for music, starting his own band, and interning with a major concert promoter.

> ❝I expect that my academic career will be balanced between liberal arts and business courses. I will elect to take the courses that interest me, the professors who inspire, and the work that will guide me into a career in the music industry. I intend to explore opportunities to get involved in the local music business, on or off campus. It may be premature to describe the 'special' talents of any seventeen year old, yet I feel my experience as a 'city kid' turned 'country kid' has given me a social facility in most settings. I have traveled modestly in Europe and more extensively in America and feel genuinely at ease socially and intellectually with diverse people and in divergent settings.❞

Doug was accepted by Wisconsin and Colorado through their rolling admissions policies, and he chose to attend Wisconsin.

## STRATEGIES FOR GOING PUBLIC

As you might guess, we do not see the public ivies as colleges of last resort, always the second choice, or simply strategic fallbacks or also-rans. We encourage students to consider them top universities and potential first choices. In addition, they may complement a student's overall college list by filling certain gaps and addressing specific interests.

Strategies for going public include building a broad and appropriate college list, as well as those intended to help students secure admission to a public ivy. For a more complete discussion of admissions to top colleges, see our book *Making It Into a Top College*. Here, we focus on fitting the public ivies into the context of your overall college admissions process and applying to the public universities in the best way possible. We talk about balancing your college list, using the rolling admissions process, achieving in-state residency, exploring your alumni legacy status, gaining advanced standing, lowering costs, staging your education, building a foundation, and pursuing distance education, among other strategies.

## Balancing Your College List

You're unsure exactly what type of college you want. You're trying for some of the top private colleges but feel that after a certain point, a public university is more worth your while. Or you have some financial need and want to use a combination of strategies to ensure that you are accepted to a school you can afford. Or you want to stay close to home, and along with several private colleges, a good choice for you is your state university. Or you're an athlete but unsure at what level you want or will be able to compete at college. Or you want to add some safety and security to your college list but are not very excited about private colleges to which you know you will be admitted, while you are almost sure you will be accepted to some public universities that seem very exciting.

For these reasons and many others, you decide to balance your college list. That means integrating one or more of the public universities into the context of your overall approach to colleges. You may visit and apply to some small, medium, and large schools, including public and private options, and then plan to visit and seriously consider your most exciting choices in April, before committing to one of them before the May 1 deadline. You may expect some financial aid offers from a few private colleges, but make sure you have an affordable public university at hand. You may reach for Division I play, but make sure you can compete at a smaller Division III college. In balancing your college list, you are taking advantage of the diversity in American higher education. You are trying to open some doors to different types of colleges. You will decide later which door you will step through next year. Because of their more quantitative approach to the admissions process, and the preference they give to in-state students, the odds in getting accepted to public universities are often more known quantities than private institutions. You may be more sure about getting in and, once you are accepted, about the cost and options available.

## Admissions: Following the Numbers

Let's look at the University of California's admissions requirements. It is worth discussing their admissions requirements at length for several reasons. First, you can see the standards you must meet to be eligible for the most selective public universities. If you meet the criteria listed here, you will almost certainly qualify for, but will not be guaranteed admission to, all of the public ivies. Second, you will begin to understand the very specific requirements and formulas the large public universities use and how they distinguish between in-state and out-of-state applicants. Third, you see how one university system is grappling with the effects of challenges to affirmative action, by guaranteeing admission to the top performers in each local high school. Fourth, you get a prize if you go to the university's website, find the specific formula in question, and figure out your scores on the eligibility index, whether or not you have fulfilled your academic course requirements, and how many points you have earned on the course requirements and GPA tables. You will encounter similar requirements and explanations in applying to most of the public ivies and should begin to learn how to read through them and find your place in the charts. Your counselor at school, your parents, and the university's admissions office may help you to do so.

To apply to the University of California, first you must determine whether you are applying as a freshman or as a transfer student. If you have graduated from high school and have not enrolled in another college or university, you are a freshman applicant. Taking a summer course right after high school is acceptable for freshman applicants, but taking fall, winter, or spring courses at another institution for college credit moves you into the transfer admission process. Next, you will be guided down the path of determining your state of residency and thus what eligibility you will have for admission to the university and what criteria you will have to meet. As a California resident, you may follow the majority of applicants by becoming eligible "in the statewide context," satisfying certain academic subject, scholarship, and examination requirements. You may be eligible for admission in a local context, if you graduated in the top 4 percent of your high school class. You must still fulfill course requirements, and this does not guarantee you admission to the campus of your choice in the University of California system. You may also obtain eligibility to the university by examination alone, if you score a 31 or higher on the ACT or 1400 on the SAT I, plus a total score of 1760 or higher on three SAT IIs, with at least a 530 on each test. Remember: being eligible in one of these ways does not guarantee you admission to the university or to the particular campus in which you are most interested.

Subject, scholarship, and examination requirements at the University of California are complex. You will be required to complete a certain minimum number of courses in a broad range of academic and nonacademic subjects: history/social science (two years required, including some form of U.S. and world history), English (four years required), mathematics (three years required; four years recommended), laboratory science (two years required; three recommended), foreign language (two years of language other than English required; three recommended), and college preparatory electives (two years required). The university sets a minimum GPA you must achieve (2.8), using a complex formula based on the course area and level. Nonresident applicants to the University of California may be eligible in a statewide context or by examination alone. They must achieve a 3.4 GPA using the university's course descriptions and formula and need a score of 31 on the ACT, a score of 1400 on the SAT I, and a total score of 1850 on the three SAT IIs.

From this example of one public ivy's admissions requirements it should be clear to you that *numbers are important.* A special talent might help you in admissions, but affirmative action, that is, consideration based on racial/ethnic status, has been threatened in many states and may not help applicants very much. The large majority of applicants, resident and nonresident alike, must fulfill baselines, minimum standards, and curricular and numeric eligibility requirements to be considered for admission. Essays and supplementary materials? The large universities may never get to them if you do not meet the minimums set out through tables, formulas, and averages. Are there exceptions to the rule? Sure there are, just as some private colleges and universities also use statistical methods, computers, formulas, and baselines in some cases to accomplish their admissions work. The rule of thumb, though, is that to help yourself gain admission to the public ivies, you need to fulfill clearly all necessary requirements and be able to "do it by the numbers." Depending on your individual strengths and on the general pattern of test taking in your area, you may choose either the ACT or SAT testing program, or may try both, to help you show your skills on a standardized test. You will note in some of the materials quoted from other public ivies in this book, that many of these universities, Virginia and North Carolina for example, do what they can to go beyond the numbers and look for those sparks of academic motivation and personal talent that can help them select the most interesting and qualified students. The president of the University of California system even announced recently that he would like to consider dropping the SAT I as an admissions component for the University of California. But for now, you will do best to make yourself eligible according to all these quantitative and qualitative measures.

---

## UNIVERSITY OF CALIFORNIA, BERKELEY, ADMISSIONS STATISTICS AND SELECTION CRITERIA: PROFILE OF THE FRESHMAN CLASS ENTERING IN FALL 1999

The following are general statistics for one recent entering class at Berkeley for all programs except engineering. For fall 2001, some procedures have changed, but this profile gives you a sense of the basic requirements for admission to this most competitive public ivy. Berkeley evaluates a student's GPA in a set of core classes and uses that for its admission purposes. Students also need to consider submitting three SAT II Subject Tests. According to the university, the overall totals in this table include any applicants with a GPA or SAT composite score that is out of the ranges listed or unavailable.

Here is what the university says, in part, about admission selection:

All achievement will be considered in the context of the opportunities the applicant has had and the ways in which he or she has responded to them. Following a complete review of each application, approximately 50 percent of students will be selected on the basis of academic performance, including high school GPA (not capped at 4.0), the depth and breadth of academic preparation, and scores on required standardized tests. The remaining percentage of freshmen will be selected on the basis of academic and personal achievement, as assessed through a comprehensive review of all information provided on the application, including academic performance as described above plus the following: extracurricular accomplishment, personal qualities such as leadership or motivation, California residency, and likely contribution to the intellectual and cultural vitality of the campus. Demonstrated interest in the major may be considered in the selection of students for professional schools and colleges.

*(continued)*

| GPA | SAT COMPOSITE | | | | | |
| --- | --- | --- | --- | --- | --- | --- |
| | 490–790 | 800–990 | 1000–1190 | 1200–1390 | 1400–1600 | Overall |
| **2.82–2.99** | | | | | | |
| No. of applicants/ no. admitted | | | 149/10 | 115/4 | 16/0 | 280/14 |
| Percentage of applicants | | | 6.7% | 3.5% | 6.7% | 5.0% |
| **3.00–3.29** | | | | | | |
| No. of applicants/ no. admitted | 61/6 | 288/23 | 831/65 | 730/48 | 138/9 | 2,048/151 |
| Percentage of applicants | 9.8% | 8.0% | 7.8% | 6.6% | 6.5% | 7.4% |
| **3.30–3.59** | | | | | | |
| No. of applicants/ no. admitted | 65/11 | 408/33 | 1,336/94 | 1,620/116 | 423/45 | 3,852/299 |
| Percentage of applicants | 16.9% | 8.1% | 7.0% | 7.2% | 10.6% | 7.8% |
| **3.60–3.89** | | | | | | |
| No. of applicants/ no. admitted | 52/4 | 421/57 | 1,726/175 | 3,025/414 | 830/259 | 6,054/909 |
| Percentage of applicants | 7.7% | 13.5% | 10.1% | 13.7% | 31.2% | 15.0% |
| **3.90–3.99** | | | | | | |
| No. of applicants/ no. admitted | 5/1 | 59/14 | 353/48 | 798/181 | 198/107 | 1,413/351 |
| Percentage of applicants | 20.0% | 23.7% | 13.6% | 22.7% | 54.0% | 24.8% |
| **4.00** | | | | | | |
| No. of applicants/ no. admitted | 21/5 | 210/59 | 1,673/506 | 4,775/2,100 | 3,179/2,405 | 9,858/5,075 |
| Percentage of applicants | 23.8% | 28.1% | 30.2% | 44.0% | 75.7% | 51.5% |
| **Overall** | | | | | | |
| No. of applicants/ no. admitted | 204/27 | 1,386/186 | 6,068/898 | 11,063/2,863 | 4,784/2,825 | 25,796/7,072 |
| Percentage of applicants | 13.2% | 13.4% | 14.8% | 25.9% | 59.1% | 27.4% |

*Source:* University of California, Berkeley, website, www.berkeley.edu.

## The Rolling Safety

One major difference between public and private universities' admissions schedules is that many public universities consider applications on a rolling basis. That is, they begin to accept applications after a certain date, normally in late August or September in the year before the fall an applicant would enter the university. After that time, the university reads and decides on applications as they come in, filling available spots and communicating their decision to the applicant usually in 6 to 15 weeks. Though some public universities have very late final deadlines for all applications, sometimes going into the summer just before entrance, others cut off admissions applications earlier in the process. The University of California system, for example, uses a common application due by November 30 the year prior to entrance. North Carolina emulates the private universities by having a deadline of January 15.

Many of the public universities do not offer any type of "regular," "early decision," or "early action" admission plans, because they consider the rolling admissions strategy more efficient and effective for them and prospective applicants. Others, like North Carolina and Virginia, offer an Early Decision option for applicants who wish to make a commitment to a first-choice school and to hear back from the school early in the process. Students should be very careful when considering the Early Decision options at the public ivies. Schools like UVA and UNC are highly selective in the admissions offers they tender in the ED process. This applicant group is usually very strong and fairly small, and includes many recruited athletes, legacies, and other students with special status. Applicants who are deferred from ED will find that they are not given first consideration again in the spring. Rather, they likely will be at the back of the pack, reviewed only after many other strong applications for regular admission have been examined and admitted. It is difficult in these big admission pools to make it out of that deferred applicant pool.

Given that most of the public ivies use some form of rolling admissions, with varying deadlines, many applicants prepare their applications early in the fall, send them in for consideration, and hear back from the schools even before they need to submit other regular-decision applications to private colleges and universities. Some students submit this application to a public university that is their serious first-choice school. Other students are looking for a *rolling safety.* They may be only moderately interested in the public university, but they have balanced their list and have good expectations of admission. If they hear back positively from the school, they have one acceptance in their pocket as they go through their senior year of high school. They still do not need to commit to the university until May 1, can apply to other colleges for regular or Early Decision action, and can even trim their overall list according to how interested they are in the public university that has accepted them. Conversely, if the applicant is rejected, he or she can reassess the overall college list, add another safety or two, and consider other ways to improve his or her applications and record through the year.

One of the most important factors associated with rolling admissions is this: apply early in the fall or as soon as you can put your best foot forward. If you are strongly prepared in September, have great grades and SAT/ACT scores from junior year, and have spent time in August working on your applications, then get your rolling admissions applications in as soon as the universities allow. This is especially true for out-of-state applicants, because the publics limit the number of nonresidents they admit and enroll and thus are careful about giving too many acceptances away to out-of-state applicants over the course of the year. Do not be lured into putting these rolling admission applications on the back burner based on a final deadline of February, March, April, or later. You not only want to hear back earlier on your admissions decision so you have time to react if you are rejected, or celebrate and relax if you are accepted, but you also want to be among the first group of applicants, who are seen as more motivated, organized, and interested.

We want to qualify this advice if you are a student who needs to improve your grades, test scores, applications, or all of the above. If you need to bring up your SAT scores and are taking the October or November SAT, wait to submit your application until those scores will be available. You want to make sure that your application will not be reviewed and summarily rejected on the basis of last year's test scores. If you need the whole semester to show a strong set of grades in a good curriculum, by all means submit your application in January if the university allows this. Your improved GPA will balance out an application submitted in the middle or end of the process. Applications? It is true that some of the public universities do not require any essays or recommendation letters. Others accept these materials but put little weight on them. Nevertheless, you, the prepared and motivated applicant, should desire to submit all the materials that are required, recommended, or accepted, and should do so in a way that is organized, thoughtful, and helpful to the admissions offices. If it takes you a little more time to make sure you have fulfilled all the necessary requirements for eligibility and admission, take your time, but do not procrastinate too long.

## Achieving In-State Residency and Declaring Independence

In-state residency is the Holy Grail of public university admissions and tuition. An in-state resident must meet less stringent admissions criteria and pays significantly lower tuition costs. In recent years, public universities have made it increasingly difficult for nonresident (out-of-state) students to gain resident status. If you are applying from another state as a first-year student, you will almost certainly be considered in the nonresident applicant pool. Exceptions to this rule are those with legacy status (see next section) and those applying from states with interstate compact or cooperative agreements with neighboring or regional states. For example, through the New England Regional Student Program, a resident of one New England state may study at reduced tuition at a university in another New England state to take advantage of programs that may not be offered at his or her own state university. The Western Interstate Commission for Higher Education offers a Western Undergraduate Exchange program that offers similar opportunities to residents of 15 different western states. In considering your own state schools, you should also do research to find out if cooperative agreements exist that may allow you preferred opportunities at other public universities.

In general, most students who go out of state to a public ivy or other state university find themselves treated as a nonresident for admissions and tuition purposes. It is then a challenge to obtain residency either before an application for admission or at some point after entrance to secure the lower in-state tuition. States have tried to make it more difficult for nonresidents to do this. Since the public universities are chartered for the benefit of in-state residents, and state taxpayers prefer to support their own sons and daughters, the universities are structured to use the higher tuition dollars of nonresidents to subsidize the lower tuitions and costs of residents and the overall budget and programs of the institution. Given that there is a cap every year on how many nonresidents the university may admit, administration officials are loath to give up four or more years of nonresident tuition on which they have counted.

Nonresidents have two choices. First, they can move to a state, alone or with their family, before applying for admission. They can then try to secure residency, which generally takes at least one full year—less if parents have moved to the state with them. Having residency before admission gives applicants the benefit of in-state admission, not just tuition status. This tactic is used mostly by families in which a parent must move for employment or other reasons. Most students and families would not move to a state just in the hopes of gaining admission to its flag-ship university. In some cases, families have moved out of a state but maintain a residence there. Students in these circumstances may find that they are treated as residents. They should inquire with the university to determine this and, like others pursuing residency status, will have to fill out an application to *apply for residency*, certifying that they meet the requirements for in-state status.

---

### THE UNIVERSITY OF NORTH CAROLINA AT CHAPEL HILL'S REQUIREMENTS FOR RESIDENCY

UNC offers the following guidelines in its admissions literature for applicants considering in-state residency, making it clear, as most public universities do, that they seek to determine that a student is applying for residency because of a serious intent to make North Carolina a permanent home, rather than a temporary student experience.

**Qualifications**

Under North Carolina law, to qualify for in-state tuition for a given term you must prove: that you established your domicile in North Carolina twelve months before the beginning of that term (first day of classes), and that you have maintained that domicile for at least twelve continuous months.

**Proof**

To prove that you established a bona fide domicile in North Carolina, you must prove: that you were physically present in the state, with the intent to make North Carolina a permanent home indefinitely, and that you were not in North Carolina solely to attend college.

*(continued)*

### Determination of Intent

Because it is difficult to determine directly someone's intention to make North Carolina their home, residency classifiers must evaluate actions taken that may indicate this 'domiciliary intent.' The Manual lists the following considerations which may be significant in determining this intent:

Do you live in your parents' home?

Where are/were you employed?

Where did you register to vote?

Where did you vote?

Where have you served on jury duty?

What are your sources of financial support?

Where have you registered/licensed a car?

Where did you get your last driver's license?

Where do you own a home or other real estate?

Where do you keep your personal property?

Where do you list personal property for taxation?

Where did you file state income tax returns?

Where do you spend your vacation time?

Where did you last attend high school?

Where did you live before enrolling in an institution of higher education?

Where do you maintain memberships in professional associations, unions, and similar organizations?

### Preponderance of Evidence

Residency classifiers weigh all the evidence furnished in an application for residence status. The preponderance (or greater weight) of the evidence must support the establishment of North Carolina domicile twelve months before the beginning of the academic term (first day of classes) for which classification is requested. If the evidence shows a cluster of significant events occurring at about the same time (within the same week, for example), the classifier will start counting from that point to determine if the twelve month requirement has been met. If instead the evidence has gradually accumulated over time, the classifier must decide at what point a preponderance of the evidence shows intent to establish North Carolina domicile, and that is the date on which the clock will begin. If this date is after the first day of classes for the term specified on the application, the classifier will be unable to render an in-state decision for the term in question. 99

*Source:* University of North Carolina at Chapel Hill website, www.unc.edu.

A nonresident's second choice is more typical and involves applying for residency while he or she is attending a university, after having moved into the state as a student. Again, it usually takes a year for students to gain residency. They usually have to show the college that they have had a driver's license, a voter registration card, a mortgage or lease, and so on, for that year, to prove their residency. For *dependent* students, those whom their parents still claim as dependents for tax purposes, it is more difficult to gain residency. These students may choose to declare independence from their parents, file their own taxes, and make sure their parents no longer claim them as dependent on their own taxes. There are books on the market today outlining just how students can go about securing residency status, and each state university has specific rules on how undergraduates can apply for and gain residency. Surprisingly, many students do not consider residency applications, even though they may live in the state where they are attending school for five years, from the age of 18 to 23, working several jobs, part-time during the academic year and full-time in the summer, voting in state elections, obtaining a driver's license and insurance, and so forth. It behooves these students to ask the university's residency officer what they need to do to gain official residency status. Of course, they should talk with their parents about the financial, tax, or legal implications of making this declaration.

Occasionally, students obtain admission to the university of their choice as nonresidents and then move into the state to which they are going while deferring admission for a year. They immediately get a job, a lease on a house, a driver's license, a voter's card, and so forth, and then apply for residency to take effect before their first year's tuition bill. Not a bad strategy for getting settled, reducing costs, and planning ahead.

## Legacy Status

Being a legacy at a public university can boost your chance for admission, just as it can when you apply to a private institution. Though universities differ in their requirements for and treatment of children of their alumni, in general the public universities treat students with legacy status the same way they treat state residents. This is most true for children of graduates of the undergraduate liberal arts colleges at the universities who are applying to the same college, but it also pertains to children of alumni of law, business, medical, and other graduate programs. If you or one of your parents graduated as an undergraduate or graduate student from a public university of potential interest for admissions, your first call should be to the undergraduate admissions office there. You should ask to speak to the counselor responsible for alumni or legacy admissions, and explain your circumstances. You might find that the advantage you gain in admissions to this particular school makes it worthwhile to add it to your overall college list as a safety or a desirable target school, even if you were not at first looking at public universities.

## Leveraging Your Strengths and Playing the Numbers

As we have seen, the requirements for admission to a public ivy are demanding and highly quantitative in nature, especially when compared to the admissions process at small, private, liberal arts colleges. The core characteristics of all strong applicants are the same: a good curriculum, strong and consistent performance throughout high school, and strong SAT/ACT scores. Successful commitment to a major extracurricular passion can also be important. We have found that many parents and students are surprised by a number of discoveries as they begin the public universities admissions process. First, admissions interviews are even rarer than at the private institutions. In fact, they are mostly nonexistent. Furthermore, recommendation letters from teachers and student application essays may not be required or encouraged. Supplementary materials—an art portfolio or writing samples, for example—may be strongly discouraged, except for the special-interest schools within the university. All the qualitative aspects of the admissions process—personal contact, narrative writing, perspectives from people who know you well, and so forth—are either not present or are weighted significantly less than are the quantitative factors in the public university admission process.

How, then, do you leverage your strengths in the process?

It is essential that you document your academic achievements in a quantitative way. This means that you need to do well on the SAT I and, for some public ivies, three SAT II Subject Tests, including the English Writing test and possibly the Math IC or IIC test, or the ACT. Your scores on one of these tests, or a combination of tests, in the case of the SAT I and II, are the primary standardized way that the admissions office compares you to other applicants around the country. These tests are more important at the state schools than at the private ones. You will want to prepare early for the standardized tests and focus on making sure that they are not a liability for you. If you are a strong student in multiple subjects, you want to take as many SAT II Subject Tests as appropriate for your curriculum. For example, you want to make sure to take the chemistry SAT II at the end of 10th or 11th grade, if you are a good science student wrapping up that course. (For more on making standardized tests work for you, see our discussion of admissions strategies in *Making It Into a Top College*.) In addition to SAT or ACT preparation and performance, you should focus on your GPA and your class rank, if this is calculated at your high school. Again, these numeric measures will be used in a formulaic way to chart your application strength compared to other students.

This brings us to the difficult and controversial subject of weighted grades and honors and AP courses. Unfortunately, if your school does not weight your grades, which means they do not raise a grade in an honors or AP class to account for the increased difficulty of that curriculum, you may be hurt in the public university admissions process. We generally tell students to challenge themselves in the most rigorous curriculum appropriate to their interests and abilities. Colleges, public and private, like to see students pushing their limits, pursuing their intellectual passions, and proving themselves at an advanced level of course work. Translating the increased difficulty of honors or AP grades into a standardized number is not so easy. If your school does not weight its grades, your potentially lower GPA in a higher level curriculum may not be as impressive to some public universities as the higher GPA of your fellow student who has taken only regular classes. This situation is an unfortunate artifact of the quantitative nature of public university admissions combined with the admirable efforts of many high schools to decrease student competition, grade inflation, and confusing GPAs by avoiding weighted grades and student rankings within their class.

As Berkeley's admissions requirements and procedures indicate, some public ivies attempt to rework a student's GPA and curriculum to take into account performance in higher level classes in grades 10 through 12. They add weight to a student's GPA for honors-level or AP classes, and determine GPA based on a preference for tougher core curriculum classes, for example, in English, in such traditional lab sciences as physics, chemistry, and biology, in U.S. history, and in advanced mathematics. Much can be lost in translation, and you must consider the possibility that you may lower your GPA too far when taking a much tougher curriculum. This is unfortunate, because of the learning experience you might be missing in more challenging courses, and because competition is still rife in schools without weighted grades or ranking. Our overall guideline for strong students considering top public universities remains the same: play to your strengths and push yourself in the advanced courses where your interests lie. If you are considering some particular public universities in your state or in other states, you should carefully examine their admissions requirements and procedures. Does the university give you credit for advanced courses in the admissions process, or do they simply look at the GPA as communicated to them by your high school? Do they look at class rank? Is there guaranteed admission for students who rank at a top percentage of their local high school as long as they meet a particular set of requirements? If so, how does your high school determine class rank for the purposes of public university admissions? Are "nonacademic" classes and your ninth-grade year included in your GPA and rank? Are your grades weighted? Will getting a B– in that AP biology class negatively affect your GPA and class rank in such a way as to suggest you should get an A in regular biology? (Of course, it is best to get the A in the AP class . . . )

We are asked these questions every day by individual students, and there is no blanket recommendation or answer we can give. You must determine your decision in consultation with your parents, your school advisor, and public university admissions offices. The answers you will find depend on your own talents and goals for college admissions. Remember, the focus is on building your strong core curriculum, excelling on standardized tests, and keeping an eye on your GPA, rank, and weighting, knowing how they are read by the universities in which you are most interested.

Leveraging your strengths means playing to your talents and abilities and learning style. If you are a competitive athlete, get in touch with the coaches at the universities you're interested in. If you are a writer, contact the English Department to ask about special programs or scholarships available to you. If you are considering an honors program, what courses should you be sure to take and what essays should you write? If you have a learning disability, you should contact the learning support programs at the universities to ask about special application procedures and requirements. Applying through such a program can ensure that you are not penalized for poor performance on standardized tests, for example, if that can be understood in the context of your learning profile. Finally, if you're interested in a special academic program, be it architecture, business, engineering, or education, you should research available admissions opportunities in those fields. It may be that your preparation and experience will give you a leg up if you apply to one of those schools instead of the college of arts and sciences.

## Course Credits and Advanced Standing

One happy result of strong performance in an advanced high school curriculum and on SAT II and AP tests is the potential for advanced standing and course credits at college. Such well-prepared students may move immediately beyond larger introductory classes, first-year English, social science, history, science, and foreign language requirements and other demands placed on the average student. They may gain entry to preferred freshmen seminars, honors and selected scholar programs, and sophomore- or even junior-level courses. With enough credits, advanced students may even enter the university with sophomore-level standing and the ability to graduate in less than four years. For those interested in gaining entry into business, communications, education, or other specialized undergraduate schools, advanced standing may allow them to apply or transfer to these schools from the liberal arts program more quickly, since many of these undergraduate schools or programs select their students to enter in their junior year.

Your first order of business is to take the advanced courses you will do well in through high school, sit for the SAT II Subject Tests and AP tests, as well as the SAT I or ACT, for which you have prepared, and, yes, take the SAT II and AP tests at the end of your *senior* year as well. Most students who enter top universities take their most advanced courses in their senior year. They may have one or two AP classes in 11th grade, but they are more likely to take several AP classes, if that is their level of performance, during their senior year. Many slide through senior year and either forget about or fail to prepare for SAT II or AP exams in May or June as they graduate high school. The last thing on most seniors' minds at graduation time is spending a few spring Saturdays in an exam room. But if they do, and achieve good results, they will be most relieved to find in the fall that they have placed out of some required classes or prerequisites, and quite possibly have gained a semester's worth of credits. Down the line this will make it easier for them to double-major, take a relaxed semester abroad, apply to an honors program, or graduate early, saving significant college tuition money.

Another way to gain college course credits is by taking college-level classes during the summer while you're in high school or alongside your high school curriculum if a class you want is not offered at your school. You may take these classes at a local community college or university, or through one of the many summer precollege programs offered on university campuses. Usually, a B or higher in an accredited college-level class will earn you some course credits down the road, and will certainly look good in the admissions process.

As you consider the public universities, take a look at their policies on course credits and advanced standing. What test scores are required? How many credits can you gain? Will you be given course credits or just relief from particular university requirements? What classes and exams will qualify you for advanced standing and credits? Are on-campus placement exams offered to gain entry into higher level courses, in English, foreign languages, or math, for example? You will need to send in official transcripts from colleges where you took classes, as well as official score reports for the SAT, AP, and ACT. You will also need to decide which courses you will want to take, even though you may have placed out of them. For example, a premedical student who has taken advanced sciences in high school may still want to take these subjects in college to prepare for medical college.

## A Summary of How You Can Lower Costs

Attending a public university can lower your overall college costs in and of itself. There are also other ways of saving money when going to a public institution. You may use your advanced standing and course credits to reduce the number of semester hours you need to pay for. You may gain in-state residency over time. You may qualify for some merit-based as well as need-based financial aid. Working as a resident assistant in a dormitory may get you on-campus housing and a stipend or tuition credits. Many work-study opportunities are available for qualified applicants to earn money and, potentially, research or work experience of more interest than that available in the cafeteria. You may decide to begin college at a local two-year college and then transfer to a public or private college or university. Lowering costs can reduce the financial burden for your family, as well as the student loan burden for yourself. This may be of more importance to you if you are also relatively sure you will attend graduate school.

## Staging Your Education (Attending More Than One School)

Viewing your college experience as a series of steps as opposed to a singular four-year event not only opens up more options for you, but also is more realistic. A very large group of students in America will attend more than one college or university. In fact, some data show that more than half of all students who graduate with a bachelor's degree have attended more than one institution. Staging your education can help lower costs and help you prepare for bigger challenges ahead. To lower your college costs, you may decide to start college at a local public college or university, which can be either a two-year or a four-year institution. You will find tuition there significantly less than at a private college or even at a flagship public university. If you want to live at home, you will also save money on room and board and travel to and from school. If you want to work, you can attend school part- or full-time by taking classes offered in the evenings and on weekends. This may allow you to save enough money and earn enough credits to make a public ivy feasible for you.

## Growing into Your Shoes

Cost is not the only reason for staging your education. You may need time to mature and grow as an individual and a student. Perhaps you were not too interested in academics in high school. Maybe you were a late bloomer. Perhaps you only "got it" as your senior year drew to a close, and you had not yet thought about college as a serious option for the following year. Maybe you were an athlete or musician who spent a lot of time pursuing your extracurricular interest and less time on your homework. An extra year or two of a lower level college could help you develop your academics and intellectual interests and prepare for admission to more selective institutions. If you are not yet ready to leave home, that is another reason to spend some time growing into your shoes at a local community college. Don't worry! This is not looked down on by the public ivies. Quite the opposite is true. If you take a year or two of growing, achieving academically at a high level and finding out what you want to study as a major, you will be seen as a *better* applicant by these universities.

## Building a Foundation

The public ivies accept a large number of transfers, more than are admitted to the small liberal arts colleges. There are just more students coming and going at these large universities, and more flexibility in terms of where, when, and how to enter. If you take some time to build a stronger foundation for college admissions, you will likely be rewarded for your efforts. If you did not have a great high school GPA or strong standardized test scores, you will probably be a stronger *transfer* applicant to a public ivy. This is predicated on the fact that you will graduate from high school and go on to study seriously in a college curriculum. You can do this at your local community college, a less competitive public university, or a private college or university. You will want to take a solid core curriculum, including the equivalent of freshman English, basic sciences, introductory history, psychology, economics, math, and other classes that colleges will look favorably on in evaluating your performance and transferring credits. The more time you spend building this college foundation, up to two full years, the less your SATs or high school grades will matter. You will have proven yourself in college courses. You may even take the two years to earn an associate degree, which looks even better to public universities considering you for transfer admission.

## Going the Distance (Off-Site Education)

Another way for you to gain course credits in high school or thereafter is to take a distance education course. Once taken through what we now call snail mail, distance courses are now available on the Internet. UCLA, for example, has extensive course offerings online for college or high school students. Colorado recently announced that all 28 of its public institutions will work together to develop a catalog of their online courses and provide more access and credit transferability for more students studying online at any one of the colleges or universities. Four state universities in different states have also formed a distance education alliance to share information and develop joint programs. The participants are the University of California at Berkeley's extension program, Pennsylvania State University's World Campus, the University of Washington, and the University of Wisconsin's Learning Innovations Program.

You may further build your foundation for college while you are in high school or after you graduate, or you may add to your college curriculum during the summers, by enrolling in some accredited distance education courses online. The public universities have become national leaders in offering distance education using developing technologies—virtual lectures, e-mail-based exams, multimedia web-based classes, and so forth. In part, their technological resources, diverse faculty, and varied student bodies have led to this development. In part, these universities are trying to overcome geographical distances, an issue in the western states in particular, and to make the specific strengths of different campuses available to students in the region or nationally. There are a number of privately financed distance education programs in the works as well. Buyers should always make sure they know who is doing the teaching, whether the course is accredited, what the academic credit is worth, and whether the credit is transferable.

## Interuniversity Transfers

Do not fret if your heart is set on a public ivy and you weren't accepted right out of high school and so went to another school, or if you felt your chances weren't good for the public ivy and so applied elsewhere, or if you headed off to a small private college and now realize you want something different. The public ivies accept transfers every year, in the fall and often in the spring or summer semesters. You will need to plan ahead, do the research on the programs that interest you, and excel in your current college or university. Transfers are successful when they have a good curriculum, good grades (at least a 3.0, or B, average, and preferably a 3.5, or A–, average, or higher), good recommendation letters from college faculty, and good reasons for wanting to transfer. Universities look for evidence of college success, academic focus, and a real understanding of what would be gained in transferring into their institution. What program would you pursue? What have you learned where you are? What do you like about your current college, and what would you like to change? Why would this university be better for you than your current school? Your application should be well prepared, mature, and direct. You should contact each university's *transfer admissions counselor* to ask about schedules, requirements, and recommendations. These individuals will often be frank about your chances for admission, the best timetable for your application, and the best curriculum to take to ready yourself. Again, you must research the programs, campuses, and unique characteristics of the different schools. These universities want to have a sense that there is a logical fit for you in their institution, that you have thought about it, and that you are not jumping from the frying pan into the fire.

As you will notice in your research on the public ivies, admissions offices list requirements and procedures specific to transfer students. Read them carefully to determine your eligibility for admission. If you are attending a junior or community college or another public university in the same state where you are applying to the flagship university, you will find that you are at an advantage. In most cases, the public college and university systems have special relationships whereby students get preferred interuniversity transfer evaluations as well as guarantees of course credit transfers, provided that they meet certain requirements. Follow those requirements carefully, and make sure you meet the eligibility for entrance as an in-state transfer student. You will be surprised how many other students in your state have followed the same path.

What about going in the other direction? You began your college life at a public university, perhaps even one of the more selective public ivies, but you have discovered a lot of things about the university that you don't like. Or you have started at your state university, with a plan to move on after a year or two. Is this possible? Absolutely. If you have two years of college work under your belt, you will probably be a stronger applicant than if you are applying after only one semester at the university. We have counseled many students who have started at a public university and moved on, having established a strong foundation and defined what they wanted for the next phase of their education. You will need to take that strong core curriculum and make an effort to get to know some of your faculty in those bigger classes by going to their office hours and talking with them after class. Proving yourself in a big and challenging environment will impress a small or middle-sized private college or more selective public university. Again, you will need to explain the logic of your move before you will be accepted as a transfer student.

## Carl: A Transfer from His State University to a Catholic University

Carl had a tough high school career. He was a bright student but got stuck in a major rut in his junior year, when significant personal conflict enveloped him at school and he became alienated from many of his teachers. He came from a family of educators and took his academics seriously, but he tuned out for several semesters before realizing in senior year that he was going to have trouble getting into a college he was excited about. He was particularly interested in some of the smaller to midsized Catholic universities, because he admired the traditional curriculum, smaller class environment, and focus on teaching and values that he desired. He came to see us in his senior year to discuss his options. He had tested well enough on the SATs and had brought his GPA up enough that we felt confident that he would be admitted to the University of Connecticut. This public university was bigger than he wanted and did not have the residential life and personality he was looking for, but we talked through a transfer strategy with him. Why not spend a year at UConn, focus on improving his academics, and begin to look into other colleges? Carl did just that. His first-year classes, which were much bigger than those at his smaller private high school, took some getting used to, and he realized that he was going to have to be assertive. He took the lead in meeting his professors, one of whom was a graduate teaching assistant who later would write him a strong recommendation. He went for tutoring and academic help with his professors when he needed it and concentrated on doing well right from the start. He earned a B+ average in his first semester. Carl visited some of the other colleges during the fall, wrote his transfer applications in the winter, and personally contacted and met with the transfer admission counselors at a few schools. He wrote movingly about his personal and academic record and made a strong argument for why he was seeking to transfer. The next year, he moved on to Providence College, after initially being told no by Boston College, his first choice. He continued his strong work at Providence but still pursued BC, which he saw as just the right balance between PC and UConn in terms of size. His work eventually paid off, and by his junior year, he was at Boston. At UConn, Carl had accomplished his goals, gained an excellent academic foundation and learning experience, and left with a positive impression of his public university experience. He was personally and academically prepared for something different by the time he made his move.

## Intrauniversity Transfers

What happens if you enter a public ivy only to find that you have chosen the wrong school or college within the university? Maybe you started in engineering and now want to be in the liberal arts. Perhaps you thought music was your thing, but now you'd prefer to major in business. Intrauniversity transfers are even easier than transfers from one in-state university to another or from an in-state public community college to the flagship university. In an intrauniversity transfer, you're changing one major thing: your identification as an enrolled student in one college within the university to your identification as an enrolled student in another college in the university. You will change your declared major as part of this transfer, and have to fulfill different course and distribution requirements associated with your new school and department. You will remain a full-time enrolled student at the university and will not lose any of the status you have as such. Sometimes, an intrauniversity transfer necessitates your taking an extra semester or two to complete course requirements you did not encounter in your previous specialty. You may have taken a lot of music theory in the music school, but now you need to take accounting, finance, and management to graduate from the business school.

Intrauniversity transfers allow you to make use of one of the great advantages of a larger public university: its variety. Without changing campuses or having to research and apply to schools near and far to find what you want, you may have discovered precisely the program you are seeking right where you started. Students within the university are accorded preference in transferring from one college or school to another. They must be in good academic standing and often must go through an application process to switch schools. This is especially true when moving from one program to a more selective or demanding school, although which schools are more competitive varies from one university to another. Often, students seek to transfer for their junior year, having met many of the universitywide academic requirements before specializing in one program. We tell students to focus on the magic B. That 3.0, or B, average is often the minimum transfer GPA, while the more selective programs may seek a 3.3 or 3.5 for admission. As long as you are doing well where you are, you will have lots of transfer opportunities.

## WHAT ARE THE BENEFITS OF GOING TO A PUBLIC INSTITUTION?

Many. We are careful not to overgeneralize for all students in all places. What is important is whether you see these aspects of public university education and life as beneficial or harmful to you. As benefits, consider the large size of almost all of the public ivies. Their resources and facilities are astounding. The faculty are encouraged to be active researchers and writers. Graduate students serve as intermediaries and role models for undergraduates in almost every field in the arts and sciences. These universities are spirited, diverse, enthusiastic places that offer every course under the sun, the sense of being part of a big, high-profile community, and recreational facilities that beat the best private clubs. Attending one of the public ivies makes you a part of that very large alumni community for the rest of your life. If, after college, you decide to remain in state for your career, as many graduates do, you will feel connected to the community, business, and political leaders who share your allegiance to your state alma mater.

# WHAT ARE THE DRAWBACKS?

"What was your name?"

"Could you please give me your student number?"

"I can't find you in the system."

"I'm sorry, that class is full."

"No, it looks like you have not fulfilled all your requirements, so you'll have to take this summer semester to graduate."

The drawbacks of the public ivies center on two major and related factors: size and research. Notice that we have cited size and research as two of the major benefits of the public universities as well. The same can be said for the elite private research universities. As negatives, size and research can make students feel lost at the larger universities. Their professors and teaching assistants may seem more interested in their own research agendas than in teaching and connecting with the undergraduates. As we discussed in *Inside the Top Colleges,* the students we surveyed at Berkeley, UNC, and Wisconsin listed the size of their classes and the quality and accessibility of their faculty among the things that they would like to change. It is no secret that the public ivies put much of their energy into research and faculty are rewarded more for publishing than for good teaching. The universities have tried to balance the negative effects of size and a research emphasis with honors colleges, teacher training programs, and the like, but the basic fact remains that the experience at a large public ivy is inherently different from that at any of the hidden ivies.

## Bigger Is Better?

Bigger means more. More of everything. More buildings and more walking to get to one part of campus from another, or from one campus to another, since some universities have a few campuses separated from one another by several miles. Some campus maps look like the Paris metro map! Size can mean physical space, and lots of it. With few exceptions, the public ivies are not schools centered around one small campus green. These are sprawling complexes where you may pass your entire academic career without ever seeing some parts of the campus. The good news is there are multiple libraries and innumerable places to study, to play, and to meet people. And with 20,000 or 30,000 compatriots around, you will always be meeting new people. Consider where you live now. Are you in a small town? What is the population? Have you ever seen them all together? If you live in a city, consider the last time you went to a big sporting or music event. What is it like to see 15,000, or 35,000, or 100,000 people together in one place? That will be your school, your environment, your football stadium, at a big flagship university.

Bigger means more classes. Look through the course bulletins for the public ivies. Hundreds upon hundreds of offerings are available to you, as well as hundreds of majors, numerous colleges, and lots of degree options. You need not worry about running out of choices. You may need to worry about getting into the classes and professors you want in time to graduate on schedule and fulfill your major requirements. You might need to sleep out at the registrars building or, more likely these days, hope you get a good number in the computerized registration lottery so that you can grab the classes you want online or by telephone.

Bigger means big classes. Consider the last small concert you went to. Were there 300 people there? Were there 500 or 1,500? Many small theaters hold 1,000 people. Many lecture classes at the public universities enroll 500. Picture your professor down on the floor, at the bottom of the room. She is lecturing on deviance in an introductory psychology class. You sit in the middle of the room, in a row with 40 other students, near the aisle, which rises from the floor toward the doors at the back of the room. The professor has a microphone pinned to her jacket to help project her voice. A techie sits in a booth at the top of the room, managing the slide projector. The screen is the size of the one at your local movie theater. The blackboard has five sections that slide up and down, and the chalk is an inch thick, but it is still hard to read. The five graduate student teaching assistants who run the individual recitation discussion sections each week sit in a group in the front row, furiously taking notes. Your mind wanders and you try to resist picking up the campus newspaper as late students drift into class and bored students walk out 10 minutes early.

Can you handle this scenario? It is a fact of life at the big universities, and one you will have to survive before moving on to the higher level seminars, honors courses, and independent research projects. If you have course credits or enter an honors program or other special program, you might be able to avoid some of these big introductory courses. Nevertheless, big classes are more prevalent at the public universities, and you need to be prepared for them.

## Research, Research, Research

The goal of almost all faculty at the universities is to gain tenure. That happens when they are promoted from assistant professor to associate professor. Then they may be promoted to full professor, and possibly to an endowed chair. Although tenure is under fire today from some critics who claim that it leads faculty to become complacent, outdated, and less productive, tenure is still with us. Tenure gives faculty the security to write and say what they want without fear of university repercussion or censure. They can pursue an independent research agenda that they feel is an important aspect of their discipline. They can be provocative, within certain bounds, in their lectures without feeling that they would be sanctioned for their views. Tenure is the ultimate reward for faculty, faculty who were once undergraduates and then graduate student teaching assistants themselves. They move on as instructors, adjunct professors, and tenure-track assistant professors, and try to build a foundation that will lead to their being granted tenure at the university of their choice. Normally, this takes anywhere from five to seven years, although obtaining tenure-track positions and eventual tenure itself is becoming more and more difficult.

It is important that undergraduates be aware of the tenure system, because it helps to explain the priorities of their teachers. Professors who want tenure or promotion to full professor need to publish their work in peer-reviewed journals and in books. To publish, they need to conduct original research. To conduct original research, they often need to apply for grants. To win grants, they need to research and write grant proposals. Winning grants brings prestige and dollars to the universities, so this is doubly beneficial for the faculty member. Tenure decisions normally are based on a combination of three criteria: research and publishing; teaching; and service to the academic department, discipline, committees, and university. At the public research universities, the decisions are influenced strongly by the first factor. Teaching matters, just not as much. Serving as department chair, on search committees, or as editor of an academic journal matters, just not as much. Junior faculty, who are seeking tenure, are obsessive about research and publishing. Senior faculty, hoping to reach full professor, are the same. And eminent faculty with endowed chairs tend not to teach many undergraduate courses. With their rank and experience, they choose to continue their research and to lead graduate seminars.

The research emphasis of the public ivies is, then, a defining aspect of the culture of these universities. Undergraduates matter, and they bring in significant tuition dollars to the university, but they are but one cog in the wheel of the larger educational system. They must fight for the attention of their instructors and for concern on the part of the university toward teaching in the undergraduate classroom. We discuss progress and measures in this direction more fully in Part Two.

The research emphasis is also one of the major attractions of the public ivies for aspiring scholars. Faculty who are leaders in their fields, whether philosophy or physics, can prove to be inspirational role models for undergraduates. Participating in a department in which groundbreaking intellectual work is taking place can be exciting. Many of the top-ranking individual undergraduate departments are situated in the public universities. That is because the scholars populating these departments are some of the most productive in their disciplines. By senior year, if not before, some undergraduates are participating in some of that research and writing, working as summer assistants or in a smaller advanced seminar on a project of interest. This experience helps them see what an academic career is all about and helps them should they decide to apply to graduate schools. The research projects at the big universities often involve multiple faculty over a number of years. A student can become involved in an ongoing project, watching it take shape over a longer period of time. They may hear lectures from the professor who wrote the book and follow advances in their field right at the source. Major conferences often take place at the campuses of the public ivies, attracting scholars from around the world. Eminent individuals come to campus to speak in well-regarded lecture series. Others stay for a semester or a year as visiting scholars. Research is a driving force, and prospective students need to learn how to work with it and gain the most from it at the public ivies.

---

### A "PRINCIPLED RESEARCH UNIVERSITY"

Writing recently on the future of doctoral education in *PMLA,* the journal of the Modern Language Association, which represents researchers and teachers in the humanities, Catharine Stimpson, dean of New York University's Graduate School of Arts and Sciences and a member of the Board of the Woodrow Wilson National Fellowship Foundation, offered a fitting metaphor for the "principled research university."[1] According to Stimpson, the 125 research universities in the United States—the bulk of which are public—constitute just 3 percent of all higher educational institutions. They award 32 percent of all bachelor's degrees in the country, and of those who received science and engineering doctorates from 1991 to 1995, 56 percent had earned their bachelor's degree at a research university. She described the modern research university as a hub:

> "The hub is the solid, central part of a wheel. So the research university can unite several spokes and sites of inquiry. In a contemporary extension of meaning, a hub is a center of airplane flights. So the research university should be a center of flights of inquiry and the imagination—in the human and natural worlds. Insistently, the hub airport is now a shopping mall as well, offering everything from apples to stuffed zebras, in addition to local delicacies (if it's Vidalia onions, it must be Atlanta). The research university can offer a mall of data, ideas, and voices instead of things. Some may fear that this abundance will lead to a hubbub, a confusion, but if the task of the research university is knowledge, then its faculty and students can spin significant patterns from these ideas and voices."
> (1151–1152)

Stimpson proposed that research universities be "principled," embodying certain values. They should "serve as the site of advanced inquiry and creativity, for the mind and imagination going at full tilt." They should focus on "teaching how

*(continued)*

to teach what we know and what we are discovering." A research university "articulates and embodies an ethics of learning and teaching." It promotes "the continued creation of a cosmopolitan meritocracy" and "should balance the human connections that have been the heart of traditional learning and teaching with the new technologies of information" (1149–1150).

This metaphor and set of proposed values for the research university should give you an idea of the diversity at the center of the public ivies and the issues that educators in these institutions are contemplating. There is a tension—many would say an inherent and invaluable interplay—between teaching and research at these universities that makes them uniquely interesting and challenging environments in which to learn.

[1]Catharine Stimpson, "Myths of Transformation: Realities of Change," *PMLA* 115 (October 2000), pp. 1142–1153.

## Facilities

Because of their size and their commitment to research and teaching at both the undergraduate and graduate levels, the public ivies are among the world's major research institutions and facilities. They host national scientific research programs, often in conjunction with federal and state governments and corporations. This can be controversial when, for example, a U.S. Department of Defense program or pharmaceutical company agenda contradicts or is perceived to contradict, some of the ideals and interests of the university and students. Yet these dollars, in addition to tuition, state budget funds, and private individual contributions, help support advanced technology programs and classrooms, science labs, lecture halls, and modern libraries.

The public university campuses are often a mix of the old and the new, and may be less wedded to or identified with the traditional, unified architectural feel of small private colleges. Some notable exceptions, of course, include the College of William and Mary and the University of Virginia.

Generally, the campuses of the public ivies are in a constant state of reinvention, with building budgets founded on growing endowments supporting new construction of facilities designed to attract not only students, but also top faculty and additional research money. Athletic facilities are big, modern, and top of the line, for varsity stars as well as the average aerobics aficionado. Dormitories? They may be mixed. Some wonderful residential facilities may be available to a select few and to freshmen. You will find that "dorms" at the big schools may include high-rise apartments, rehabilitated motels and hotels that have been purchased by the university over the years, and local condominium complexes. Most of the public ivies have high rates of off-campus living. Junior and senior students in particular typically find housing arrangements with friends in private or college-owned houses and apartments near campus. Some join fraternities and sororities mainly for the residential living opportunities they present. Housing facilities are a key aspect of the public ivies that you want to explore carefully.

When you visit a public university, especially a larger one, you will be impressed by the expanse and range of academic, residential, and social facilities on or near campus. Make sure you explore closely the liberal arts libraries and departmental buildings. That is where you will likely spend most of your time, unless you intend to enroll in another school or program. Talk with undergraduates in the program in which you are interested to find out how and where they spend their days and examine those facilities most intently.

## The Sciences

When one hears the words "doctoral and research university," one may be inclined to think of the stereotypical scientist, with white lab coat, pocket protector, and a beaker of chemicals in hand. The sciences are indeed strong at the public ivies, as we have discussed. The facilities are there for their exploration, and the budgets are larger for what some call the "hard sciences"—physics, chemistry, biology, engineering, and so on—than they are for the "soft sciences"—economics, political science, sociology, psychology, etc.—and for the humanities. There is certainly a great deal of writing and speaking today on the value of the social sciences, languages, and humanities in American education and at the public universities in particular, and a sense of needing to defend these programs against more "practical" or "pragmatic" hard science or business fields. The fact that the sciences are rich and seemingly dominant at the research universities should not blind the prospective student to the wealth of opportunities in English, philosophy, political science, French literature, or other major intellectual disciplines. You will be amazed upon leaving your fairly narrow high school curriculum to discover the array of interdisciplinary and multidisciplinary programs at your disposal in the universities.

## Graduating with Graduate Students

Let's face it. Graduate students do not have a great public image. They struggle for higher wages, better recognition, and union organization today. The average parent or student reacts negatively to the idea of the graduate teaching assistant (TA), with little experience and perhaps even less command of the English language, standing in front of the university classroom or grading essays and exams. The TA or graduate part-time instructor (GPTI) appears overworked, undervalued, too young, and poorly informed. Most say, "This is not what we expected to pay for or find in a university education." This stereotype may fit in some ways, but it hides significant diversity and strengths and ignores some of the realities of education at a major university.

A doctoral and research university, as defined by the Carnegie classifications, grants a significant number of *advanced* degrees, that is, master's degrees and doctorates (see the box titled

"Carnegie Classification of Institutions of Higher Education" in the Introduction). They award these degrees across the spectrum of the liberal arts and sciences. In almost every department on campus, undergraduates study alongside and under the tutelage of graduate students. The undergrad in philosophy may take a seminar or work with a TA who is working on a Ph.D. in philosophy. That TA is not only teaching a class or four under the guidance of a professor but also reading the major literature in philosophy, focusing on one specific area, and conducting original research as part of a doctoral dissertation on an author or idea. The biology undergrad will see that his TA in the organic lab is working on her Ph.D. in molecular sciences and is being funded through part of her advisor's National Science Foundation multiyear grant.

The benefits of exposure to advanced students are many for the undergrad. You see what it takes to secure a higher level degree and may discover an area of knowledge that compels you to follow in the TAs' footsteps. Perhaps a young TA is more able to serve as a role model for an undergraduate who is only three or four years younger. Possibly, that TA is more energetic and motivated, fresher to the subject, and thus a better teacher than some of the older faculty in the department. The presence of graduate students also implies the availability of graduate classes, and motivated and advanced undergraduates may find exciting the opportunity to take a few master's-level courses in their final year of school.

Graduate students operate on both parallel and vertical tracks with undergraduates. The grad students may teach their junior counterparts, but they are also students in their own right. Typically, academic departments are designed to accommodate these distinctions, having a chair of the department, a director of undergraduate studies for the department, and a director of graduate studies. Graduate students are a fact of life in research universities. Undergraduate students should go beyond simple stereotypes to evaluate the good and bad elements of working with them. Just as they can judge faculty, undergraduates can evaluate which TAs are better or worse to work with and how TAs will affect their education.

## Affirmative Action and Diversity

In recent years public universities have faced more challenges to their efforts to ensure diversity on their campuses than have private institutions. This is because they are governed publicly and are more indebted to state legislation that controls their budgets, policies, and procedures. As public entities, they must comply more directly with the wishes of their states' citizens, as expressed through legislation, regulations, or orders from the governor's office and state education department or higher education commission and through public referenda or initiatives.

Lately, a number of court cases have challenged the public universities' use of race or ethnicity in making admissions decisions, charging that the use of such criteria violates the rights of White or Asian students who may have had higher grades and test scores than those of Black, Hispanic, or American Indian students who were admitted. These cases are, at heart, seeking to overturn the 1978 *Regents of the University of California v. Bakke* decision of the U.S. Supreme Court, which allowed the use of affirmative action, or the consideration of race and ethnicity in admitting promising minority students whose overall academic profile could be lower than that of the average admitted student, with the intended goal of providing educational opportunities to historically disadvantaged groups. These opportunities would redress past discrimination and give these students the chance to move significantly forward with the aid of a university education and foundation.

Without going into the details or controversies surrounding the use of affirmative action on college campuses, what critics brand as unfair quotas and supporters argue is a necessary step to redress the underrepresentation of certain racial and ethnic groups in higher education, we wish to say only that the debate will continue for some time yet. Changes that have been occurring in many states—California, Washington, Texas, and Michigan, to name a few—should neither discourage minority applicants from applying nor send negative signals to nonminority candidates. The public universities are diverse places. Could they be more so? Probably. In the next fifty years, America as a nation will no longer have one majority race or ethnic group. Some states will

---

### CHANGES IN AFFIRMATIVE ACTION IN CALIFORNIA

The verdict is not yet in on the impact of policy changes at the state universities on using race and ethnicity in admissions. California, the largest public university system in the United States, dropped an official affirmative action policy in 1995. Recent figures show that of 41,790 Californians admitted for fall 2000, 17.6 percent were members of what are called underrepresented groups: American Indians, Blacks, and Hispanics. This compares to 16.9 percent for 1999 and 16.7 percent for 1998, after affirmative action was abandoned, and 18.8 percent for 1997, the last year racial preferences were in place. Asian Americans have made up for most of the drop in these other groups' admissions spaces, constituting 34.2 percent of the fall 2000 total, compared to 33.2 percent for 1997. More applicants today, 8.1 percent, are declining to state their race at all. This number has risen from 5.1 percent in 1997 and is believed to be made up largely of Asians or Whites. The major negative data for underrepresented groups appears when one looks at the more selective campuses in California. At Berkeley, only 43 of 7,107 admissions offers were made to Black students. Only 16.4 percent of the total admitted pool at Berkeley consisted of underrepresented minorities, compared with 25.3 percent in 1997. A similar pattern has occurred at UCLA and the University of California, San Diego, where a rise in Hispanic and Black admissions from 1999 to 2000 has not made up for drops since 1997. The University of California now spends $250 million a year to try to increase the number of qualified minority applicants.

*Source:* "Affirmative Action in California: Passed," *The Economist,* April 8, 2000, p. 29.

be more polyglot than others, particularly those on the coasts or borders: California, New York, Texas, Arizona, Florida. Affirmative action has helped many students gain the opportunities that have led them to successful careers and advanced degrees. Today, many educators are turning the debate away from affirmative action in higher education to the provision of better education and college preparation for all students at the K–12 levels. In fact, many are talking about education as a K–16 process, with the expectation that all students should be prepared to earn some type of college degree and that universities need to play a role in ensuring that their applicant pool will be qualified, diverse, and able to succeed in their changing environments. The long-term evidence is not yet in on how policy changes in such states as California or Washington will affect minority enrollment and graduation. To any interested applicant, our advice is to prepare as strongly as possible in the ways that will help you gain admission to a university of your choice. If diversity of any sort—racial, ethnic, geographic, international, academic, political—is important to you, be sure to do the research and ask the questions—of admissions officers, minority affairs deans, residential life deans, current students, and others on campus—that will help you compare and contrast the public ivies on this variable.

## Being a Number

Many high school students tell us they do not want to go someplace "where I'll just be a number." Others who want to leave a big school often say the same thing. "They treat me like a number here. I want to go someplace where professors know my name."

No one likes being a number. Unfortunately, we are increasingly identified today by our Social Security number, which often doubles as a student identification number at college. This is true at tiny private colleges, not just big state schools. Everybody has a number. The difference is, of course, that at the big state schools, you are likely to use that number more often and less likely to have personal relationships with teachers, administrators, and staff. You are more likely to be treated as one of many than as an individual sometimes, and that can be difficult. There is a certain amount of anonymity at a large university. Some students love this. Others detest it.

As you progress through a big university, you will begin to form attachments, first with your roommate, your hallmates, your teammates. As you declare a major and spend more and more time in a particular department, you will start to establish bonds with TAs and professors. You will get to know the department secretaries and the chair. You might spend some time at the career planning office and get to know your advisor. As we discuss in Part Four, you must be the assertive one in making these relationships. There is little likelihood of people tapping you on the shoulder to ask where your homework is, whether you registered for classes, and if you have fulfilled necessary requirements.

As you wander across campus to correct a course registration problem, go to the student health center, or meet with an assistant dean to try to get some funding for your campus organization, you will feel a part of a big system, a bureaucracy that takes some getting used to and a good deal of negotiating skills. That is not necessarily a bad thing; it's more a matter of degree than a matter of substance. At a small college, the same independent tasks are required of you. They may just be a little bit easier to accomplish.

Being a number at a larger public university also means taking more multiple-choice tests and having them graded by computer. Some classes may even curve your grades across four hundred students in the course, making it still more difficult for you to stand out. In small seminar-style classes, you will write more papers and essay exams, which will be personally graded by your professor. As your teachers get to know you, you will be able to develop a relationship with them, and they will get a sense of your intellectual style and talents. That is not being just a number, and it can happen at the public ivies, though you may not reach that state until the third year if you are not in an honors program or scholars program.

## Reflective Learning

Do you learn well by listening? Do you like to hear a lecture, see an outline on the board, and think about the meaning of what has been told to you? Can you take notes as the class goes on, jotting down key points and questions that you would like answered? Are you able to go to your textbooks to look up areas that were unclear and to ask your questions later, during your professor's office hours or during a discussion section? Do you find that you don't mind not having the opportunity to participate in class, while you ponder what is being said, and that your best thoughts and questions arise after careful consideration?

If you answer yes to a lot of these questions, you are likely a reflective learner, or at least can function in that capacity in certain situations and still learn the relevant material. Reflective learners do well in some of those large lecture classes at the big public universities. They get less frustrated with the requirements of dealing with many students and a style of education that emphasizes listening rather than questioning. If you are not a reflective learner by nature, you need to develop the skills to operate as one in those courses where ten people discussing the course readings around a seminar table is not the norm.

## Go Big Red (or Blue, or Gold, or . . . )

Not every student shares it, but each of the public ivies has a healthy sense of school spirit. From football games, tailgate parties, and alumni gatherings, these universities have traditions that encourage students to share the school identity and bonds. If you are excited by the prospect of sitting among tens of thousands of rabid fans, or watching your teams on television year in and year out, or identifying yourself with a state as well as a school, one of the public ivies might be for you. Or you do not have to be thrilled with football and being part of the pep rally culture that exists at most of these schools. You will find alternative social venues and groups at each one. The public ivies have literally hundreds of clubs and organizations on campus that will provide you with any outlet you choose to pursue.

## HOW DO YOU CHOOSE?

The best way to get at the research universities is to research them. In Part Two, we discuss some of the criteria you should consider in deciding, first of all, whether a public ivy or another public university is right for you and, second, which of these institutions best match your interests and abilities. We intend these criteria to be used as general guidelines for you to evaluate schools. We hope that your information gathering will be an educational process that helps you determine where your needs will be best met and where you will be most successful in college and beyond. In addition to researching these schools, you need to get on the road and visit some campuses. There is no way to get a sense of what a big public university is like from a computer. You need to visit a few to begin to understand the environments. You may apply to other schools that you have not seen, and then visit them later if you are admitted. To know if you should add some public ivies to your list, visit one or two. Combine that with your reading, with spending a lot of time at these universities' websites, and with your own reflections on what you want out of college, and you will know what is right for you.

# [PART TWO Criteria for Evaluating a Public College or University

Evaluating a university is an ongoing personal task. You must assess the relative merits and particular aspects of the university as they apply to your own interests and preferences. We are not strong advocates for the many rankings systems that exist today, primarily because we believe they obscure many of the important individual qualities of the universities and quantify such elements of the universities as test scores, average class size, and selectivity, which present "best" and "worst" in a categorically misleading way. We prefer to identify the criteria that are important in evaluating a college or university and have students use those criteria as a personal compass in navigating the complex and varied universe of universities. In other words, you as an individual will decide which criteria are most important to you and then examine a number of schools to discern which best fit your ideal environment and academic program. Finally, certain qualities of colleges and universities are quite intangible and difficult to define or quantify. What is the feel of the place to you? Is it socially right? How far is it from home, and how important is this to you? How serious are the students, and how do you fit in? These and many other questions will affect your choice of college, in addition to the hard data available on class size, areas of study, selectivity, financial aid availability and cost—and, yes, rankings.

## DEALING WITH THE RANKINGS GUIDES

Many parents and students enter our offices with guidebook or magazine in hand, quoting rankings statistics as justification for a particular college choice or asking why a particular university has moved up or down. "Look, this university is number 12, and that one's number 20," they point out. "So, obviously, we [note the use of the word "we"] want to go for number 12."

Or, "We thought that university was an excellent school, but we noticed that it dropped last year from 15th to 25th. What happened?" This kind of thinking drives college administrators, admissions officers, guidance counselors, and even the students and parents themselves crazy.

---

### PRINT AND ONLINE RESOURCES FOR COLLEGE AND UNIVERSITY RANKINGS AND DESCRIPTIONS

The following is a selected list of books, links, and resources in which you'll find a variety of college and university rankings and evaluations.

**Print Sources:**

"America's Best Colleges," a special issue of *U.S. News & World Report* that comes out annually. This is the one that started the rankings mania, and it is still the most cited source around. Beyond the rankings, the magazine offers tips and useful data.

*The College Handbook,* published annually by the College Board. A reliable and comprehensive source for information on U.S. colleges and universities.

*Educational Rankings Annual,* edited by Lynn Hattendorf Westney, published by the Gale Group. An expensive, comprehensive, annotated book presenting all sorts of rankings and evaluation information.

*The Fiske Guide to Colleges,* edited by Edward Fiske, published by Three Rivers Press. A responsible annual guide that provides detailed college descriptions, as well as such ratings as "best values."

*The Gourman Report,* by Jack Gourman, published by the Princeton Review. A controversial and nonscientific source, because its author refuses to reveal his methodology. Offers readers a glimpse into specific majors offered at a wide range of schools.

*Rugg's Recommendations on the Colleges,* by Frederick Rugg, published by Rugg's Recommendations. An annual guide based primarily on surveys of students.

**Internet Sources:**

*College and University Rankings.* An excellent online resource on rankings and guides, with multiple links, hosted by the University of Illinois at Urbana-Champaign. www.library.uiuc.edu/edx/rankings.htm.

"Rankings and Ratings," a summary article in the *Enrollment Management Review* from the College Board. www.collegeboard.org/index_this/aes/emr/emrsu97/html/rank.html.

Universities have learned that they cannot completely ignore rankings guides. They simultaneously play down a bad ranking or a drop in rank and tout those numbers that reflect positively on their university or particular programs. Let's not get bogged down in the whys of rankings, or the ethics of the process. Instead, we would like to offer some advice to prospective students on how to use the rankings, before presenting selected data that show where some of the public ivies stand.

First, *please* do not take the rankings as gospel—especially when you are comparing colleges or universities that are close in rank. There is probably much less difference between a school ranked 6th and one ranked 10th than there is between the school ranked 10th and the one ranked 50th. You should view rankings as one piece of rather generalized information about a university's reputational standing, relative place in the pecking order, and, to some degree, quality. Even our grouping of 30 universities as "public ivies" is a generalized presentation of institutions we believe represent public universities of best quality overall. We have followed with data on the criteria we discuss in this part. We have also based our judgments on reputation, experience with students going to and from these institutions, conversations with academics and educators, and an eye toward some of the varied rankings available. Our list is not totally exclusive. Other public universities will look stronger or comparable on a number of the criteria. We hope that students will use our criteria in addition to the rankings guides in examining all the universities that interest them, whether they are profiled in this book or not. *The Public Ivies* is not a rankings guide, and we do not rate the 30 schools relative to one another. This is a select group of institutions, and there are differences within the group. Some of the universities are more selective, some are better endowed, some are ranked more highly, and some draw less of a national applicant pool. We hope that you use this list as a helpful starting

### U.S. News & World Report's Top 50 Public National Universities

| University | 2001 | 2000 |
|---|---|---|
| University of California, Berkeley | 1 | 1 |
| University of Virginia | 1 | 2 |
| University of California, Los Angeles | 3 | 3 |
| University of Michigan, Ann Arbor | 3 | 3 |
| University of North Carolina at Chapel Hill | 3 | 5 |
| College of William and Mary | 6 | 6 |
| University of California, San Diego | 7 | 7 |
| Georgia Institute of Technology | 8 | 10 |
| University of Wisconsin—Madison | 8 | 8 |
| University of California, Davis | 10 | 12 |
| University of California, Irvine | 10 | 16 |
| University of Illinois at Urbana-Champaign | 10 | 8 |
| Pennsylvania State University (University Park) | 13 | 10 |
| University of California, Santa Barbara | 14 | 13 |

## U.S. News & World Report's Top 50 Public National Universities (continued)

| University | 2001 | 2000 |
| --- | --- | --- |
| University of Washington | 14 | 13 |
| University of Texas at Austin | 16 | 13 |
| Texas A&M University (College Station) | 17 | 18 |
| University of Florida | 18 | 16 |
| University of Minnesota, Twin Cities | 18 | 18 |
| Ohio State University (Columbus) | 20 | 28 |
| Purdue University | 20 | 18 |
| University of Georgia | 20 | 22 |
| University of Iowa | 20 | 21 |
| Rutgers, The State University of New Jersey (New Brunswick) | 24 | 22 |
| University of Maryland (College Park) | 24 | 22 |
| Colorado School of Mines | 26 | 28 |
| Indiana University Bloomington | 26 | 31 |
| Miami University (Oxford, Ohio) | 26 | 22 |
| University of California, Santa Cruz | 26 | 31 |
| University of Colorado at Boulder | 26 | 31 |
| University of Delaware | 26 | 22 |
| Virginia Tech | 26 | 28 |
| Michigan State University | 33 | 31 |
| North Carolina State University (Raleigh) | 33 | 38 |
| State University of New York at Binghamton | 33 | 22 |
| University of California, Riverside | 33 | 31 |
| University of Missouri—Columbia | 33 | 48 |
| Clemson University | 38 | 38 |
| Iowa State University | 38 | 38 |
| University of Connecticut | 38 | 31 |
| University of Pittsburgh | 38 | 38 |
| Auburn University | 42 | 38 |
| University of Kansas | 42 | 38 |
| Ohio University | 44 | 31 |
| University of Arizona | 44 | 48 |
| University of Tennessee, Knoxville | 44 | 45 |
| Florida State University | 47 | 45 |
| University of Massachusetts at Amherst | 47 | 48 |
| University of New Hampshire | 47 | 45 |
| University of Vermont | 47 | 38 |
| Washington State University | 47 | not ranked |
| Michigan Technological University | not ranked | 48 |

Source: U.S. News & World Report, "America's Best Colleges," 2000 and 2001 issues (no dates).

point for your college search and use the criteria and initial data we provide to further your exploration.

Second, you should carefully understand the basis for any ranking. What are the authors' credentials? What data are they using in establishing the ranks? Where do the data come from, and are they reliable? Several of the publishers of major rankings are using what's called the Common Data Set, in which universities participate to provide accurate and consistent data. Criticisms have been lodged at colleges for massaging their data to influence rankings formulas. What are the data measuring? Are they subject to influence, for example, withholding the test scores of some students or including graduate research data when undergraduate programs are under consideration? How do the data chosen affect the output of the rankings? What formula is used to rank or combine the data, and how have changes in the formula, and the data reported, affected individual college rankings over time? How much difference is there between schools of various ranks? How important is it, for example, that a school is not in the "top 25" if it is ranked 26th? Again, all references for establishing rank need not be quantitative. Reputational data are a legitimate way to judge a university's quality and impact in education. Anecdotal evidence can provide understanding of a school's environment, character, and mission. Quantitative data can obscure as well as enlighten, so try to be a critical and well-informed user of rankings guides.

Rankings are one way of placing universities in a particular ballpark. They are a beginning to compare the many schools in the United States and abroad. Curious about computer technology? Then you might find the Yahoo! Internet Life survey helpful in the way that it captures some aspects of technology usage on campuses. Don't worry about whether the 20th-ranked university is much better or worse than its near neighbors, and don't discount a university that has not been ranked. Look at the specific data used to describe computer technology on each

## Yahoo! Internet Life's Top 50 Most Wired Universities, 2000

1.  Carnegie Mellon University
2.  University of Delaware
3.  New Jersey Institute of Technology
4.  Indiana University
5.  Dartmouth College
6.  Massachusetts Institute of Technology
7.  Rensselaer Polytechnic Institute
8.  University of Virginia
9.  Washington State University
10. University of California, Los Angeles
11. State University of New York at Buffalo
12. Pennsylvania State University (University Park)
13. University of Idaho
14. Rochester Institute of Technology
15. Georgia Institute of Technology

## Yahoo! Internet Life's Top 50 Most Wired Universities, 2000 (continued)

16. Drexel University
17. Ball State University
18. Florida State University
19. Wake Forest University
20. Iowa State University of Science and Technology
21. University of Dayton
22. North Carolina State University
23. Worcester Polytechnic University
24. George Mason University
25. Virginia Tech
26. University of Pennsylvania
27. Illinois Institute of Technology
28. University of Colorado at Boulder
29. New York University
30. Seton Hall University
31. University of Missouri—Rolla
32. University of Cincinnati
33. Kansas State University
34. University of Missouri—Columbia
35. Oregon State
36. University of Texas at Austin
37. Stevens Institute of Technology
38. Ohio State University
39. University of California, Santa Cruz
40. University of Maryland College Park
41. Northwestern University
42. University of Miami (Florida)
43. University of Scranton
44. University of Illinois at Chicago
45. University of North Carolina at Chapel Hill
46. Indiana University—Purdue University at Indianapolis
47. Villanova University
48. James Madison University
49. University of Oregon
50. Rutgers, The State University of New Jersey

*Source: ZDNet Ultimate College Guide.* See www.zdnet.com/yil/content/college/college2000/criteria.html.

campus to discern the differences. Clearly, a university that is ranked in the top 10 probably has a strong emphasis on computer technology, but you will still want to ascertain whether it fits your needs overall.

Throughout this book, you will note a variety of rankings and statistics on the universities. We hope they will give you an indication of how the public ivies stand in relation to one another and in comparison to other colleges and universities. We encourage you to examine these and other data to put together a comprehensive picture of the schools that interest you. You might consult *Kiplinger's* magazine, for example, for their ranking of public universities using a variety of data, including cost and performance. You can view the various rankings as just one of the criteria you will use in evaluating universities.

## *Kiplinger's* Best Public University Values, 1998

1　University of North Carolina at Chapel Hill

2　University of Virginia

3　College of William and Mary

4　University of Illinois at Urbana-Champaign

5　University of Florida

6　University of Wisconsin—Madison

7　University of California, Berkeley

8　University of California, Los Angeles

9　Georgia Institute of Technology

10　State University of New York at Binghamton

11　State University of New York College at Geneseo

12　University of Texas at Austin

13　University of Michigan, Ann Arbor

14　College of New Jersey

15　Rutgers The State University of New Jersey (New Brunswick)

16　Virginia Tech

17　University of Washington

18　Florida International University

19　Pennsylvania State University

20　University of Georgia

21　New College of the University of South Florida

22　Mary Washington College

23　Michigan Technological University

24　James Madison University

25　University of Maryland College Park

26　Colorado State University

26b　University of Missouri—Columbia

28　University of Iowa

28　North Carolina State University

30　Miami University (Oxford, Ohio)

31　University of California, Davis

32　Indiana University Bloomington

33　Appalachian State University

34　University of Colorado at Boulder

35　University of Minnesota, Morris

36　University of Delaware

37　St. Mary's College of Maryland

38　Ohio University

39　Washington State University

40　University of California, San Diego

40　Texas A&M University (College Station)

42　Rutgers, The State University of New Jersey (Camden)

43　Eastern Illinois University

44　University of Hawaii at Manoa

45　University of Minnesota, Twin Cities

46　University of California, Irvine

47　Florida State University

48　University of Kansas

49　Rutgers, The State University of New Jersey (Newark)

50　State University of New York at Albany

*Source:* www.kiplinger.com/magazine/archives/1998/September/college.htm.

# LOOKING FOR PARTICULAR PROGRAMS

When you head off to college, you may have some idea of what you would like to study, or no idea at all, or a very clear idea. Perhaps you are interested in several major areas, but want some flexibility. Perhaps you have seriously explored engineering, or medicine, or art history, and know that will likely be your eventual major. Whether you are certain of your direction or only mildly curious, looking into one or more academic or "co-curricular" programs at the universities should be a part of your college exploration process. One of the criteria important in comparing universities is the relative strength of individual academic departments, interdisciplinary majors, experiential education opportunities such as study abroad and service learning programs, and residential advising systems, to name only a few areas. Begin to research each university by examining some of the aspects of particular interest to you. You will note that the public ivies are renowned for the reputation and opportunities offered by quite a few of the specific undergraduate academic departments and programs. Beyond the overall reputation of a university, its campus, or even its highly regarded graduate degree programs, you need to examine its undergraduate offerings in your definite or possible areas of concentration in and out of the classroom. Here are some of the statistics or aspects you should look at:

- The number of undergraduate majors in a department or program you're interested in

- The number of courses offered regularly in the department

- The career recruiting and graduate admissions record for students graduating with that major

- Interdisciplinary, multidisciplinary, double-major, and major–minor opportunities associated with your academic interests

- The number of full-time faculty associated with your interests and their involvement in teaching undergraduates

- Evidence of recent faculty turnover or strife

- Campus happenings or conflicts or atmosphere, as indicated, perhaps, in the online student newspaper

- The number of graduate students focusing in your areas of interest

- The teaching responsibilities of these graduate students, as well as part-time faculty— who is teaching the courses you might be taking?

- The size of the classes you will likely enroll in, and how they are structured

- Research opportunities in your possible departments

- Funding for these departments by the university as a whole, and any evidence that your program might be on the way out

- The attrition rate of students in the program—how many students start but do not graduate from the program

- The requirements and opportunities, curricular and otherwise, related to the program.

How do you find out these things? By reading college literature, browsing the college website, reading available guidebooks, and, especially as you begin to narrow down your choices through your senior year, talking to university and departmental representatives. As we discuss in Part Four, you can take the personal initiative to contact faculty and program directors in your areas of interest to learn more about potential concentrations and, initially, to interest them in your application.

## The Lombardi Program's Top Public Research Universities, 2000

Nine criteria are measured:

- Total research expenditures
- Federal research expenditures
- Endowment assets
- Annual giving
- National academy members
- Faculty awards
- Doctorates awarded
- Postdoctoral appointees
- SAT scores

The university is followed by the number of Lombardi's measures on which it is in the top 25 of the research universities the program has evaluated.

University of California, Berkeley, 9
University of California, Los Angeles, 9
University of Michigan, Ann Arbor, 9
University of North Carolina at Chapel Hill, 9
Pennsylvania State University (University Park), 8

University of Florida, 8
University of Illinois at Urbana-Champaign, 8
University of Minnesota, Twin Cities, 8
University of Washington (Seattle), 8
University of Wisconsin—Madison, 8
Texas A&M University, 7

## The Lombardi Program's Top Public Research Universities, 2000 (continued)

University of California, San Francisco, 7
University of Iowa, 7
University of Texas at Austin, 7
Georgia Institute of Technology, 6
Ohio State University (Columbus), 6
Purdue University, 6
University of Arizona, 6
University of California, Davis, 6
University of California, San Diego, 6
University of Pittsburgh, 6
University of Virginia, 6
University of Maryland College Park, 5
University of Utah, 5
Rutgers, The State University of New Jersey (New Brunswick), 4
University of Colorado at Boulder, 4
University of Texas SW Medical Center—Dallas, 4
University of Alabama at Birmingham, 3
Indiana University Bloomington, 2
Michigan State University, 2
North Carolina State University, 2
State University of New York at Stony Brook, 2
University of California, Irvine, 2
University of Georgia, 2
University of Nebraska—Lincoln, 2
Iowa State University, 1
State University of New York at Buffalo, 1
University of California, Santa Barbara, 1
University of Cincinnati, Cincinnati, 1
University of Colorado Health Sciences Center, 1
University of Delaware, 1
University of Illinois at Chicago, 1
University of Kansas (Lawrence), 1
University of Texas MD Anderson Cancer Center, 1
University of Texas Medical Branch—Galveston, 1
Virginia Polytechnic Institute and State University, 1
Washington State University (Pullman), 1

*Source:* John V. Lombardi et al., "The Top American Research Universities." Lombardi Program on Measuring University Performance, July 2000, The Center, University of Florida. thecenter.ufl.edu.

## THE FACULTY

As we have learned from our research and our conversations with college students and graduates, the faculty at the school you attend is one of the biggest factors determining whether you are satisfied with your college experience. Along with the quality of your fellow students and how well you fit in with them and the availability of the courses you want to take, the availability and talent of your teachers will stand as the defining element of your university education. You will encounter better and worse instructors, but if you find overall that you had strong faculty and were able to connect closely with one or two key mentors, you will generally be happy about the education you have pursued. As we discussed in Part One, achieving this last goal—bonding with a few professors—is easier said than done at a large research university, but it can happen. Through research assistantships, internships, senior honors seminars, and initiative on your part within your department and academic major, you can link up with professors who share your academic and personal interests and may serve as future references and advisors.

You can assume that faculty at the public ivies, with few exceptions, have a strong research interest or two and have a goal to produce articles and books, secure research grants, earn tenure or a promotion, and keep their teaching load as light as possible. They tend to prefer teaching graduate seminars and junior- or senior-level undergraduate courses. Lowest on the totem pole for faculty are introductory lecture classes, just as they are for students. Nevertheless, some faculty, and some graduate students, are outstanding teachers. It will be one of your jobs in college to seek them out. One of your tasks in admissions is to try to determine which universities seem to have strong faculty overall in your particular areas of interest.

The public ivies employ some of the most prominent faculty in the nation. They often battle with one another to retain these scholars, as one university makes an offer of tenure, or an endowed chair, or a full professorship, to entice a professor at another school to change horses. Top professors, like professional athletes, have become free agents, so there is no guarantee that a professor from whom you are most interested in learning will be there when you enter the university in the fall or when you start your senior year. Since state legislatures have kept public funding of their universities at the lowest levels that are politically acceptable within their tight budgetary constraints, public universities have increasingly turned to private

---

### PROJECTED NUMBERS OF GRADUATING SENIORS IN THE UNITED STATES AND SELECTED STATES

The number of seniors graduating from high school in the United States is projected to grow during the next decade, but this growth is not occurring evenly across the country. The 2001 high school graduating class is expected to total 2,852,533 in the United States. The states with the largest numbers of graduating seniors are California (319,870), Texas (211,165), New York (174,757), Pennsylvania (133,810), Florida (127,905), Ohio (125,802), Illinois (125,438), and Michigan (104,391). In some states the numbers are growing, and in others they're declining. Florida's class will be 4 percent larger than in 2000, and Ohio's will be 2 percent lower. Nevada, with just 14,941 graduates, will show a 4 percent increase over the previous year. West Virginia (5 percent decline), Utah (4 percent decline), and Mississippi (7 percent decline) will show the largest decreases in numbers over the one-year period, while Vermont (4 percent increase), Arizona (3 percent increase), Georgia (3 percent increase), Missouri (3 percent increase), and New Hampshire (3 percent increase) will see growth. These changes will reflect the states' university enrollments, tax base, and legislative outlook on funding for higher education.

*Source:* "SAT Trend Report, October 2000," College Board, www.collegeboard.com.

fundraising to supplement their budgets, many of which are supplied by more than 50 percent private dollars. Combined with the fact that the amount public universities can raise their tuitions is constrained by state rules, this has led to an increasing imbalance in faculty compensation for top professors at the public and private universities. In recent years, public universities have raised their tuitions, but not as much as private universities have. Because of state rules and control, they are less able to compete against their private counterparts in recruiting and retaining top faculty. According to King Alexander, a University of Illinois economist, the salary gap between full professors at the top private universities and those at the top public universities has grown from $1,300 in 1980 to $21,700 in 1998.[2] The major new capital campaigns underway at the public universities are intended to help rectify this imbalance by allowing the public universities to offer more enticements to their teaching and research staffs. Many states are now trying to increase the levels of funding for higher education, since they recognize the role that their public colleges and universities are playing in their economies.

Faculty retention rates and length of tenure in some departments are indicators of whether the university and specific departments are able to keep their professors happy. The number of new hires of talented junior faculty indicates whether the university and its departments are attractive to rising scholars in the field. Here are some elements you will want to concentrate on regarding faculty:

- Faculty salaries relative to similar universities

- Proportions of full-time, part-time, tenured, endowed chair, nontenured, and visiting faculty and the classes that are taught by these groups

- The numbers of graduate teaching assistants and how many classes they teach

- Recent evidence of conflict between faculty and administration, or of large numbers of faculty leaving campus

- Evidence that the university is committed to hiring major scholars or high-profile rising stars

- Amounts of research grants awarded to faculty at the university and in what areas

- Students' opinions of their professors, which can be found in the campus paper, online faculty course evaluations, and discussions with current students

- Major awards (Fulbright grants, MacArthur grants, Nobel Prizes, etc.) given to faculty in recent years and in what areas

- Major publicity associated with star faculty, and the programs they have been able to promote and furnish

[2]"University Education: The Gap Widens," *The Economist*, April 22, 2000, pp. 24–26.

## Faculty Salaries at Selected Institutions

| Institution | Professor | Associate Professor | Assistant Professor | Instructor |
|---|---|---|---|---|
| Harvard University | $128.9 | 71.6 | 66.5 | 48.0 |
| Princeton University | 120.0 | 71.9 | 56.0 | 49.2 |
| Yale University | 119.0 | 67.3 | 54.7 | 45.8 |
| University of Pennsylvania | 114.8 | 80.5 | 67.0 | |
| Columbia University | 113.4 | 72.2 | 57.0 | 68.8 |
| University of California, Berkeley | 108.7 | 69.6 | 60.1 | |
| University of California, Los Angeles | 106.1 | 67.4 | 58.3 | |
| University of Virginia | 101.2 | 68.9 | 53.7 | 41.2 |
| University of Michigan, Ann Arbor | 100.9 | 71.8 | 57.7 | 50.2 |
| University of California, San Diego | 99.7 | 65.0 | 55.6 | |
| Rutgers, The State University of New Jersey (New Brunswick) | 98.8 | 70.8 | 53.1 | 33.7 |
| Cornell University Endowed Colleges | 97.9 | 72.3 | 61.4 | 51.9 |
| Dartmouth College | 97.4 | 69.6 | 54.1 | 42.5 |
| University of California, Irvine | 96.8 | 66.6 | 56.8 | |
| University of California, Santa Barbara | 96.7 | 63.4 | 53.2 | |
| University of North Carolina at Chapel Hill | 93.8 | 67.4 | 55.2 | 58.1 |
| University of Connecticut | 93.5 | 68.7 | 53.9 | 49.2 |
| College of William and Mary | 93.4 | 64.9 | 51.6 | 36.9 |
| University of Delaware | 91.9 | 65.0 | 52.1 | 39.0 |
| University of Illinois at Urbana-Champaign | 91.6 | 63.4 | 54.1 | |
| University of California, Davis | 91.3 | 64.2 | 53.9 | |
| Pennsylvania State University (University Park) | 89.9 | 60.4 | 50.2 | 34.2 |
| University of Iowa | 89.6 | 60.8 | 52.7 | 42.2 |
| University of Minnesota, Twin Cities | 89.5 | 63.9 | 53.6 | 45.6 |
| University of Texas at Austin | 89.4 | 58.2 | 54.2 | 39.7 |
| University of Maryland College Park | 88.8 | 63.5 | 57.5 | 43.3 |
| Ohio State University Main Campus | 88.8 | 61.1 | 51.0 | 44.3 |
| Indiana University Bloomington | 85.0 | 58.8 | 48.4 | 32.8 |
| University of Wisconsin—Madison | 84.5 | 64.8 | 55.4 | 43.7 |
| University of Georgia | 82.8 | 58.9 | 50.2 | 35.7 |
| University of Colorado at Boulder | 82.6 | 59.4 | 50.2 | 36.9 |
| University of Arizona | 81.9 | 57.2 | 49.8 | |
| Michigan State University | 81.5 | 60.4 | 49.1 | 32.6 |
| University of Washington (Seattle) | 80.6 | 58.4 | 51.4 | 34.9 |

## Faculty Salaries at Selected Institutions (continued)

| Institution | Professor | Associate Professor | Assistant Professor | Instructor |
|---|---|---|---|---|
| State University of New York at Binghamton | 79.4 | 58.8 | 49.4 | 38.4 |
| Miami University (Oxford, Ohio) | 78.3 | 57.5 | 44.1 | 30.4 |
| University of Florida | 76.9 | 56.9 | 49.9 | |

These salaries are for 1999–2000 American Association of University Professors Category I institutions. Salaries are in thousands of dollars, rounded to the nearest hundred, and are adjusted to a nine-month work year. The figures cover full-time members of each institution's faculty, except those in medical schools. Note these salary figures reflect the earnings of graduate faculty engaged primarily in research and graduate instruction, as well as undergraduate professors.

Adapted from *Chronicle of Higher Education*, April 14, 2000, www.chronicle.com/state/aaup.

## CLASS SIZE

Class size seems an obvious factor to consider, but it is not an easy one to determine. It is measured in many ways: overall average class size at the university, percentage of classes with fewer than 20 students or more than 50, largest and smallest classes, and so forth. Within these categories, there is much disagreement on how reliable or consistent the data are. Class size is important, because there is a connection between learning opportunities and contact with faculty, and between faculty contact and class size. Remember that professor facing the 500 students seated in tiers in the lecture hall? Consider the impact on your getting to know your teacher and what you learn sitting through that course a few times per week. Think about the largest class you have at your high school. Is it 50 students? Fifteen? At what point is a big class too big for you? There is much less difference between a class of 40 students and a class of 60 than there is between a class of 20 students and one of 200. The public ivies are, for the most part, large universities where, as we have said, you will encounter some lecture halls that seat 400+ students. Some of the professors lecturing in these classes are star faculty, researchers who wrote the very books they are teaching. This can inspire you. The public ivies are also places where, especially by your third year, you will be primarily in 30- to 50-student classes, with some smaller seminars and larger 150-student lectures mixed in. Do examine the class size data. At each university try to get a sense of the following:

- The percentage of undergraduate classes with more than 50 students
- The percentage of undergraduate classes with fewer than 20 students
- The average class size

- The median class size

- The average class size of introductory courses

- The biggest class

- Special seminar or honors program classes and their entrance requirements

- Maximum allowable size of discussion or recitation sections taught by graduate teaching assistants

- Average class size in your particular college (arts and sciences, for example) and in your potential major

## ENDOWMENTS OF THE MAJOR UNIVERSITIES

The 1990s were good years overall for endowment builders at both public and private universities and colleges. The markets performed well, investments rose, and donors gave generously. Many public ivies compare favorably to some of the wealthiest private colleges and universities in terms of their overall endowments. Since many public ivies are larger than some of the small and middle-sized private universities, their endowments do not appear as high when looked at on an endowment-per-student basis. When you examine endowment figures, take into account that some of these figures cover an entire public university system, and not just one campus or institution. In 1999 Harvard had by far the largest endowment of any university in the United States, more than $14.2 billion. The University of Texas system was a distant second, with over $8.1 billion, Yale University ranked third, with $7.1 billion, Princeton was fourth at almost $6.5 billion, and Stanford was fifth at just over $6 billion. From there, individual universities and

---

### UNIVERSITY LEADERS IN VOLUNTARY GIVING

The Council for Aid to Education estimates that in 1998–99, nongovernmental sources gave $20.4 billion to public and private colleges and universities. The largest proportion of this money, 29 percent, came from alumni. Twenty-four percent came from other individuals, 22 percent from foundations, 18 percent from corporations, 2 percent from religious organizations, and 6 percent from other sources. The institutions used one-third of this money for restricted endowment funds, more than one-third for restricted current operations, and about 14 percent

*(continued)*

## UNIVERSITY LEADERS IN VOLUNTARY GIVING

for property, buildings, and equipment. A number of the public ivies ranked at the top of the total voluntary giving, as well as alumni and other individual giving. The public institutions are doing their best to raise funds for their operations and endowment outside the public sector and the state legislature. Voluntary giving includes donations from alumni and other private individuals who want to invest in education or contribute to a research institute or financial aid fund, for example, and corporations wishing to sponsor research or enhance their public image. These additional funds help them expand their facilities and financial aid, strengthen their research programs, and attract and retain top faculty.

**Public universities in the top 20 in total voluntary giving**

| | |
|---|---|
| University of Wisconsin—Madison | $245,382,486 |
| University of Nebraska | $218,746,396 |
| University of Washington | $210,744,638 |
| University of California, Los Angeles | $208,203,671 |
| University of California, Berkeley | $184,230,886 |
| University of Michigan | $176,993,402 |
| University of Minnesota | $161,966,013 |
| Indiana University | $159,436,782 |

**Public universities in the top 20 in alumni giving**

| | |
|---|---|
| University of Nebraska | $151,703,706 |
| University of California, Berkeley | $80,132,456 |
| University of Michigan | $79,626,322 |
| University of California, Los Angeles | $62,397,182 |
| University of North Carolina at Chapel Hill | $48,662,581 |

**Public universities in the top 20 in giving from nonalumni individuals**

| | |
|---|---|
| University of California, San Francisco | $44,273,331 |
| University of California, Los Angeles | $43,105,049 |
| University of Texas Anderson Cancer Center | $33,556,727 |
| Indiana University | $32,945,709 |
| University of Texas at Austin | $31,725,008 |
| University of Washington | $31,498,318 |

*Source:* Kit Lively, "Giving to Higher Education Breaks Another Record," *Chronicle of Higher Education,* May 5, 2000, p. A41; "Voluntary Support of Higher Education, 1998–99," *Chronicle of Higher Education,* May 5, 2000, no page, www.chronicle.com/weekly/v46/i35/4635voluntary_support.htm.

systems, including most of the public ivies, range from $4 billion down to several hundred million dollars. The bulk of the public universities have endowments in the $300 million to $1 billion range. See our individual school data sheets in Part Three for exact figures for each of the public ivies or their systems.

Tracing endowment figures and their connection to undergraduate studies in the liberal arts is a complicated task. One must rely on publicly reported data from the universities and comparisons made by academic sources and popular guides. Try to find out the overall endowment, its proportion to the number of graduate and undergraduate students on campus, and the growth of the endowment in recent years. Are the reported figures limited to the university campus in which you are interested, or do they cover a state's university system as a whole? Do the figures include money held specifically by such graduate institutions as medical or law schools, or are these amounts reported separately? Can you determine the endowment funds related to the college of the liberal arts and sciences, where most undergraduates are enrolled?

---

### BIG MONEY GIFTS AND CAPITAL CAMPAIGNS

Money flowed into the coffers of public universities at the end of the twentieth century and beginning of the twenty-first, in the form of both huge individual gifts and capital from major fundraising campaigns. Here are some highlights. At the end of 2000, of the 18 colleges and universities in the United States that are seeking to raise $1 billion or more (yes, billion), 6 had reached their goal and 12 were well on their way. Eight of these are public universities or university systems:

- The Pennsylvania State University system raised $886 million toward its goal of $1 billion by 2003.
- The University of Arizona raised $529.6 million toward its goal of $1 billion by 2005.
- The University of California, Berkeley, raised $1.28 billion, higher than its goal of $1.1 billion by December 31, 2000.
- The University of California, Los Angeles, raised $1.399 billion toward its goal of $1.6 billion by 2002.
- The University of Illinois system raised $1.498 billion, over its goal of $1 billion by December 31, 2000.
- The University of Minnesota raised $1.001 billion toward its goal of $1.3 billion by 2003.
- The University of Texas at Austin raised $765 million toward its goal of $2 billion by 2004.
- The University of Virginia raised $1.268 billion, over its goal of $1 billion by December 31, 2000.

*(continued)*

## BIG MONEY GIFTS AND CAPITAL CAMPAIGNS

In addition to these capital campaign accumulations, the public universities have been the recipients of some of the largest single private gifts to higher education in the last decade. The University of Utah and the University of Nebraska each received cash gifts of $125 million in 1998. Iowa State University received $80 million in stock in 1999. The University of Virginia received $60 million in stock in 1999, and the University of North Dakota received $100 million in cash, stock, and assets in 1998. The University of Colorado received a $250 million gift, the largest single gift ever to any public college or university, in 2001.

*Source:* "Largest Private Gifts to Higher Education since 1967," *Chronicle of Higher Education,* December 15, 2000, www.chronicle.com/stats/biggifts.htm; "Updates on Billion-Dollar Campaigns at 18 Universities," *Chronicle of Higher Education,* February 2, 2000, www.chronicle.com/daily/2001/02/2001020205n.htm.

In addition to endowment funds, government grants for research or specific educational programs are a major source of university income. Note these figures at the public ivies and other institutions to see their impact on university functions. Again, see if you can trace the grants to particular undergraduate programs in your areas of interest.

## VOLUNTARY GIFTS TO RESEARCH UNIVERSITIES

The amount of voluntary giving to public and private research universities in the United States is astounding, and it has been increasing. Take a look at these figures to get a sense of how much nonpublic support the universities, both public and private, receive each year:

| Year | Number of institutions | Amount | Average per institution | Increase |
|---|---|---|---|---|
| 1997–98 | | | | |
| All research universities | 199 | $10,872,831,000 | $54,913,000 | |
| Private | 71 | $5,238,538,000 | $73,782,000 | |
| Public | 128 | $5,634,293,000 | $44,018,000 | |
| 1998–99 | | | | |
| All research universities | 195 | $12,223,617,000 | $62,685,000 | 14.2% |
| Private | 69 | $5,902,214,000 | $85,539,000 | 15.9% |
| Public | 126 | $6,321,403,000 | $50,170,000 | 14.0% |

*Source:* "Voluntary Support of Higher Education, 1998–99," *Chronicle of Higher Education,* May 5, 2000, no page, www.chronicle.com/weekly/v46/i35/4635voluntary_support.htm.

# COLLEGE COSTS

According to figures from the College Board, public universities have increased the amount they charge for in-state tuition in recent years (to an average of $3,510 at four-year public institutions in 2000, a 4.4 percent increase over the previous year), but not as much as have private universities (to an average of $16,332 at four-year private institutions, a 5.2 percent increase). The amount that public universities charge out-of-state students as a "tuition surcharge" on top of the in-state tuition base has actually declined (from $8,706 at four-year institutions to $5,510). Average room-and-board costs increased in 2000. They were up 4.2 percent at four-year private institutions and 5.1 percent at four-year public colleges and universities. Offsetting these average increases, some public universities systems, notably California and New York, have tried to keep their tuition levels relatively constant, and financial aid provision has risen. In 1999, Virginia even approved a 20 percent cut in tuition at public colleges and universities, sparking concerns among private colleges over the increase in the disparity between their higher costs and those at state-supported institutions. Overall, the cost picture for students in the United States has not been rosy. The average aid for full-time students increased only 79 percent in the last 20 years, while tuition and fees have risen more than 100 percent and family income has increased on average just 20 percent. Loans now represent 59 percent of a student's financial aid package, up from the 41 percent they constituted in 1980. The tuition increases at public universities in recent years, in the 3 to 5 percent range, are significantly lower than the 10 to 12 percent rises in tuition seen during the late 1980s and early 1990s.

Keeping students' costs under control, while competing with private colleges and universities to retain faculty and provide the kind of education and amenities that students expect today will continue to be a major issue for state and federal legislators, governors, and educators at the public ivies. Citing General Accounting Office statistics, Senators Joseph Lieberman and Fred Thompson noted in 2000 that from 1990 to 1996, the average tuition for a full-time undergraduate student rose 44 percent, while the Consumer Price Index, which measures inflation, rose just 15.4 percent and median household income increased only 13.8 percent.[3] In 2001, the Bush administration advanced proposals to increase the amount of the federal Pell Grants to help students pay for college tuition. Students will continue to have to contend with high tuition, fee, and room-and-board costs and the impact of federal and state budget changes and university capital campaigns. It is essential that students carefully consider the costs associated with attending different colleges and universities, public and private, and the potential ways they can keep their initial costs and potential loan debt down. Track how the public universities you are considering are doing in terms of tuition, fees, room and board, and need- and merit-based financial aid. See what each university's state legislature is up to in terms of increasing or decreasing state funds for higher education. And take a look at the university's fundraising efforts in the private sector.

[3]Stephen Burd, "Lawmakers Warn Colleges to Keep Their Prices within Reach," *Chronicle of Higher Education,* February 18, 2000, p. A40.

---

### THE RISE IN MERIT-BASED FINANCIAL AID

---

According to the National Association of State Student Grant and Aid Programs, overall state support for student aid has increased dramatically in recent years, and more merit-based aid is being awarded to students. For the 1998–99 academic year, the amount that states spent on student aid rose by about 8.8 percent over the previous year. Spending on merit-based aid rose even more dramatically. States awarded some $718 million in merit-based scholarships, an increase of about 19 percent over the 1997–98 amount and 47 percent over the 1996–97 amount. Merit-based aid constituted 19 percent of state spending on student aid in 1998–99, compared to 15 percent four years before. Almost all need-based financial aid from the states went to undergraduates, who also received about 93 percent of all merit-based aid. In addition, more states have begun to offer merit awards and forgivable loans as part of programs to recruit students into such occupations as teaching, medicine, nursing, engineering, and computer science.

*Source:* Peter Schmidt, "Boom in Merit-Based Scholarships Drives 8.8% Rise in State Funds for Student Aid," *Chronicle of Higher Education*, April 21, 2000, p. A39.

## FACILITIES

A big endowment at a university supports the construction and maintenance of academic and other facilities on campus: dormitories, athletic complexes, cafeterias, counseling and learning centers, arts pavilions, theaters, computer technology labs, and research centers. Universities build these facilities to attract and retain top faculty, staff, and students with a wide variety of interests. The public ivies have some of the most extraordinary university campuses in the country, small cities in their own right, with the most modern, accessible facilities available. What some may lack in residential offerings they make up in scientific research laboratories. Though they may not have a central campus green with Georgian architecture, they have huge student recreation centers, computer integrated library systems, and art studios. Each is different; you should tour the campuses that most interest you and the departments or facilities where you might spend a lot of your time. If you plan to major in French literature, philosophy, or classics, the research lab for the program in quantum mechanics is of little relevance. You will want to visit the departmental buildings for these humanities majors and go to the library, or libraries, where the humanities readings are housed. What computer facilities are available to you, a nontech major? Where will you be able to do your research and studying? What do your classrooms look like? Where do the aspiring philosophers hang out?

## SOCIAL AND RESIDENTIAL LIFE

Where and how students live is an important matter to universities. That is why they have deans of social and residential life who concern themselves with student housing and often with students' social life, counseling programs, mentoring programs, and health services. Here are some questions to ask these deans and others at the university about undergraduates' residential and social life:

- Where do first-year students live? Are they guaranteed housing? If so, where?

- How many first-year students live on campus? Are they required to do so? If so, what are their choices?

- Are there special housing programs available, with suite-style apartments, single rooms, faculty-in-residence advising, student mentoring, or affinity living (for example, an international house, an African American house, a substance-free dorm, single-sex dorms or floors, family housing, and athletes' dorms)? How does one get into these facilities?

- Where do students eat and congregate? What meal programs are offered? What student recreational and social spaces are provided? What access do athletes and nonathletes have to athletic facilities, tickets to major games, and physical trainers and therapists?

- What housing opportunities are available for those with physical disabilities or other special needs? What dining facilities are available for those with vegetarian, kosher, Muslim, or other dietetic needs?

- Is there a Greek system on campus? How many students, male and female (and in what years are they), are affiliated with fraternities and sororities? When do students rush, or join, these organizations? Do students live in Greek houses? What proportion do, and when can they move into them? Does the university count fraternity and sorority houses as on-campus living? Do students eat their meals in their fraternity or sorority house?

- How many undergraduates live on campus? Where? Are first-year students mixed in with upper class students? Are there special dorms and opportunities (single rooms or resident advisor positions, for example) for juniors and seniors? If upper class students move off campus, where do they live? Does the university help them find housing in the area? What are rents like?

- What physical and mental health programs are available for students? What kind of student health insurance is provided, and what does it cover? Are confidential counseling services provided? Are student mentoring programs, anonymous hotlines, crisis centers, substance abuse education and treatment programs, violence awareness and prevention programs, nutritional counseling, and campus mediation programs available?

Social and residential life is a big part of your college experience. How a university meets your needs greatly affects your overall satisfaction with the school, your happiness, and your success. Of course, you cannot predict whether you will use or need all of the great diversity of social programs, but you should understand that they exist should you want them or need to refer a friend to them. Awareness and action on the part of a university in the areas mentioned suggest that the institution is interested in and capable of providing the range of services that college students need and expect today.

## HONORS PROGRAMS

Public universities have done a great deal in the last decade to attract top students, from both in state and out of state. Along with prestigious merit scholarships they now offer a variety of honors programs. Some are distinct honors colleges, major components of the academic structure at the university, whereas others are programs reaching across disciplinary boundaries within the university. Often the honors colleges have a dean who controls them administratively, while the programs typically have a director in charge. Many feel that an honors college represents a more serious commitment on the part of the university to the maintenance and expansion of the program. An honors program may carry less weight on the campus and be less institutionalized. Most public ivies have honors programs that integrate special aspects of the main university, rather than an honors college.

Honors programs and honors colleges offer academically talented students smaller classes, better advising systems, interdisciplinary study, and more opportunities for advanced academic enrichment. Sometimes they involve preferred housing opportunities, research grants, merit scholarships, a senior thesis, community service, service learning, independent study or work, or other advantages and requirements. Honors scholars are recognized in some way at the university and at graduation, and they will likely enjoy some prestige and advantage in their career search or graduate school admissions.

Not all honors programs are alike. Here are some questions you will want to ask in researching available honors programs:

- What level of funding does the university provide for the program?

- How many students are enrolled, how are they selected, and when do they enter the program?

- Do students apply during the regular first-year admissions process or once they reach campus? Or are students selected by the admissions committee without having to complete any additional application?

- When do the advantages of the honors program begin? Are special small classes offered right away, or are they available only to juniors and seniors?

- What is special about the honors program? What are the curriculum, courses, and other study, service, and work opportunities it offers?

- How many faculty are involved in the program? What is their teaching and advising availability for honors students? What incentives are faculty given to participate? Are they granted a higher salary, reduced teaching elsewhere at the university, or other advantages?

- Who is the dean or director of the program, and what is his or her background? What is the office's position in the academic hierarchy? Does the dean or director report directly to the president or chancellor of the university, for example?

- How long has the program been in place, and what is its record of involving and graduating students? Where do honors graduates go after college? Do they win prestigious graduate

---

### SOME TOP HONORS PROGRAMS IN 1994

University of California, Los Angeles, Honors Programs

University of Delaware, University Honors Program

University of Georgia, Honors Program

University of Maryland, University Honors Program

University of Michigan, Honors Program (also at Ann Arbor is the Residential College)

University of North Carolina, Honors Program

Pennsylvania State University, University Scholars Program (since 1997 the Schreyer Honors College)

University of Texas, Plan II Honors Program (also at Austin are the Business Honors Program, College of Pharmacy Undergraduate Honors Program, Dean's Scholars Program, Engineering Honors Program, Humanities Honors Program, Liberal Arts Honors Programs, and the Senior Fellows Program)

University of Virginia, Echols Scholars Program (also see the Rodman Scholars Program in engineering, and the Honors Program in philosophy)

The author used a mixture of vague qualitative and quantitative items in four categories—Town and Campus, Intellectual Setting, Entrance Requirements, and Program Quality—to rate 55 public college and university honors programs on a scale of one to three stars. The universities listed here were the only ones to receive the top three-star rating.

*Source:* Robert R. Sullivan, *Ivy League Programs at State School Prices* (Englewood Cliffs, NJ: Prentice Hall, 1994).

fellowships, or get admitted to top law, medical, business, or academic graduate programs? Are honors students recognized by the university during their tenure and at graduation? If so, how?

- What are the characteristics of students in the honors program versus those in the rest of the university, and in particular the liberal arts college? Is there a difference between in-state and out-of-state enrollment, male/female participation, financial aid, and so forth?

- What kind of housing or facilities are associated with the honors program? Will you live in a separate dorm or part of the campus as an honors student?

- Will you receive research grants, guaranteed merit-based financial aid, or other monetary incentives as an honors student? Or does the honors program in fact cost you more?

- How is the honors program integrated into the university? What is its governance structure, and will you as a student have input into how the program is run?

- What are the opportunities to transfer in and out of the honors program, and what are the curricular and other requirements of being enrolled in it?

---

### CURRICULAR REQUIREMENTS, OPPORTUNITIES, AND SPECIAL PROGRAMS

In your research on public universities and their honors programs and colleges, be sure to look out for other special programs, honors opportunities, and curricular opportunities and requirements. Not all honors, or scholars, choices come under the rubric of a universitywide honors college or program. Just take a look at the offerings of the University of Texas at Austin or the University of Virginia, for example. Special programs that are not well publicized may exist precisely in your areas of interest and may make the difference for you in choosing one university over another.

Interdisciplinary or multidisciplinary programs may be of interest to you. These combine study in a variety of areas, allowing you to gain knowledge in different academic subjects. Some of these, including science and ethics, women's studies, environmental studies, peace and conflict studies, and African American studies, arrived on the scene mostly in the late 1960s and 1970s. Others, gay and lesbian studies or biotechnology for example, are later inventions. Such programs represent efforts by the university and the faculty to cross disciplinary boundaries to provide a more stimulating and creative academic foundation for students.

The university will have publications about the honors college or program, which will also have a separate page on the university website. You should examine these. Remember: an honors program is only one aspect of the overall environment, and a fantastic honors program may not make the wrong university right for you. A great honors program can be one of the criteria you use in determining the strength of a university, and the presence of a well-regarded, well-funded, and strongly enrolled program on campus may positively affect the rest of academic and social life at the university. If you are part of an honors program on campus, it may connect you with strong faculty, other motivated and talented students, and interesting intellectual opportunities. These opportunities will not completely change the fact that you, in most cases, are at a large research university, but they will compensate for some of the negatives we have

---

### STUDY ABROAD AT PUBLIC DOCTORAL AND RESEARCH INSTITUTIONS IN THE UNITED STATES, 2000

The following are the public doctoral and research universities with the most students studying abroad and the number of students doing so at each.

| Institution | Number of Students Studying Abroad |
| --- | --- |
| Michigan State University | 1,565 |
| University of Texas at Austin | 1,452 |
| University of Wisconsin–Madison | 1,204 |
| Miami University (Oxford, Ohio) | 1,110 |
| University of North Carolina at Chapel Hill | 1,061 |
| University of Arizona | 1,040 |
| University of Colorado at Boulder | 1,019 |
| University of Illinois at Urbana-Champaign | 1,005 |
| University of Michigan, Ann Arbor | 995 |
| Indiana University Bloomington | 983 |
| Pennsylvania State University (University Park) | 917 |
| University of Georgia | 900 |
| Ohio State University (Columbus) | 889 |
| University of Delaware | 874 |
| George Mason University | 671 |
| University of New Hampshire | 438 |
| Ball State University | 432 |
| Georgia State University | 380 |
| State University of New York at Binghamton | 368 |
| University of Southern Mississippi | 355 |
| College of William and Mary | 352 |
| Illinois State University | 328 |
| Northern Arizona University | 300 |

*Source:* "U.S. Institutes with the Largest Numbers of Students Studying Abroad, by Type of Institution," *Chronicle of Higher Education*, November 17, 2000, p. A75.

discussed in relation to the larger universities and will make these institutions feel more like a smaller liberal arts college in some important areas. For more information on honors colleges and programs, and links to regional collegiate honors councils as well as institutions with honors programs, contact the National Collegiate Honors Council at www.runet.edu/~nchc.

A college curriculum comes with requirements and opportunities. In evaluating a university, determine not only how many courses, and in what areas, are available to you, but also what the curricular requirements are in mathematics, sciences, humanities, languages, non-Western studies, and so forth so you know whether they are acceptable to you. Universities vary widely in terms of what they require, although the public ivies generally ask students to complete distribution requirements across the arts and sciences, without specifically naming the courses they must take.

## SELECTIVITY

Selectivity matters, but less for prestige than for the quality of the student body that a university is able to create and maintain. When a university has many more applicants than it has available spaces, it can afford to be selective in its offers of admission. It can set admission standards and criteria higher and can select students to create a more diverse and interesting class. For those who are accepted and choose to go, this means a class full of brighter, more accomplished peers overall. A key point is that a university's selectivity, that is, the percentage of applicants who are admitted, is closely related to its yield, or the percentage of admitted applicants who choose to enroll. Most universities in this country, even those considered highly desirable and selective, have admissions yields well below 50 percent. That means they still must admit twice as many students as they want to enroll, so that they obtain close to the class size they seek. This is a difficult game for all colleges to play, and certainly so for large universities, since having even a slightly higher or lower percentage of admitted students enrolling in any year can dramatically change the number of first-year students.

Selectivity can help you determine which universities are more or less likely to admit you. This statistic can also help you to evaluate which universities are able to be more discerning in their admissions process. Thus selectivity should be taken as a general indicator of the level of interest in a university compared to its available spaces, the demand for entrance into the university, and the university's ability to maintain a high level of quality in its student body and overall programs.

## OUT-OF-STATE STUDENTS

You may be on the outside looking in or on the inside looking out, but either way, you should consider the situation of nonresident, or out-of-state, students at a public university. What is the overall percentage of nonresidents in the university as a whole, in the undergraduate student body, and in the college or program you are considering? Where do these nonresidents come from? Are they drawn mainly from surrounding states, creating more of a regionalized student body, or do they come from states across the country and countries around the world? Out-of-state students bring talent, money, and a wide range of interests to a public university. Since admissions standards are higher for nonresidents, these students have been judged in a more demanding fashion during the admissions process and tend on average to have stronger credentials than in-state students. They may bring significant talents in athletics, music, arts, and specific academic areas to programs at the university in which they are particularly interested. Since out-of-state students pay significantly higher tuition than state residents, they also subsidize the tuition of residents and help support university programs. There is often a tense negotiating process among university administrators, state legislators, and state higher education commissioners about the percentage of nonresident undergraduates allowed to enroll at the state's public universities. The school administrators often seek the individual merits and higher tuition dollars the out-of-state students bring with them, while legislators and commissioners listen to state taxpayers and voters, many of whom favor keeping the state university

---

### GRADING THE STATES ON THEIR HIGHER EDUCATION

Recently, the National Center for Public Policy and Higher Education awarded letter grades to the states in five categories. The center used the following criteria to grade the states:

**PREPARATION:** Measured by the percentage of 18- to 24-year-olds with a high school credential; the percentage of high school students who have taken upper level math and science courses; the percentage of eighth-grade students who have taken algebra and scored at or above "proficient" on national assessment examinations in math, reading, and writing; the percentage of low-income eighth-grade students who scored at or above "proficient" on national assessment examinations in math; the number of scores in the top 20 percent on the SAT or ACT per 1,000 high school graduates; and the number of scores that are 3 or higher on AP subject tests per 1,000 high school juniors and seniors.

**PARTICIPATION:** Measured by the percentage of high school freshmen who enroll in college in any state within four years; the percentage of 18- to 24-year-olds enrolled in college in the state; and the percentage of 25- to 44-year-olds enrolled part time in some type of postsecondary education.

*(continued)*

## GRADING THE STATES ON THEIR HIGHER EDUCATION

**AFFORDABILITY:** Measured by the percentage of a family's income needed to pay for college expenses minus financial aid at both two- and four-year colleges; the percentage of state grants awarded to low-income families compared with federal Pell grants given to low-income families in the state; the share of their income that poorest families need to pay for tuition at the lowest priced colleges in the state; and the average loan amount that students borrow each year.

**COMPLETION:** Measured by the percentage of first-year students who return for their second year; the percentage of first-time, full-time students completing a bachelor's degree within five years; and the number of certificates, degrees, and diplomas awarded at all colleges per 100 undergraduate students.

**BENEFITS:** Measured by the percentage of 25- to 65-year-olds with a bachelor's degree or higher; the percent difference in total personal income between those with a bachelor's degree and those without a bachelor's degree; the percentage of eligible residents voting in the 1996 and 1998 national elections; the percentage of residents who declare charitable gifts among those who itemize their federal income taxes; and the percentage of adults who demonstrate high literacy skills.

No state received straight As, but here are some of the states that did best across all or most of the five criteria:

| State name | Preparation | Participation | Affordability | Completion | Benefits |
|---|---|---|---|---|---|
| Colorado | B | B– | B– | C | A |
| Connecticut | A | B+ | C | B+ | A |
| Illinois | A | A | A | C+ | B– |
| Iowa | B | B | B | A– | C+ |
| Kansas | B | A | B | B | B |
| Maryland | B+ | A | D | B– | A |
| Massachusetts | A | A– | D | A– | A– |
| Minnesota | C+ | B– | A | B+ | A |
| New Jersey | A | B+ | B | B– | A |
| North Dakota | B | B | C | B | C+ |
| Virginia | B | B– | C | B | B+ |
| Wisconsin | A– | B | B+ | B | B– |

*Source:* Jeffrey Selingo, "Grading the States on Higher Education," *Chronicle of Higher Education,* December, 8, 2000, p. A24.

accessible to their children. Meanwhile, these same voters like to keep in-state tuition low, which is helped by charging out-of-state students more and admitting them in higher numbers.

You will see that each state strikes its own balance between in-state and out-of-state students. The public ivies in California have nonresident percentages that are quite low, below 10 percent, while Michigan and Colorado, for example, have out-of-state enrollments over 30 percent. If you are an out-of-state applicant, the university's having a higher percentage of nonresidents may tell you that you have a better chance for admission. It may also reassure you that you will not be lost among a crowd of students having similar geographic backgrounds. In addition to examining the overall percentage of out-of-state students, be sure to consider where these students come from, as well as the overall diversity of the student body, resident as well as nonresident.

## DIVERSITY IN ALL ITS FORMS

When you hear the word "diversity," you often think of racial or ethnic groups. Diversity at a university represents many factors, however. You should consider the accessibility and composition of a university's student body not only in racial or ethnic terms, but also in relation to religious identification, national heritage, geographic background, academic interests, intellectual orientation, political beliefs, age, sexual orientation, socioeconomic background, disabilities, extracurricular involvements, and so on. Consider the impact that a diverse student body and faculty and administration will have on your own growth and development. Think about how interacting with people different from yourself in many ways will push your boundaries and force you to ask and answer new questions. That, of course, is one of the purposes of education. Regardless of your views on affirmative action as a public policy, you can acknowledge that there is an inherent value to engaging in dialogue with others who have perspectives different from your own.

It's up to you to consider how important these various types of diversity are to you and determine the balance between comfort and challenge. If diversity is very important to you, make sure to explore some of these issues by talking with the admissions office, reading the college's literature, exploring noncollege sources for students with particular interests or backgrounds, and contacting the college's representatives for diversity awareness or recruiting. Here are some questions to ask about the university's diversity:

- What is the university's policy on affirmative action? Have there been recent changes, or are changes currently under discussion? How have changes affected the enrollment of particular groups?

- What is the university doing to attract a diverse student body? Does it have a mission statement and particular policies in this area? What kinds of resources are directed toward diversity?

---

### aMAGAZINE: INSIDE ASIAN AMERICA'S TOP 25 UNIVERSITIES
### FOR ASIAN AMERICANS, 2000

---

1. University of Hawaii at Manoa
2. University of California, Riverside
3. University of California, Los Angeles
4. University of California, Davis
5. Polytechnic University (Brooklyn, New York)
6. University of California, Irvine
7. Rutgers, The State University of New Jersey (New Brunswick)
8. University of Pennsylvania
9. University of California, San Diego
10. University of Maryland College Park
11. Cornell University
12. Stanford University
13. Massachusetts Institute of Technology
14. University of California, Santa Barbara
15. Georgia Institute of Technology
16. University of Texas at Dallas
17. Wayne State University
18. University of Texas at Austin
19. Stevens Institute of Technology
20. Ohio State University
21. University of Colorado at Boulder
22. Washington State University
23. Michigan State University
24. University of Florida
25. North Carolina State University

---

- Does the university have an admissions officer in charge of multicultural recruiting and admissions?

- Does the university have an office with administrative staff to advise and support diverse students and plan multicultural awareness and education programs on campus?

- Are there multicultural student groups on campus? If so, what are their activities, and what kind of support do they receive from the university?

- Is affinity housing available for students with specific backgrounds, beliefs, or interests?

- What is the percentage of undergraduate enrollment for various groups of students?

- What are the percentages of faculty or administrative staff with various backgrounds?

- Are there departmental or interdisciplinary majors dealing with multicultural studies, or distribution requirements or courses in non-Western studies?

- Has there been any evidence of tension between ethnic, racial, religious, or other groups? Racist violence or threats? Anti-Semitism? Anti-gay/lesbian violence? Hazing of students seen as different?

- What is the university's retention record regarding various groups, particularly those underrepresented at the university level?

- Are there special scholarships or programs designed to attract, enroll, and retain different groups of students?

Diversity is not a simple issue by any means. It matters a great deal to some, and not at all to others. Some people believe diversity is not an important aspect of university life. Others argue strongly that affirmative action hurts minority groups more than it helps them, by stigmatizing those who make it to campus and fostering resentment among majority students. Some point out that a deliberate focus on differences between groups of students can promote continued separation between them on campus and after college, and may further dampen individual identity and intellectual growth. Nevertheless, diversity means diversity of individuals, and many individuals identify more or less with various aspects of their background, race, ethnicity, culture, upbringing, academic passion, country of origin, athletic talent, or religious faith. In many respects, diversity is in the eye of the beholder, and in the college search process, that beholder is you.

## FINANCIAL AID FOR MERIT AND NEED

Even if you personally do not need financial aid, you should consider how much merit- and need-based aid the university provides. Another form of diversity is socioeconomic diversity, and strong universities are able to recruit and retain talented students from any place and any background, even if they require significant financial support. Top universities attract talented students by granting them merit awards. This is how many of the public ivies compete with Ivy League and other top private colleges and universities. They make offers that are too good to refuse to the best students, both residents and nonresidents of the state. Four years of total tuition, room and board, travel, and summer research money? That sounds all right to many students, even those without much financial need. And those with need are attracted to universities that are able to keep their tuition and fee structures low and can afford to cover most financial need with grants and scholarships, which do not need to be repaid, as opposed to federally guaranteed loans. A strong commitment to financial aid represents a positive step on the part of the university to further its academic mission—and, OK, often its athletic mission. Some questions you want to ask about financial aid:

- What percentage of the undergraduate student body is receiving financial aid? How many students are receiving need-based aid, and how many are getting merit-based aid?

- What is the average size of the financial aid award? How much of the aid is typically in the form of grants and scholarships or loans?

- What is the average debt of graduating students?

- What special merit-based university scholarships are available, and how do you apply for them?

- To what extent does the university try to disregard need in its admissions process? To what extent does it try to cover all the demonstrated need of a student?

- What is the university's budget for need- or merit-based aid, and where does the money come from? Is it drawn primarily from endowment income, which may be a more stable and guaranteed source, or from current tuition dollars, which may mean larger tuition increases in the future?

- How does the university determine financial need, and what levels of federal and state funding are available to support students?

- What work-study opportunities are available at the university, and what other local jobs may be accessible?

- What is the cost of room and board on campus as well as in the local community? How high will your cost of living be?

## RETENTION RATES

*Retention* is how long students maintain their enrollment at the university, and it reflects the ability of the university to help students be successful and happy.

Students drop out of or transfer from a university for a variety of reasons, including academic failure, a search for a better fit or a more challenging academic environment, substance abuse or mental health issues, lack of financial means, lack of interest, a family move, or a desire to go to work. We know that two-thirds of high school graduates go on to some form of higher education. We also know that fewer than half of the students who begin college return to campus the following year. Most drop out of college completely, at least for the time being. Others transfer to a four-year university from a two-year college, from a big school to a small school, from a less prestigious school to one with a more prominent name. Whatever the reason, overall retention rates at colleges and universities are quite low. You should look at the university's retention rate in relation to the national average, as well as in comparison to other similar institutions. The public ivies vary in their retention rates. You will also find a difference between some of the public ivies and the private hidden ivies and Ivy League schools in terms of retention: most of the top small to middle-sized private and larger public institutions have retention rates of 80 to 90 percent.

More students move in and out of the public universities. One sees more transferring, more time taken out of school, and more years taken to complete a degree. Explore the retention rate of a university. What percentage of students return for their second year of study? What happens to those who leave, and why do they not return? What efforts are made to retain students? Are there time-out programs, plans to reintegrate or help students who have been placed on academic or disciplinary probation, and adequate counseling services to help those in crisis?

## GRADUATION RATES

Graduation rates tell you what percentage of students who enter the university graduate from it. They also indicate how long it takes the average student to graduate. Many universities now report *six-year* graduation rates. That's right, six years. The rates go up when students are given two years beyond the traditional four-year period to complete their degree. Students and parents are often mystified and skeptical when we tell them that the old four-year college plan is a thing of the past for many students. More are taking time out during college to pursue a job, travel, or service experience. They are combining part-time and full-time study over a longer period of time, taking reduced course loads, or double-majoring. They are also, at the big universities in particular, having a tougher time getting into the courses they need to graduate. You should not feel pressed to have to graduate in four years. Many universities charge students on a per-credit basis, so you can take the lightest full-time course load if that works better for you, without incurring substantial financial penalties (see "Quality over Quantity" in Part Four).

If possible, find out the four-, five-, and six-year graduation rates at a university. This will tell you how many students graduate in the accustomed four years, how many take a year or two more, and how many will likely never graduate from the university.

The following table shows graduation rates for athletes and other students at the public ivies. There are several interesting things in these data. First, notice the fairly wide range of graduation statistics among the public ivies. Also notice that in almost all cases, athletes graduate at lower rates than does the average student on campus (see Delaware and Minnesota for exceptions). These statistics capture the six-year graduation rate of all students at these particular universities during their academic career. It may be that they left the university in question, but graduated elsewhere, and these statistics do not show that. In a sense, these statistics are also measuring retention among these schools by showing the percentage of students the universities were able to retain each year through graduation. Finally, you should see that the graduation rates at the public ivies are generally higher on average than the rates for male and

## Graduation Rates at the Public Ivies for Athletes and Other Students Who Entered College in 1993–94

| Institution | All Students | | Athletes | |
|---|---|---|---|---|
| | No. | % | No. | % |
| College of William and Mary (Division I-AA, Colonial Athletic Association) | | | | |
| Class entering 1993–94 | 1,200 | 88% | 57 | 88% |
| Classes entering 1990–91 to 1993–94 | 4,866 | 89% | 211 | 83% |
| Indiana University Bloomington (Division I-A, Big Ten Conference) | | | | |
| Class entering 1993–94 | 5,813 | 68% | 68 | 66% |
| Classes entering 1990–91 to 1993–94 | 21,862 | 68% | 310 | 69% |
| Miami University (Oxford, Ohio) (Division I-A, Mid-American Conference) | | | | |
| Class entering 1993–94 | 3,264 | 79% | 95 | 73% |
| Classes entering 1990–91 to 1993–94 | 12,857 | 80% | 345 | 68% |
| Ohio State University (Division I-A, Big Ten Conference) | | | | |
| Class entering 1993–94 | 5,283 | 56% | 84 | 50% |
| Classes entering 1990–91 to 1993–94 | 22,301 | 56% | 343 | 51% |
| Pennsylvania State University (University Park) (Division I-A, Big Ten Conference) | | | | |
| Class entering 1993–94 | 4,262 | 80% | 89 | 78% |
| Classes entering 1990–91 to 1993–94 | 17,559 | 79% | 335 | 78% |
| Rutgers, The State University of New Jersey, University College—New Brunswick (Division I-A, Big East Conference) | | | | |
| Class entering 1993–94 | 4,513 | 73% | 93 | 65% |
| Classes entering 1990–91 to 1993–94 | 17,256 | 73% | 323 | 63% |
| University of Arizona (Division I-A, Pacific-10 Conference) | | | | |
| Class entering 1993–94 | 4,287 | 52% | 58 | 52% |
| Classes entering 1990–91 to 1993–94 | 16,156 | 52% | 228 | 58% |
| University of California, Berkeley (Division I-A, Pacific-10 Conference) | | | | |
| Class entering 1993–94 | 3,233 | 82% | 66 | 62% |
| Classes entering 1990–91 to 1993–94 | 13,091 | 81% | 243 | 59% |
| University of California, Irvine (Division I-AAA, Big West Conference) | | | | |
| Class entering 1993–94 | 2,367 | 74% | 28 | 86% |
| Classes entering 1990–91 to 1993–94 | 10,199 | 74% | 92 | 63% |

## Graduation Rates at the Public Ivies for Athletes and Other Students Who Entered College in 1993–94 (continued)

| Institution | All Students | | Athletes | |
|---|---|---|---|---|
| | No. | % | No. | % |
| University of California, Los Angeles (Division I-A, Pacific-10 Conference) | | | | |
| Class entering 1993–94 | 3,387 | 79% | 72 | 68% |
| Classes entering 1990–91 to 1993–94 | 14,276 | 78% | 294 | 59% |
| University of California, Santa Barbara (Division I-AAA, Big West Conference) | | | | |
| Class entering 1993–94 | 3,239 | 67% | 49 | 63% |
| Classes entering 1990–91 to 1993–94 | 12,213 | 70% | 222 | 71% |
| University of Colorado at Boulder (Division I-A, Big 12 Conference) | | | | |
| Class entering 1993–94 | 3,440 | 64% | 49 | 57% |
| Classes entering 1990–91 to 1993–94 | 14,412 | 64% | 191 | 54% |
| University of Connecticut (Division I-AA, Big East Conference) | | | | |
| Class entering 1993–94 | 2,026 | 68% | 71 | 66% |
| Classes entering 1990–91 to 1993–94 | 8,608 | 67% | 244 | 65% |
| University of Delaware (Division I-AA, America East Conference) | | | | |
| Class entering 1993–94 | 3,181 | 70% | 43 | 77% |
| Classes entering 1990–91 to 1993–94 | 12,132 | 71% | 132 | 77% |
| University of Florida (Division I-A, Southeastern Conference) | | | | |
| Class entering 1993–94 | 5,074 | 67% | 67 | 48% |
| Classes entering 1990–91 to 1993–94 | 18,112 | 65% | 277 | 52% |
| University of Georgia (Division I-A, Southeastern Conference) | | | | |
| Class entering 1993–94 | 3,808 | 63% | 69 | 72% |
| Classes entering 1990–91 to 1993–94 | 14,617 | 63% | 269 | 58% |
| University of Illinois at Urbana-Champaign (Division I-A, Big Ten Conference) | | | | |
| Class entering 1993–94 | 5,654 | 75% | 55 | 65% |
| Classes entering 1990–91 to 1993–94 | 22,592 | 77% | 262 | 65% |
| University of Iowa (Division I-A, Big Ten Conference) | | | | |
| Class entering 1993–94 | 3,132 | 62% | 72 | 71% |
| Classes entering 1990–91 to 1993–94 | 11,693 | 63% | 286 | 71% |

### Graduation Rates at the Public Ivies for Athletes and Other Students Who Entered College in 1993–94 (continued)

| Institution | All Students | | Athletes | |
|---|---|---|---|---|
| | No. | % | No. | % |
| University of Maryland College Park (Division I-A, Atlantic Coast Conference) | | | | |
| Class entering 1993–94 | 3,153 | 64% | 61 | 61% |
| Classes entering 1990–91 to 1993–94 | 12,303 | 63% | 260 | 58% |
| University of Michigan (Division I-A, Big Ten Conference) | | | | |
| Class entering 1993–94 | 5,016 | 82% | 74 | 68% |
| Classes entering 1990–91 to 1993–94 | 19,580 | 83% | 305 | 68% |
| University of Minnesota, Twin Cities (Division I-A, Big Ten Conference) | | | | |
| Class entering 1993–94 | 2,273 | 51% | 89 | 65% |
| Classes entering 1990–91 to 1993–94 | 8,728 | 51% | 352 | 57% |
| University of North Carolina at Chapel Hill (Division I-A, Atlantic Coast Conference) | | | | |
| Class entering 1993–94 | 3,310 | 80% | 90 | 78% |
| Classes entering 1990–91 to 1993–94 | 12,899 | 82% | 358 | 68% |
| University of Texas at Austin (Division I-A, Big 12 Conference) | | | | |
| Class entering 1993–94 | 5,872 | 65% | 72 | 51% |
| Classes entering 1990–91 to 1993–94 | 23,282 | 65% | 292 | 55% |
| University of Virginia (Division I-A, Atlantic Coast Conference) | | | | |
| Class entering 1993–94 | 2,661 | 91% | 69 | 78% |
| Classes entering 1990–91 to 1993–94 | 10,529 | 92% | 303 | 79% |
| University of Washington (Division I-A, Pacific-10 Conference) | | | | |
| Class entering 1993–94 | 3,206 | 72% | 75 | 64% |
| Classes entering 1990–91 to 1993–94 | 13,630 | 70% | 307 | 63% |
| University of Wisconsin—Madison (Division I-A, Big Ten Conference) | | | | |
| Class entering 1993–94 | 4,585 | 74% | 69 | 55% |
| Classes entering 1990–91 to 1993–94 | 18,303 | 73% | 310 | 60% |
| Male athletes and other male students at NCAA Division I Colleges | 249,609 | 54% | 8,911 | 51% |
| Female athletes and other female students at NCAA Division I Colleges | 273,819 | 59% | 6,017 | 68% |

*Source:* NCAA, *Chronicle of Higher Education,* www.chronicle.com/stats/ncaa.

female students at the most competitive level of National Collegiate Athletic Association play, NCAA Division I colleges and universities.

---

## UNIVERSITY MEMBERSHIP IN THE ASSOCIATION OF AMERICAN UNIVERSITIES

The Association of American Universities (AAU) was founded in 1900 by 14 doctorate-granting universities. Today, the group consists of 59 American and 2 Canadian academic research universities, about half of which are public. The AAU develops policy positions on higher educational issues involving research and graduate education and provides its members with a network to discuss these and other relevant issues. Membership is prestigious and limited to those universities that are nationally known and active in advancing research at the highest level. Most of the public university members are flagship institutions in their states. Note all the public ivies who are members. You can find the AAU at www.aau.edu.

The following are AAU member institutions (and their year of admission):

Brandeis University (1985)
Brown University (1933)
California Institute of Technology (1934)
Carnegie Mellon University (1982)
Case Western Reserve University (1969)
Catholic University of America (1900)
Columbia University (1900)
Cornell University (1900)
Duke University (1938)
Emory University (1995)
Harvard University (1900)
Indiana University (1909)
Iowa State University (1958)
Johns Hopkins University (1900)
Massachusetts Institute of Technology (1934)
McGill University (1926)
Michigan State University (1964)
New York University (1950)

Northwestern University (1917)
Ohio State University (1916)
Pennsylvania State University (1958)
Princeton University (1900)
Purdue University (1958)
Rice University (1985)
Rutgers, The State University of New Jersey (1989)
Stanford University (1900)
Syracuse University (1966)
Tulane University (1958)
University of Arizona (1985)
State University of New York at Buffalo (1989)
University of California, Berkeley (1900)
University of California, Davis (1996)
University of California, Irvine (1996)
University of California, Los Angeles (1974)

*(continued)*

## UNIVERSITY MEMBERSHIP IN THE ASSOCIATION
## OF AMERICAN UNIVERSITIES

University of California, San Diego (1982)

University of California, Santa Barbara (1995)

University of Chicago (1900)

University of Colorado at Boulder (1966)

University of Florida (1985)

University of Illinois at Urbana-Champaign (1908)

University of Iowa (1909)

University of Kansas (1909)

University of Maryland College Park (1969)

University of Michigan (1900)

University of Minnesota, Twin Cities (1908)

University of Missouri, Columbia (1908)

University of Nebraska, Lincoln (1909)

University of North Carolina at Chapel Hill (1922)

University of Oregon (1969)

University of Pennsylvania (1900)

University of Pittsburgh (1974)

University of Rochester (1941)

University of Southern California (1969)

University of Texas at Austin (1929)

University of Toronto (1926)

University of Virginia (1904)

University of Washington (1950)

University of Wisconsin—Madison (1900)

Vanderbilt University (1950)

Washington University in St. Louis (1923)

Yale University (1900)

## CORPORATE PARTNERSHIPS AND RESEARCH FACILITIES

In addition to state and federal support for research at the public universities, private corporations and foundations sponsor research activities and engage in corporate–university and foundation–university partnerships in a variety of areas. For example, the Lilly Endowment recently gave Indiana University's School of Medicine $105 million to create the Indiana Genomics Initiative. In California, private industry was set to begin three major initiatives in 2000: the California NanoSystems Institute at the University of California (UC) at Los Angeles and UC Santa Barbara; the California Institute for Telecommunications

*(continued)*

and Information Technology at UC San Diego and UC Irvine; and the California Institute for Bioengineering, Biotechnology, and Quantitative Biomedicine at UC Berkeley, UC San Francisco, and UC Santa Cruz. In addition to the $75 million the state planned to put in to support these institutes, some $1.4 billion was pledged in federal grants and support from 237 different companies, such as Microsoft, IBM, and Hewlett-Packard. Such partnerships are nothing new in academia, and are sometimes controversial on campus, whether they involve U.S. Department of Defense research projects, genetic research programs, or sports apparel contracts. Nevertheless, they are prominent on today's public university campuses, and students should keep their eyes open for research opportunities and available facilities in their areas of interest.

## THE FLAGSHIP CAMPUS

In this book we are concerned mainly with the flagship public university campuses. The term *flagship* derives from the most powerful ship in a naval fleet, which carries an admiral and his or her flag. A flagship campus is the premier academic center in a state, the locale of the most competitive liberal arts programs and many other academic areas and the primary doctoral-granting research institution in the state. Some states, such as Georgia, Colorado, and Wisconsin, have one clear flagship institution. Others, such as California and New York, have a larger university system with more and less selective public universities but not necessarily a clear flagship model. Still others, like Virginia and Ohio, have a flagship campus and one or more highly competitive and prestigious freestanding public colleges or universities. In this book, we do not discuss the specialized public technical colleges and universities, such as Purdue or the Georgia Institute of Technology. We have also, for the most part, left out the historic land-grant colleges and universities, which were chartered to provide more technical education in agricultural sciences, engineering, mining, and animal sciences.

State systems of higher education are varied and not perfectly comparable to one another, and there is a great deal of difference among the public ivies we have included here. In one way or another, all of the public ivies are flagship schools. They are the major public institutions in a state to which the most talented and competitive students are drawn, from inside and outside the state. They are the institutions that draw a nationally diverse student body and have a major emphasis in the liberal arts. As you explore public universities in general, you will see that other than the public ivies and other public flagship campuses, public universities and colleges tend to be more localized, regionalized, specialized, and less impressive on all the criteria we have discussed here.

## Selected Top Institutions in Federal Research and Development
## Expenditures, Over $100 Million, Fiscal Year 1998

| Institution | Expenditure |
| --- | --- |
| Stanford University | $342,426,000 |
| *University of Washington | $336,748,000 |
| *University of Michigan | $311,450,000 |
| *University of California, San Diego | $262,303,000 |
| Harvard University | $251,876,000 |
| University of Pennsylvania | $247,914,000 |
| *University of Wisconsin—Madison | $240,513,000 |
| *University of California, Los Angeles | $233,702,000 |
| Columbia University | $229,723,000 |
| *University of Colorado | $228,342,000 |
| Yale University | $205,046,000 |
| *University of Minnesota | $204,741,000 |
| Cornell University[†] | $204,187,000 |
| *Pennsylvania State University | $186,274,000 |
| *University of North Carolina at Chapel Hill | $171,505,000 |
| *University of California at Berkeley[†] | $171,135,000 |
| *University of Illinois at Urbana-Champaign | $168,871,000 |
| *University of Texas at Austin | $165,082,000 |
| *University of Arizona | $161,999,000 |
| *University of Maryland College Park | $129,198,000 |
| *Ohio State University | $124,177,000 |
| *University of Iowa | $115,312,000 |
| *University of California, Davis | $114,912,000 |
| *University of Florida | $106,510,000 |

* Public university.
[†]Excludes expenditures at university-associated, federally financed research and development centers.

*Source:* National Science Foundation, "Top Institutions in Total Research and Development Spending, Fiscal 1998," *Chronicle of Higher Education,* September 1, 2000, www.chronicle.com/weekly/almanac/2000/facts/5002money.htm.

# PROGRAMS FOR STUDENTS WITH LEARNING DISABILITIES OR SPECIAL NEEDS

Contrary to what one might expect, many of the large public universities have some of the best learning support programs for students with special needs. Because they are bigger, and because they are more directly governed by state and federal regulations, many public universities have developed strong, comprehensive learning centers. They are found under the rubrics "academic support programs," "learning resource centers," "learning disabilities support services," and so forth. For students with learning disabilities or other special needs, the availability of these programs is a must if they are to succeed in the larger and more challenging public university. Although large classes, big systems, and lecture-based teaching might work against students with attentional difficulties or learning styles better suited to discussion and explanation, comprehensive learning support programs can help make a big university smaller by providing appropriate services for students who need them. A learning program can't do away with all of the negatives we have mentioned about large public universities, or change the fundamental nature of the program or institution, but it can help a student learn to negotiate the university system, take advantage of what is available academically and socially, and compensate for some of the challenges he or she will face. Here are some questions to ask to evaluate a learning or special needs program:

- How many students does the program serve?

- Is there an extra fee for using available resources?

- Is there a separate admissions process for the program, and if so, what are the entrance requirements and procedures?

- What services does the program provide, and for whom?

- How is the program integrated into the university as a whole? Is there a separate learning center, or are program components distributed throughout the university?

- Is there a program director, and what is his or her background? How many full- and part-time staff work with the program, and what is their experience level? Are students involved in running the program?

- Is the program considered a comprehensive support program, providing a full range of services and institutionalized fully into the university, or does it provide only a moderate level of support?

- Does the program fulfill your individual needs, given what you know about yourself and the accommodations you have taken advantage of in high school, or might need to make use of in college?

- How is the program funded? At what level?

- What is the university's overall treatment of students with learning differences or other special needs? Is there any history of conflict or bias? Is there a legacy of real commitment?

- How involved are faculty with the program and its implementation? Do advisors in the learning program contact faculty on behalf of students with special needs? Do faculty help run the program and work as mentors with students?

- Is there a program facility where students can meet with tutors, take exams on a computer or in a quiet space, and interact with other students?

What you want is a real commitment from the university not just to accommodate, but also to support and educate students with learning disabilities and other special needs. You want an environment that is open and caring, experienced with handling your needs, and capable of providing the services you require. The public ivies are not "special schools," but many of them happen to have outstanding support programs.

## ACADEMIC SUPPORT PROGRAMS FOR ATHLETES

One area where the public universities have committed a large amount of resources is in the support of varsity athletes. Of course, they have a great deal at stake in making sure their top athletes remain eligible to compete in intercollegiate athletics. That means these students need to make adequate academic progress and maintain a solid GPA. The universities have also faced criticism for using and then throwing out their recruited athletes without making an effort to see that they are well educated. To ensure that athletes succeed and "remain on the job," the universities have developed specialized athletic academic support programs. These are typically well-funded, highly developed, very focused programs intended to help athletes choose courses, write papers, complete homework assignments, and negotiate the wilds of the university. They employ student mentors, graduate student tutors, and academic specialists. Sometimes they are linked with other learning support programs on campus. We can acknowledge that the universities are serving their own interests in implementing these services for athletes, while simultaneously applauding their efforts at retaining and graduating these students. If you are a prospective athlete, ask these questions:

- Is there an academic support program specifically for athletes?

- What are the graduation and retention rates of varsity athletes?

- What level of commitment has the university made to its athletes? What kind of funding does the support program have? Who works for it?

- Is participation in the program mandatory or voluntary, and at what levels?

- Are support services limited to athletes in a major sport (football, basketball, etc.) or available to all intercollegiate athletes?

- What types of services are offered? Will you receive specialized academic counseling and advising? Will you have an advocate to help you reschedule exams when you are away at a game or help you plan your homework assignments and term papers? Will you have a study space available with tutors on hand and other athletes who have similar needs?

- What are the requirements, in addition to those mandated by the NCAA or another athletic association, that the university dictates governing your eligibility for athletic participation? What do you need to do to stay in the game?

## INTERSTATE AGREEMENTS ON ACADEMIC PROGRAMS

As we mentioned earlier, many states have regional agreements to allow students to take advantage of programs not offered in their state at the universities of neighboring states. These regional agreements (in New England, the South, and the West, for example) help to broaden the curricular offerings of a university, as well as the base for the student body. If you are looking for a specific program that is not offered in your home state, see if you are eligible to pursue that program in another state as part of an interstate agreement. You will be treated and charged as an in-state student.

## IMPORTANT STATISTICS, AND HOW TO FIND AND USE THEM

Getting information about schools on the criteria we have discussed in the preceding sections will require you to find and evaluate a lot of statistics, some of which are more reliable than others. Many universities are participating in the Common Data Set, which helps to standardize the reporting of statistics in which students are most interested. You may find Common Data Set information in publications of the College Board, for example. Other statistics are found on university websites, often on the admissions office pages, or in the documents provided by the university's institutional research office. You may need to call or e-mail a department or program directly to find out information of special interest to you. Other sources of information include guidebooks, news magazines, the U.S. Department of Education (www.ed.gov), state departments of education, and education journals such as the *Chronicle of Higher Education* (www.chronicle.com). The Internet has a wealth of information at your fingertips; in fact, the biggest challenge you face with the Net is learning how to sort through all of that knowledge, evaluate what you are looking at, and make sense of the big picture. And you will need the time to explore carefully the choices you are making. Consider this your first big college research project.

Here are some tips for using statistics:

- Take the numbers with a grain of salt. Don't rely too heavily or become fixated on statistics.

- Try to evaluate the source of the data, the age of the statistics, and the comparability of the numbers among different institutions.

- Try to use statistics from several sources, to get a variety of perspectives on your target universities.

- Be persistent in trying to obtain information in the areas that matter most to you.

- Don't be afraid to call a university as you seek to learn more about it. Often you will be directed to the right office, person, web page, or pamphlet to find out what you want to know.

## HOW TO USE THE CRITERIA WE HAVE DISCUSSED IN PART TWO

The criteria we've discussed in this part are major points you want to address in your search for and evaluation of universities and colleges that may be right for you. Some of the criteria will matter more to you personally; others will seem totally irrelevant. Nevertheless, walk through each of them as you explore different schools. You may also add other criteria that are important to you and we have not addressed, for example, the physical qualities of the campus, such as its proximity to the wilderness or a city. See these criteria as guideposts in your approach to universities. Try not to either quantify everything or go by gut feeling alone. A combination of intuition and rational evaluation is often how students end up choosing their college.

In Part Three we give brief informational and statistical overviews of the thirty public ivies. These overviews are by no means comprehensive and do not include all the factors you will want to research. See this list as a starting point. You will surely be reading other guidebooks, university materials, and websites. In putting together this list, we decided to avoid a superficial narrative that tried to capture the personality of each of these mostly large and very diversified public ivies. At the same time, we did not want to bog down in the minutia associated with each university at the expense of an overall perspective on the group. Our aim is to give key statistics associated with the criteria we have discussed in Part Two and list some of the programs available at the universities in which students might be particularly interested.

# PART THREE

# The Public Ivies

## Thirty Top Universities and Colleges in America

Here we present data on the thirty institutions we consider public ivies. We offer a snapshot of each school, detailing just some of the statistics important for you to consider as you evaluate the different institutions. We provide you with contact information, the most important of which is the university's website. That is where you will find the most complete view of the university, before and after a visit to campus. In the "Programs, Highlights, and Developments" entries, we give you a glimpse into some of the colleges, schools, and programs at each university and some guidance as to where you will enter the university as a first-year student. We encourage you to see this list as a guidepost and a starting point, from which excursions to campus and virtual tours will take you farther down the road on your journey to the right college.

## A WORD ABOUT THE DATA

We have done our best to provide accurate, complete, and comparable data. If we were unable to find appropriate or readily available figures, we indicate "n/a." In some cases, universities do not report the data called for or do so in a substantially different manner from most of the other universities. We encourage you to pursue data of interest at the several schools and programs you're focusing on, and not to make your decisions primarily on one set of numbers.

**Total students**: Degree-seeking graduates and undergraduates.

**Total undergraduates**: Degree-seeking undergraduates.

**First-year retention rate**: Percentage of undergraduate students who return as sophomores.

**Graduation rate**: The first figure is the percentage of entering students who graduate sometime within six years. When available, we also give the percentages of students who graduate in four, five, or six years exactly. Percentages may not total 100% because of rounding.

**Ratio of males to females**: As percentage of undergraduates in the student body.

**In-state students**: As percentage of the freshman class admitted for fall 2000, unless otherwise noted.

**Admission statistics**: For class admitted for fall 2000, unless otherwise noted. Includes in-state and out-of-state applicants. "Mid-50%" SAT and ACT scores represents the middle range of scores on these standardized tests. In other words, half of entering students scored within the range listed, 25 percent scored higher, and 25 percent scored lower. Note again that the public ivies generally give preference to in-state residents in the admissions process, particularly in terms of the GPA and SAT/ACT scores they set as baselines or guidelines, but each does so in a different way. Also, particular colleges and programs at the universities have varying degrees of selectivity. Carefully examine procedures, requirements, and admissions standards for the particular programs you're looking into.

**In-state and out-of-state admissions statistics**: Offered where available and clearly identified by the university.

**Students living on campus**: As percentage of first-year class admitted for fall 2000, unless otherwise noted.

**Students enrolled full-time**: As percentage of degree-seeking undergraduates.

**Total endowment**: As of June 30, 1999, from the National Association of College and University Business Officers. Figures are for individual universities or university systems, as noted.

**Public funding**: The 2000–01 state appropriations total and change from the previous year. We obtained this information from "State Appropriations for Higher Education, 2000–1," written by James C. Palmer and Sandra H. Gillilan of Illinois State University, in the *Chronicle of Higher Education*, December 15, 2000, no page. The figures for Arizona, Connecticut, Indiana, Minnesota, North Carolina, Ohio, Texas, Virginia, Washington, and Wisconsin may be skewed because of biennial budgeting. In addition, some figures, for Colorado and Connecticut, for example, may represent multiple campus appropriations. In cases so acknowledged by the researchers, such figures are noted as "system" figures. Overall, these figures indicate the overall amounts the different states are budgeting for their public universities and how these budgets have fared over a two-year period.

# THE PUBLIC IVIES

University of Arizona

University of California, Berkeley

University of California, Davis

University of California, Irvine

University of California, Los Angeles

University of California, San Diego

University of California, Santa Barbara

University of Colorado at Boulder

University of Connecticut

University of Delaware

University of Florida

University of Georgia

University of Illinois at Urbana-Champaign

Indiana University Bloomington

University of Iowa

University of Maryland College Park

Miami University (Oxford, Ohio)

University of Michigan, Ann Arbor

Michigan State University

University of Minnesota, Twin Cities

State University of New York at Binghamton

University of North Carolina at Chapel Hill

Ohio State University (Columbus)

Pennsylvania State University (University Park)

Rutgers, The State University of New Jersey (New Brunswick)

University of Texas at Austin

University of Virginia

University of Washington

College of William and Mary

University of Wisconsin—Madison

# UNIVERSITY OF ARIZONA

Robert L. Nugent Building
Tucson, AZ 85721-0040
(520) 621-3237
www.arizona.edu

Total students: 32,322
Total undergraduates: 25,356
First-year retention rate: 77%
Graduation rate: 52% (six years); 21% in four years, 25% in five years, 7% in six years
Ratio of students to faculty: 18:1
Ratio of males to females: 47:53
In-state students: 70%

## Tuition and fees for 2000–01:

In-state: $2,348
Out-of-state: $9,804

## Admission statistics:

17,700 applied, 84% were accepted, 5,365 enrolled (36% yield)
Mid-50% SAT verbal: 490–610
Mid-50% SAT math: 490–610
SAT verbal scores over 700: 5%
SAT verbal scores over 600: 28%
SAT math scores over 700: 6%
SAT math scores over 600: 32%
Mid-50% ACT: 20–26
ACT scores over 30: 7%
ACT scores over 24: 48%

Average high school GPA: 3.33
GPA 3.0 or higher: 75%
GPA 2.0–2.9: 25%
Rank in top 10% of high school class: 32%
Rank in top 25% of high school class: 59%

## In-state admissions statistics (fall 1999):

Mid-50% SAT combined scores: 970–1220
Mid-50% ACT: 20–27
Average high school GPA: 3.40

## Out-of-state admissions statistics (fall 1999):

Mid-50% SAT combined scores: 1000–1190
Mid-50% ACT: 21–26
Average high school GPA: 3.22

Students living on campus: 80%
Students enrolled full-time: 85%
Total endowments: $272,950,000 (University of Arizona and Foundation)
Public funding: $327,952,000 (+2.6%)

## Programs, Highlights, and Developments:

The Honors College automatically considers all university applicants and admits qualified students without a separate application (www.honors.arizona.edu/prospective.html). The college enrolls more than 1,000 students, who can take advantage of more than 200 honors courses with an average class size of 15 students. To remain in the Honors College, students must maintain a GPA over 3.5. The SALT (Strategic Alternative Learning Techniques) Center for Learning Disabilities (www.salt.arizona.edu) is a comprehensive learning support center. Students apply to both the university and the SALT program during the admissions process, and should apply early in the year. The Eller College of Business and Public Administration, the College of Science, the College of Humanities, and the College of Social and Behavioral Sciences offer most of the tremendous array of programs available to undergraduates at Arizona.

# UNIVERSITY OF CALIFORNIA, BERKELEY

110 Sproul Hall, #5800
Berkeley, CA 94720-5800
(510) 642-3175
www.berkeley.edu

Total students: 31,337
Total undergraduates: 22,593
First-year retention rate: 94%
Graduation rate: 81% (six years); 48% in four years, 30% in five years, 5% in six years
Ratio of students to faculty: 17:1
Ratio of males to females: 49:51
In-state students: 90%

### Tuition and fees for 2000-01:

In-state: $4,047
Out-of-state: $14,221

### Admission statistics:

31,108 applied, 27% were accepted, 3,727 enrolled (44% yield)
Mid-50% SAT verbal: 580–700
Mid-50% SAT math: 620–730
SAT verbal scores over 700: 30%

SAT verbal scores over 600: 71%
SAT math scores over 700: 44%
SAT math scores over 600: 81%
Mid-50% ACT: n/a
ACT scores over 30: n/a
ACT scores over 24: n/a
Average high school GPA: 3.90
GPA 3.0 or higher: n/a
GPA 2.0–2.9: n/a
Rank in top 10% of high school class: 96%
Rank in top 25% of high school class: n/a

Students living on campus: 89%
Students enrolled full-time: 93%
Total endowments: $4,315,219,000 (University of California System)
Public funding: $525,955,000 (+11.7%)

## Programs, Highlights, and Developments:

Berkeley has some 300 academic programs. For undergraduates, the College of Environmental Design (which houses the architecture programs), the College of Chemistry, the College of Engineering, the College of Letters and Science, and the College of Natural Resources will be first homes. Undergraduates may then apply as upper class students to the Haas School of Business. Berkeley offers a Freshman Seminar Program, as well as a well-developed Education Abroad Program connected to more than 100 foreign institutions.

# UNIVERSITY OF CALIFORNIA, DAVIS

175 Mak Hall
Davis, CA 95616
(530) 752-2971
www.ucdavis.edu

Total students: 24,196
Total undergraduates: 19,393
First-year retention rate: 90%
Graduation rate: 76% (six years)
Ratio of students to faculty: 19:1
Ratio of males to females: 44:56
In-state students: 96%

### Tuition and fees for 2000–01:

In-state: $4,072
Out-of-state: $14,316

### Admission statistics:

23,126 applied, 62% were accepted, 3,819 enrolled (27% yield)
Mid-50% SAT verbal: 510–630
Mid-50% SAT math: 550–650
SAT verbal scores over 700: 9%
SAT verbal scores over 600: 39%

SAT math scores over 700: 13%
SAT math scores over 600: 54%
Mid-50% ACT: 21–27
ACT scores over 30: 6%
ACT scores over 24: 51%
Average high school GPA: 3.73
GPA 3.0 or higher: 99%
GPA 2.0–2.9: 1%
Rank in top 10% of high school class: 95%
Rank in top 25% of high school class: 100%

Students living on campus: 87%
Students enrolled full-time: 89%
Total endowments: $4,315,219,000 (University of California System)
Public funding: $492,760,000 (+22.0%)

## Programs, Highlights, and Developments:

Davis has historically strong programs in the agricultural and environmental sciences, and undergraduates enter the College of Agricultural and Environmental Sciences, the College of Engineering, or the College of Letters and Science. The university also offers a number of intercollege programs. The Integrated Studies Program invites 70 first-year students into its residential honors interdisciplinary program. The university has an Experimental Farm and an Independent Study Program for upper class students. An Undergraduate Research Expeditions Program gives students the opportunity to conduct field research with an academic team around the world.

# UNIVERSITY OF CALIFORNIA, IRVINE

[ 204 Administration Building
Irvine, CA 92697-1075
(949) 824-6703
www.uci.edu ]

Total students: 18,375
Total undergraduates: 15,235
First-year retention rate: 91%
Graduation rate: 75% (six years)
Ratio of students to faculty: 18:1
Ratio of males to females: 47:53
In-state students: 98%

## Tuition and fees for 2000–01:

In-state: $4,061
Out-of-state: $14,675

## Admission statistics:

22,040 applied, 60% were accepted, 3,629 enrolled (27% yield)
Mid-50% SAT verbal: 495–600
Mid-50% SAT math: 540–655
SAT verbal scores over 700: n/a
SAT verbal scores over 600: n/a

SAT math scores over 700: n/a
SAT math scores over 600: n/a
Mid-50% ACT: n/a
ACT scores over 30: n/a
ACT scores over 24: n/a
Average high school GPA: 3.72
GPA 3.0 or higher: 99%
GPA 2.0–2.9: 1%
Rank in top 10% of high school class: 90%
Rank in top 25% of high school class: 100%

Students living on campus: 60%
Students enrolled full-time: 95%
Total endowments: $4,315,219,000 (University of California System)
Public funding: $269,307,000 (+22.8%)

## Programs, Highlights, and Developments:

Irvine offers the School of Biological Sciences, the School of Arts, the School of Social Ecology, the Samueli School of Engineering, the School of Humanities, the Department of Information and Computer Science, the School of Physical Sciences, the School of Social Sciences, and interdisciplinary studies for undergraduates. Its Campuswide Honors Program is interdisciplinary and enrolls about 3 percent of undergraduates. One hundred forty honors students live in special houses on campus. In addition to completing a research thesis and honors classes, a student must maintain a GPA of 3.2 to graduate from the Honors Program.

# UNIVERSITY OF CALIFORNIA, LOS ANGELES

[ 1147 Murphy Hall
Los Angeles, CA 90095
(310) 825-3101
www.ucla.edu ]

Total students: 34,675
Total undergraduates: 24,668
First-year retention rate: 97%
Graduation rate: 79% (six years); 38% in four years, 35% in five years, 5% in six years
Ratio of students to faculty: 18:1
Ratio of males to females: 45:55
In-state students: 95%

### Tuition and fees for 2000–01:

In-state: $3,683
Out-of-state: $14,297

### Admission statistics:

35,681 applied, 29% were accepted, 3,751 enrolled (36% yield)
Mid-50% SAT verbal: 570–680
Mid-50% SAT math: 600–720
SAT verbal scores over 700: 18%

SAT verbal scores over 600: 64%
SAT math scores over 700: 35%
SAT math scores over 600: 77%
Mid-50% ACT: 23–29
ACT scores over 30: 20%
ACT scores over 24: 74%
Average high school GPA: n/a
GPA 3.0 or higher: 99%
GPA 2.0–2.9: 1%
Rank in top 10% of high school class: 97%
Rank in top 25% of high school class: n/a%

Students living on campus: 95%
Students enrolled full-time: 95%
Total endowments: $4,315,219,000 (University of California System); $402,537,000 (UCLA Foundation)
Public funding: $642,033,000 (+17.6%)

## Programs, Highlights, and Developments:

Undergraduate programs are found in the College of Letters and Science, the School of Engineering and Applied Science, the School of Film, Theater, and Television, the School of the Arts and Architecture, the School of Nursing, and the School of Public Policy and Social Research. Students may pursue honors courses through UCLA's honors programs in the College of Letters and Science. Extensive foreign study opportunities at 11 study centers are available through the Office of International Studies and Overseas Programs. UCLA has 81 academic departments and 30 interdepartmental programs that schedule more than 2,000 courses per quarter. Undergraduates may pursue research through the Student Research Program, which serves about 2,500 students per year, as well as through the Center for Academic and Research Excellence, the Ocean Discovery Center, the UCLA Summer Research Program, and the OMEGA Research Scholars Program in engineering.

# UNIVERSITY OF CALIFORNIA, SAN DIEGO

9500 Gilman Drive, 0021
La Jolla, CA 92093-0021
(619) 534-4831
www.ucsd.edu

Total students: 19,918 (total students, not necessarily degree-seeking)
Total undergraduates: 15,763
First-year retention rate: 93%
Graduation rate: 79% (six years)
Ratio of students to faculty: 19:1
Ratio of males to females: 51:49
In-state students: 98% of total student body

## Tuition and fees for 2000-01:

In-state: $3,851
Out-of-state: $14,465

## Admission statistics:

32,539 applied, 41% were accepted, 5,328 enrolled (40% yield)
Mid-50% SAT verbal: 520–640
Mid-50% SAT math: 550–650
SAT verbal scores over 700: n/a
SAT verbal scores over 600: n/a
SAT math scores over 700: n/a
SAT math scores over 600: n/a
Mid-50% ACT: 21–27
ACT scores over 30: n/a
ACT scores over 24: n/a
Average high school GPA: 3.98
GPA 3.0 or higher: 100%
GPA 2.0–2.9: n/a
Rank in top 10% of high school class: 95%
Rank in top 25% of high school class: n/a

Students living on campus: 80%
Students enrolled full-time: 99% (1997)
Total endowments: $4,315,219,000 (University of California System); $130,384,000 (UCSD Foundation)
Public funding: $343,031,000 (+18.3%)

## Programs, Highlights, and Developments:

Students apply to one of five colleges at UCSD, which have the same admissions requirements but different personalities and programs. The colleges are Revelle, John Muir, Thurgood Marshall, Roosevelt, and Warren. From the base of these colleges, students can pursue engineering, interdisciplinary courses, and studies at the Scripps Institute of Oceanography. Academic Enrichment Programs at UCSD offer students research and mentoring programs through the Faculty Mentor Program, the Summer Research Program, the UCSD Undergraduate

Research Conference, the CAMP Science Program for underrepresented minority students, and the McNair Program for budding researchers or teachers, for example. UCSD ranks fifth in the nation and first in the University of California system for the spending of federal research money on research and development. The university boasts that its science faculty was rated first in the nation among science faculty at public institutions in a Johns Hopkins University study.

# UNIVERSITY OF CALIFORNIA, SANTA BARBARA

PO Box 2881
Santa Barbara, CA
93106
(805) 893-2881
www.ucsb.edu

Total students: 20,036
Total undergraduates: 17,685
First-year retention rate: 89%
Graduation rate: 67% (six years)
Ratio of students to faculty: 20:1
Ratio of males to females: 46:54
In-state students: 54%

## Tuition and fees for 2000-01:

In-state: $3,831
Out-of-state: $14,448

## Admission statistics:

26,931 applied, 53% were accepted,
3,781 enrolled (26% yield)
Mid-50% SAT verbal: 530–630
Mid-50% SAT math: 550–660
SAT verbal scores over 700: 7%
SAT verbal scores over 600: 44%

SAT math scores over 700: 12%
SAT math scores over 600: 55%
Mid-50% ACT: 22–27
ACT scores over 30: n/a
ACT scores over 24: n/a
Average high school GPA: 3.69
GPA 3.0 or higher: 99%
GPA 2.0–2.9: 1%
Rank in top 10% of high school class:
95%
Rank in top 25% of high school class:
n/a

Students living on campus: 46%
Students enrolled full-time: 97%
Total endowments: $4,315,219,000
(University of California System)
Public funding: $230,531,000 (+21.6%)

## Programs, Highlights, and Developments:

Students enter mainly the College of Engineering or the College of Letters and Science, which lists 48 different departments, programs, and units and offers some 80 different majors. The College of Creative Studies offers a flexible curriculum for 160 students in the arts, math, or sciences. There are eight national research centers on campus, including the Institute for Theoretical Physics, the National Center for Geographic Information and Analysis, and the National Center for Ecological Analysis and Synthesis. The University of California's Education Abroad Program is based at UCSB. The Interdisciplinary Humanities Center encourages scholarship and instruction across academic boundaries. The College of Letters and Science Honors Program enrolls students who commit themselves as scholars. They may live in Scholars Halls, designated floors in university residence halls; may pursue interdisciplinary programs, internships, and mentoring opportunities; and must complete at least 10 hours of community service per year as upper division students. Freshman applicants usually must have a minimum high school GPA of 3.75 and scores of 1350 on the SAT or 30 on the ACT.

# UNIVERSITY OF COLORADO AT BOULDER

125 Regent
Administrative Center
Boulder, CO 80309
(303) 492-6301
www.colorado.edu

Total students: 26,593
Total undergraduates: 21,781
First-year retention rate: 84%
Graduation rate: 64% (six years); 35% in
   four years, 24% in five years, 5% in six
   years
Ratio of students to faculty: 14:1
Ratio of males to females: 52:48
In-state students: 58%

### Tuition and fees for 2000–01:

In-state: $3,223
Out-of-state: $16,541

### Admission statistics:

14,617 applied, 85% were accepted,
   4,596 enrolled (37% yield)
Mid-50% SAT verbal: 520–620
Mid-50% SAT math: 540–640
SAT verbal scores over 700: 6%

SAT verbal scores over 600: 38%
SAT math scores over 700: 8%
SAT math scores over 600: 45%
Mid-50% ACT: 22–27
ACT scores over 30: 10%
ACT scores over 24: 64%
Average high school GPA: 3.41
GPA 3.0 or higher: 88%
GPA 2.0–2.9: 12%
Rank in top 10% of high school class:
   24%
Rank in top 25% of high school class:
   57%

Students living on campus: 95%
Students enrolled full-time: 92%
Total endowments: $325,975,000
   (University of Colorado Foundation)
Public funding: $209,000,000 (+3.7%)

## Programs, Highlights, and Developments:

Applicants enter the College of Arts and Sciences, the College of Business and Administration, the College of Engineering and Applied Science, or the College of Music. They may later enter the School of Education, the College of Architecture and Planning (usually after completing a Bachelor of Environmental Design degree), or the School of Journalism and Mass Communications. Special programs include the Environmental Residential Academic Program, which offers students interdisciplinary opportunities in environmental studies and related areas in a small college environment within the university; the Chancellor's Leadership Residential Academic Program, which focuses on the study of leadership, again with an emphasis on creating a more intimate campus environment; the Farrand and Sewall Residential Academic Programs, serving over 700 students; the Kittredge Honors Program; and the Engineering and Science Residential Program. The Undergraduate Research Opportunities Program allows undergraduates across all disciplines to pursue research with a faculty mentor and a university grant. Summer Undergraduate Research Fellowships are also available. A comprehensive learning support program is available through CU's Disability Services. CU recently received the largest private gift ever made to a public university—$250 million—to endow the University of Colorado Coleman Institute for Cognitive Disabilities. Students at CU recently voted to create a student-run honor code to encourage honesty and responsibility among students and allow students to review academic misconduct cases.

# UNIVERSITY OF CONNECTICUT

2131 Hillside Road, Box U-88
Storrs, CT 06269
(860) 486-3137
www.uconn.edu

Total students: 17,604
Total undergraduates: 11,987
First-year retention rate: 86%
Graduation rate: 68% (six years); 40% in four years, 23% in five years, 4% in six years
Ratio of students to faculty: 15:1
Ratio of males to females: 47:53
In-state students: 71%

## Tuition and fees for 2000-01:

In-state: $5,596
Out-of-state: $14,370

## Admission statistics:

11,781 applied, 70% were accepted, 2,956 enrolled (36% yield)
Mid-50% SAT verbal: 510–610
Mid-50% SAT math: 520–620
SAT verbal scores over 700: 5%

SAT verbal scores over 600: 31%
SAT math scores over 700: 6%
SAT math scores over 600: 37%
Mid-50% ACT: n/a
ACT scores over 30: n/a
ACT scores over 24: n/a
Average high school GPA: n/a
GPA 3.0 or higher: n/a
GPA 2.0–2.9: n/a
Rank in top 10% of high school class: 20%
Rank in top 25% of high school class: 58%

Students living on campus: 96%
Students enrolled full-time: 95%
Total endowments: $142,884,000 (University of Connecticut Foundation)
Public funding: $252,727,000 (+1.1%)

## Programs, Highlights, and Developments:

UConn's Honors Scholars Program offers students about 40 honors courses per year (for freshmen and sophomores), with an average class size of 16. Juniors and seniors focus on honors courses in their major and work toward a senior thesis. Interdisciplinary courses, a Washington Internship Program, and a summer internship program are also available within the Honors Scholars Program. The First Year Experience Program helps high school students transfer to the university by exposing them to special seminars taught by senior faculty. The university offers more than 90 undergraduate majors and is the only public university in New England with its own Schools of Law, Social Work, Medicine, and Dental Medicine. The Undergraduate Research office at UConn coordinates a wide array of opportunities for undergrads to pursue their interests. First-year students have a variety of choices entering UConn: the College of Agriculture and Natural Resources, the Ratcliffe Hicks School of Agriculture, the School of Business Administration, the School of Engineering, the School of Family Studies, the School of Fine Arts, the College of Liberal Arts and Sciences, or the School of Nursing. They may then go on to the School of Allied Health, School of Education, or School of Pharmacy. UConn offers significant merit scholarships for incoming freshmen, from the Nutmeg Scholarship and the Day of Pride Scholarship, each valued at $12,500 and offered to in-state students, to the Achievement Scholarships and Leadership Scholarships offered to all students. The Achievement Scholarships are automatically awarded to admitted students with at least a 1300 SAT and a top 15 percent class rank. The Leadership Scholarships are automatically given to those who have shown commitment to diversity awareness and leadership, have at least an 1100 SAT and a top 15 percent class rank. These two scholarships cover from half to full tuition for up to four years. The UConn 2000 initiative offered $1 billion of state financing to improve the university.

# UNIVERSITY OF DELAWARE

116 Hullihen Hall
Newark, DE 19716
(302) 831-8123
www.udel.edu

Total students: 18,445

Total undergraduates: 15,463

First-year retention rate: 87%

Graduation rate: 70% (six years); 51% in four years, 16% in five years, 2% in six years

Ratio of students to faculty: 13:1

Ratio of males to females: 41:59

In-state students: 32%

### Tuition and fees for 2000-01:

In-state: $5,004

Out-of-state: $13,754

### Admission statistics:

14,107 applied, 63% were accepted, 3,503 enrolled (39% yield)

Mid-50% SAT verbal: 520–610

Mid-50% SAT math: 520–630

SAT verbal scores over 700: 5%

SAT verbal scores over 600: 32%

SAT math scores over 700: 7%

SAT math scores over 600: 40%

Mid-50% ACT: 22–26

ACT scores over 30: 6%

ACT scores over 24: 55%

Average high school GPA: 3.50

GPA 3.0 or higher: 82%

GPA 2.0–2.9: 18%

Rank in top 10% of high school class: 26%

Rank in top 25% of high school class: 62%

Students living on campus: 89%

Students enrolled full-time: 92%

Total endowments: $777,349,000

Public funding: $101,531,000 (+5.1%)

## Programs, Highlights, and Developments:

Delaware offers over more than 163 academic programs of study, over 120 majors, and a huge Undergraduate Research Program. Seven colleges make up the university: Agriculture and Natural Resources; Arts and Science; Business and Economics; Engineering; Health and Nursing Sciences; Human Services, Education and Public Policy; and Marine Studies. Delaware lists 31 interdisciplinary academic areas, from cognitive science to operations research to legal studies. Delaware offers a large amount of merit-based financial aid, with about a third of the class of 2004 offered an academic merit scholarship in addition to their offer of admission. Amounts ranged from $1,000 per year to the Eugene du Pont Memorial Distinguished Scholar Award full scholarships. The LIFE (Learning: Integrated Freshman Experience) Program links academic and residential aspects of the university for freshmen through residential clusters, interdisciplinary courses, and collaborative research work. Delaware's Honors Program offers honors degrees in some 80 majors across the university's colleges, residential and extracurricular opportunities, and faculty research networking. New students apply to admission to the program while they are applying to the university, and about 500 first-year students join each year. The Academic Services Center offers comprehensive Learning Disabilities Services and other academic support programs on campus.

# UNIVERSITY OF FLORIDA

201 Criser Hall
Gainesville, FL 32611-4000
(352) 392-1365
www.ufl.edu

Total students: 41,903

Total undergraduates: 30,883

First-year retention rate: 91%

Graduation rate: 67% (six years); 31% in four years, 28% in five years, 8% in six years

Ratio of students to faculty: 17:1

Ratio of males to females: 48:52

In-state students: 95%

### Tuition and fees for 2000–01:

In-state: $2,256

Out-of-state: $9,244

### Admission statistics:

13,967 applied, 60% were accepted, 5,462 enrolled (65% yield)

Mid-50% SAT verbal: 570–670

Mid-50% SAT math: 600–690

SAT verbal scores over 700: 18%

SAT verbal scores over 600: 66%

SAT math scores over 700: 22%

SAT math scores over 600: 75%

Mid-50% ACT: 26–29

ACT scores over 30: 25%

ACT scores over 24: 89%

Average high school GPA: n/a

GPA 3.0 or higher: 99%

GPA 2.0–2.9: 1%

Rank in top 10% of high school class: 69%

Rank in top 25% of high school class: 92%

Students living on campus: 90%

Students enrolled full-time: 92%

Total endowments: $601,813,000 (University of Florida Foundation)

Public funding: $517,939,000 (+5.8%)

## Programs, Highlights, and Developments:

Florida consists of 23 colleges and schools and more than 100 research, service, and academic centers and units. More than 100 majors are offered, and more than 1,500 first- and second-year students are involved in its Honors Program, which lists about 70 courses each semester open to no more than 25 students each. The University of Florida Brain Institute is a major, federally funded research institute. Most entering students will join the College of Liberal Arts and Sciences, the Warrington College of Business, the Fisher School of Accounting, the College of Engineering, the College of Journalism and Communications, or the College of Agricultural and Life Sciences. The University Scholars Program offers research opportunities to undergraduates throughout the university.

# UNIVERSITY OF GEORGIA

212 Terrell Hall
Athens, GA 30602
(706) 542-2112
www.uga.edu

Total students: 30,244
Total undergraduates: 23,689
First-year retention rate: 89%
Graduation rate: 63% (six years); 46% in four years, 16% in five years, 4% in six years
Ratio of students to faculty: 8:1
Ratio of males to females: 46:54
In-state students: 90%

## Tuition and fees for 2000-01:

In-state: $3,276
Out-of-state: $10,794

## Admission statistics:

13,402 applied, 63% were accepted, 4,398 enrolled (52% yield)
Mid-50% SAT verbal: 550–640
Mid-50% SAT math: 550–650
SAT verbal scores over 700: 10%

SAT verbal scores over 600: 50%
SAT math scores over 700: 8%
SAT math scores over 600: 50%
Mid-50% ACT: 24–28
ACT scores over 30: n/a
ACT scores over 24: n/a
Average high school GPA: 3.64
GPA 3.0 or higher: 90%
GPA 2.0–2.9: 10%
Rank in top 10% of high school class: 61%
Rank in top 25% of high school class: n/a

Students living on campus: 80%
Students enrolled full-time: 90%
Total endowments: $334,534,000
    (University of Georgia and Foundation)
Public funding: $410,651,000 (+3.5%)

## Programs, Highlights, and Developments:

Some 500 merit scholarships are available at Georgia, ranging from $1,000 per year to the price of full tuition. The Georgia Hope Scholarships cover full tuition and are awarded to about 95 percent of first-year students from Georgia. These scholarships are renewable every year for those who maintain a B average. Georgia's Honors Program offers honors classes, the freedom to design interdisciplinary majors, faculty advising opportunities, and a thesis or project requirement during the senior year. About 180 smaller, more demanding honors classes are offered every year. Potentially qualified honors students admitted to the university are sent an application, and others may request one. In 1998, admitted honors students averaged a 3.97 GPA and a score of 1380 on the SATs. Georgia's Center for Undergraduate Research Opportunities helps students pursue research projects with faculty mentors. Georgia offers over 170 different academic programs. Students generally begin academic life at Georgia in the General Studies Division of the Franklin College of Arts and Sciences, the Terry College of Business, the Tull School of Accounting, the Grady College of Journalism and Mass Communication, or the College of Agricultural and Environmental Sciences. Other schools at Georgia include the School of Environmental Design, the Warnell School of Forest Resources, the School of Social Work, and the College of Veterinary Medicine. Georgia broke ground in the fall of 2000 for a new $43 million, 200,000-square-foot Student Learning Center, due to be completed in 2003. The building will house 25 classrooms, an electronic teaching library with 500 public-access computers, Internet connections, 95 group-study rooms, and a coffee house.

# UNIVERSITY OF ILLINOIS AT URBANA-CHAMPAIGN

901 West Illinois
Urbana, IL 61801
(217) 333-0302
www.uiuc.edu

Total students: 36,674
Total undergraduates: 27,492
First-year retention rate: 92%
Graduation rate: 77% (six years); 49% in four years, 23% in five years, 4% in six years
Ratio of students to faculty: 14:1
Ratio of males to females: 53:47
In-state students: 93%

## Tuition and fees for 2000-01:

In-state: $4,752
Out-of-state: $12,200

## Admission statistics:

17,867 applied, 71% were accepted, 6,479 enrolled (51% yield)
Mid-50% SAT verbal: 550–650
Mid-50% SAT math: 590–710
SAT verbal scores over 700: 11%

SAT verbal scores over 600: 51%
SAT math scores over 700: 26%
SAT math scores over 600: 69%
Mid-50% ACT: 25–28
ACT scores over 30: 23%
ACT scores over 24: 84%
Average high school GPA: n/a
GPA 3.0 or higher: n/a
GPA 2.0–2.9: n/a
Rank in top 10% of high school class: 50%
Rank in top 25% of high school class: 86%

Students living on campus: 100%
Students enrolled full-time: 98%
Total endowments: $816,573,000 (University of Illinois and Foundation)
Public funding: $853,080,000 (+5.6%)

## Programs, Highlights, and Developments:

Illinois has eight undergraduate colleges and one school, which together offer over 150 academic programs of study: Liberal Arts and Sciences; Engineering; Education; Agricultural, Consumer and Environmental Sciences; Applied Life Sciences; Fine and Applied Arts; Commerce and Business Administration; Communications; and Engineering. These will be home to most undergrads. The Campus Honors Program at Illinois admits about 125 new students each year—not many out of 6,000 freshmen. Those maintaining at least a 3.25 GPA and fulfilling other requirements remain in the program as Chancellor's Scholars and are not segregated from the rest of the university population in separate housing. They may take honors courses of their choice. Talented students admitted to Illinois are asked to apply for admission to the Honors Program, although others may ask to apply on their own.

# INDIANA UNIVERSITY BLOOMINGTON

> **107 S. Indiana Avenue**
> **Bloomington, IN 47405-7000**
> **(812) 855-4848**
> **www.iub.edu**

Total students: 34,730
Total undergraduates: 27,461
First-year retention rate: 87%
Graduation rate: 67% (six years)
Ratio of students to faculty: 21:1
Ratio of males to females: 46:54
In-state students: 73%

### Tuition and fees for 2000-01:

In-state: $4,362
Out-of-state: $13,418

### Admission statistics:

20,095 applied, 81% were accepted,
6,583 enrolled (41% yield)
Mid-50% SAT verbal: 490–600
Mid-50% SAT math: 490–610
SAT verbal scores over 700: n/a
SAT verbal scores over 600: n/a

SAT math scores over 700: n/a
SAT math scores over 600: n/a
Mid-50% ACT: 22–27
ACT scores over 30: n/a
ACT scores over 24: n/a
Average high school GPA: n/a
GPA 3.0 or higher: n/a
GPA 2.0–2.9: n/a
Rank in top 10% of high school class:
   23%
Rank in top 25% of high school class:
   55%

Students living on campus: n/a
Students enrolled full-time: 95%
Total endowments: $802,395,000
   (Indiana University and Foundation)
Public funding: $447,733,000 (+3.4%)

### Programs, Highlights, and Developments:

Most first-year students enter first into the IU's University Division, before declaring a major. Other strong undergraduate opportunities include the Kelley School of Business, the School of Music, the Kinsey Institute for Research in Sex, Gender, and Reproduction, and the School of Education. In the Honors College at IU, students are offered honors sections in traditional courses, plus opportunities for independent study, fieldwork, research, meetings with faculty, community service, and research and teaching grants. Qualified students are automatically asked to join and have at least a 1300 combined SAT score or a 30 on the ACT, and a top 10 percent class rank.

# UNIVERSITY OF IOWA

107 Calvin Hall
Iowa City, IA 52242
(319) 335-3847
www.uiowa.edu

Total students: 27,309
Total undergraduates: 18,770
First-year retention rate: 82%
Graduation rate: 62% (six years); 33% in four years, 26% in five years, 5% in six years
Ratio of students to faculty: 14:1
Ratio of males to females: 46:54
In-state students: 63%

## Tuition and fees for 2000-01:

In-state: $3,204
Out-of-state: $10,966

## Admission statistics:

11,358 applied, 83% were accepted, 3,859 enrolled (41% yield)
Mid-50% SAT verbal: 520–660
Mid-50% SAT math: 540–660
SAT verbal scores over 700: 14%

SAT verbal scores over 600: 45%
SAT math scores over 700: 15%
SAT math scores over 600: 50%
Mid-50% ACT: 22–27
ACT scores over 30: 10%
ACT scores over 24: 61%
Average high school GPA: 3.45
GPA 3.0 or higher: 87%
GPA 2.0–2.9: 13%
Rank in top 10% of high school class: 21%
Rank in top 25% of high school class: 50%

Students living on campus: 90%
Students enrolled full-time: 90%
Total endowments: $476,800,000 (University of Iowa and Foundation)
Public funding: $281,344,000 (+2.9%)

## Programs, Highlights, and Developments:

Iowa offers over 100 areas of study, including about 57 different majors. Well-known programs include the International Writing Program and the Writer's Workshop. Undergraduates may find courses in the Health Sciences Center, with its Colleges of Medicine, Pharmacy, Dentistry, and Nursing. They may also study in the College of Liberal Arts (the largest of Iowa's 11 colleges), the College of Business (generally admitted after two years of study in Liberal Arts), the College of Education, and the College of Engineering. Eight interdisciplinary programs are available, from Biosciences to Literature, Science and the Arts. Iowa offers numerous study centers and projects through its international programs. The Honors Program on campus serves more than 3,500 students with small class sections, 30 lower division honors classes, independent study opportunities, teaching intern arrangements, a special honors study center and honors residential floors. Students who matriculate at Iowa are automatically admitted to the Honors Program if they are in the top 10 percent of their high school class and have an ACT score of 29 or comparable SAT, are in the top 15 percent and have an ACT score of 30–32, or are in the top 20 percent and have an ACT of 33 or higher, or if they are a National Merit Scholar, a Presidential Scholar, a Dean's Scholar, a National Achievement Scholar, or an Opportunity at Iowa Academic Scholar. Students must maintain a 3.2 GPA to remain in the program. Annually, Iowa offers more than 350 scholarships based on merit, need, or both. First-year students may take advantage of a First-Year Seminar program, giving them the opportunity to work with faculty members on their areas of research or expertise. Iowa's Courses in Common program helps make the transition to a big university easier by letting first-year students group with 20 or so other students to take a few of the same classes together. Iowa recently completed the $21 million Levitz Center for Advancement, home to the alumni association and University of Iowa Foundation. The College of Liberal Arts building also underwent a major renovation.

# UNIVERSITY OF MARYLAND COLLEGE PARK

Mitchell Building
College Park, MD 20742-5235
(301) 314-8385
www.maryland.edu

Total students: 21,889
Total undergraduates: 14,466
First-year retention rate: 90%
Graduation rate: 64% (six years); 32% in four years, 26% in five years, 6% in six years
Ratio of students to faculty: 14:1
Ratio of males to females: 51:49
In-state students: 67%

**Tuition and fees for 2000-01:**

In-state: $5,136
Out-of-state: $12,668

**Admission statistics:**

18,731 applied, 54% were accepted, 3,916 enrolled (39% yield)
Mid-50% SAT verbal: 560–660
Mid-50% SAT math: 580–680
SAT verbal scores over 700: 13%
SAT verbal scores over 600: 56%
SAT math scores over 700: 21%
SAT math scores over 600: 67%
Mid-50% ACT: n/a
ACT scores over 30: n/a
ACT scores over 24: n/a
Average high school GPA: 3.61
GPA 3.0 or higher: 93%
GPA 2.0–2.9: 6%
Rank in top 10% of high school class: 45%
Rank in top 25% of high school class: 83%

Students living on campus: 83%
Students enrolled full-time: 84%
Total endowments: $498,703,000 (University of Maryland system and Foundation)
Public funding: $798,293,000 (+10.9%) (UMD system)

## Programs, Highlights, and Developments:

Maryland has 13 colleges and schools: the College of Arts and Humanities, the College of Behavioral and Social Sciences, the Smith School of Business, the Clark School of Engineering, the College of Life Sciences, the College of Journalism, the College of Computer, Mathematical, and Physical Sciences, the College of Education, the School of Public Affairs, the College of Architecture, the College of Agriculture and Natural Resources, the College of Health and

Human Performance, and the College of Library and Information Services. Multicollege programs include Computer Engineering and Environmental Science and Policy. In the College Park Scholars program, first- and second-year students choose from among 12 residential learning programs with special themes. They take specifically designed courses and live together in residence halls. Most students are talented Maryland applicants who are invited to participate in the College Park Scholars program during the admissions process. Maryland's University Honors Program serves top first- and second-year students with smaller classes, interdisciplinary topics, and advanced courses. Some 2,000 students take part in the program, with the 700 most talented Maryland freshmen invited to join each year. The Maryland College of Journalism was recently renamed for Philip Merrill, who donated $10 million to the school. A new Riggs Alumni Center will begin construction in 2002 with a price tag of $21 million. The building will be designed by Maryland alumnus Hugh Jacobsen. A $1.7 million gift started a new program at Maryland called the Hinman Campus Entrepreneurship Opportunities (CEO) program. This business education program offers a limited number of students the chance to live in a technology-rich residential learning environment focusing on integrating the wired world and studies of entrepreneurship, venture capital, and operating businesses.

# MIAMI UNIVERSITY (OXFORD, OHIO)

301 South Campus Avenue
Oxford, OH 45056-3434
(513) 529-2531
www.muohio.edu

Total students: 16,359
Total undergraduates: 15,168
First-year retention rate: 90%
Graduation rate: 79% (six years); 63% in four years, 16% in five years, 2% in six years
Ratio of students to faculty: 18:1
Ratio of males to females: 45:55
In-state students: 73%

### Tuition and fees for 2000-01:

In-state: $6,403
Out-of-state: $13,443

### Admission statistics:

11,993 applied, 79% were accepted, 3,605 enrolled (38% yield)
Mid-50% SAT verbal: 540–630
Mid-50% SAT math: 550–660
SAT verbal scores over 700: 7%

SAT verbal scores over 600: 45%
SAT math scores over 700: 10%
SAT math scores over 600: 57%
Mid-50% ACT: 24–28
ACT scores over 30: 12%
ACT scores over 24: 76%
Average high school GPA: n/a
GPA 3.0 or higher: n/a
GPA 2.0–2.9: n/a
Rank in top 10% of high school class: 32%
Rank in top 25% of high school class: 70%

Students living on campus: 98%
Students enrolled full-time: 94%
Total endowments: $201,080,000 (Miami University and Foundation)
Public funding: $70,584,000 (+6.7%)

### Programs, Highlights, and Developments:

Miami offers almost 100 undergraduate degrees. A high percentage of students study abroad at Miami, and the university maintains the John E. Dolibois European Center in Luxembourg. Most students at Miami will enter the College of Arts and Science. Other schools on campus are the Farmer School of Business Administration, the School of Education and Allied Professions, the School of Engineering and Applied Science, the School of Fine Arts, and the School of Interdisciplinary Studies. The large majority of Miami's students are undergraduates and pursue studies in the liberal arts. The Office for the Advancement of Scholarship and

Teaching provides opportunities for undergraduates to pursue research projects with faculty supervision. Summer Scholars and Research Awards are available, as is the STARS (Student Achievement in Research and Scholarship) Program for talented African American, Hispanic, and Native American students. Miami's Honors Program requires participating students to maintain a 3.2 GPA for their first two years and a 3.3 for their third and fourth years of college. They participate in a Faculty Mentoring Program during their first year and may earn up to eight tuition hours of credit by maintaining a 3.5 GPA over two years and completing eight honors experiences, including courses, internships, and summer scholars programs. Strong students admitted to Miami may be invited to join the Honors Program. Others may apply to the program during summer orientation.

# UNIVERSITY OF MICHIGAN, ANN ARBOR

1220 Student Activities Building
Ann Arbor, MI 48109-1316
(734) 764-7433
www.umich.edu

Total students: 37,846

Total undergraduates: 24,493

First-year retention rate: 95%

Graduation rate: 82% (six years); 62% in four years, 19% in five years, 2% in six years

Ratio of students to faculty: 11:1

Ratio of males to females: 50:50

In-state students: 72%

### Tuition and fees for 2000–01:

In-state: $6,513

Out-of-state: $20,323

### Admission statistics:

21,324 applied, 59% were accepted, 5,559 enrolled (44% yield)

Mid-50% SAT verbal: 560–670

Mid-50% SAT math: 600–710

SAT verbal scores over 700: 15%

SAT verbal scores over 600: 60%

SAT math scores over 700: 29%

SAT math scores over 600: 76%

Mid-50% ACT: 25–30

ACT scores over 30: 30%

ACT scores over 24: 88%

Average high school GPA: 3.6

GPA 3.0 or higher: 96%

GPA 2.0–2.9: 4%

Rank in top 10% of high school class: 63%

Rank in top 25% of high school class: 90%

Students living on campus: 94%

Students enrolled full-time: 94%

Total endowments: $2,525,612,000

Public funding: $409,495,000 (+5.9%)

### Programs, Highlights, and Developments:

Applicants to the University of Michigan are admitted directly to 1 of 12 undergraduate schools and colleges, the largest of which is the College of Literature, Science, and the Arts (LS&A). High school students can apply to this college or one of six other schools: Art and Design; Engineering; Kinesiology, the Residential College of LS&A; Music (which offers dual enrollment options with LS&A, Engineering, or the Residential College); Nursing; and Natural Resources and Environment. Undergraduates can then apply as upper division students to the Taubman College of Architecture and Urban Planning, the Business School, the College of

Dental Hygiene, the School of Education, or the College of Pharmacy. Michigan offers numerous special programs, including First-Year Seminars; both residential and nonresidential Learning Communities, which create groups of students working together in and out of class, the Residential College program, a small liberal arts college environment within LS&A; and more than 70 international programs in 36 countries and 6 continents through the Office of International Programs. The Honors Program in LS&A invites 10 to 12 percent of LS&A admitted students to enroll. In the fall of 1998, the average honors student had a 3.8 GPA and an ACT score of 32 or SAT score of 1400. Those not invited may request to be admitted in writing. Special honors courses are offered across many disciplines, as are advanced honors sections of regular courses and independent study courses with faculty advisors. Honors housing is available to all honors students, but they are not required to live there. Michigan's Undergraduate Research Opportunity Program (UROP) offers first- and second-year students the chance to conduct research under the direction of university faculty. About 900 students and 600 faculty are engaged in research partnerships. UROP allows sophomores to undertake a second year of research. Students may also participate in the UROP in Residence program to bring a residential aspect to their research interests and may apply for sponsored summer fellowship programs. The Ford School of Public Policy recently received an anonymous $3 million gift to help establish the Life Sciences Policy Center.

# MICHIGAN STATE UNIVERSITY

250 Administration Building
East Lansing, MI 48824-1046
(517) 355-1855
www.msu.edu

Total students: 41,439
Total undergraduates: 33,687
First-year retention rate: 88%
Graduation rate: 64% (six years); 32% in four years, 29% in five years, 6% in six years
Ratio of students to faculty: 18:1
Ratio of males to females: 47:53
In-state students: 93%

### Tuition and fees for 2000-01:

In-state: $5,210
Out-of-state: $12,875

### Admission statistics:

22,623 applied, 71% were accepted, 6,716 enrolled (42% yield)
Mid-50% SAT verbal: 490–610
Mid-50% SAT math: 490–630

SAT verbal scores over 700: 7%
SAT verbal scores over 600: 30%
SAT math scores over 700: 9%
SAT math scores over 600: 37%
Mid-50% ACT: 21–26
ACT scores over 30: 7%
ACT scores over 24: 52%
Average high school GPA: 3.44
GPA 3.0 or higher: 89%
GPA 2.0–2.9: 11%
Rank in top 10% of high school class: 23%
Rank in top 25% of high school class: 56%

Students living on campus: 96%
Students enrolled full-time: 87%
Total endowments: $265,238,000
Public funding: $388,780,000 (+7.3%)

## Programs, Highlights, and Developments:

MSU's traditional strengths, due to its founding as a land-grant university, have been in the agricultural and veterinary sciences. In addition to majors in the College of Agriculture and Natural Resources and the College of Veterinary Medicine, however, MSU students may study in the College of Arts and Letters, the College of Business, the College of Communication Arts and Sciences, the College of Education, the College of Engineering, the College of Human Ecology, the College of Natural Science, the College of Nursing, James Madison College, and the College of Social Science. James Madison offers an integrated bachelor's program in the social sciences, focusing on public affairs, public policy, and international relations. The Lyman Briggs School in the College of Natural Science offers science students an interdisciplinary residential program. Other than those entering Lyman Briggs and James Madison, all new first- and second-year students at MSU enter the Undergraduate University Division, where they take a broad range of courses in the liberal arts and sciences before entering one of the other bachelor-degree-granting colleges, typically after two years of study. In all the colleges undergraduates may pursue research opportunities independently, with a group, or with a faculty advisor. MSU's Honors College offers independent and flexible study options for talented students, who may live in honors floors. Some 1,600 students are enrolled in the Honors College, which has no separate application process but invites admitted students who are in the top 5 percent of their high school class and have an ACT score of 30 or higher, or an SAT of 1360 or higher. Students must maintain a 3.2 average to stay in the Honors College. The Liberty Hyde Bailey Scholars Programs allows students to engage in "active, experiential, progressively self-directed, increasingly complex, and reflective learning," according to MSU's materials. In-class academic learning in the College of Agriculture and Natural Resources is combined with service, work, and mentoring to integrate university learning with ethical practice in a student's field. MSU also offers freshman seminars, RISE (Residential Initiative on the Study of the Environment) for those interested in environmental studies, ROIAL (Residential Option in Arts and Letters) for first- and second-year Arts and Letters students interested in a residential learning program, and ROSES (Residential Option for Science and Engineering Students) for those in the Colleges of Agriculture and Natural Resources, Engineering, and Natural Science. MSU's Office of Study Abroad coordinates programs in 48 countries and 6 continents, and the participation in and variety of choices are impressive.

# UNIVERSITY OF MINNESOTA, TWIN CITIES

240 Williamson Hall
231 Pillsbury Drive SE
Minneapolis, MN 55455-0115
(612) 625-2008
www.umn.edu/tc

Total students: 39,186
Total undergraduates: 26,968
First-year retention rate: 82%
Graduation rate: 51% (six years)
Ratio of students to faculty: n/a
Ratio of males to females: 48:52
In-state students: 59%

### Tuition and fees for 2000–01:

In-state: $4,879
Out-of-state: $13,465

### Admission statistics:

15,319 applied, 73% were accepted,
5,141 enrolled (46% yield)
Mid-50% SAT verbal: 540–660
Mid-50% SAT math: 550–620
SAT verbal scores over 700: 13%
SAT verbal scores over 600: 52%

SAT math scores over 700: 19%
SAT math scores over 600: 61%
Mid-50% ACT: 22–27
ACT scores over 30: 11%
ACT scores over 24: 61%
Average high school GPA: n/a
GPA 3.0 or higher: n/a
GPA 2.0–2.9: n/a
Rank in top 10% of high school class:
29%
Rank in top 25% of high school class:
60%

Students living on campus: 74%
Students enrolled full-time: 77%
Total endowments: $1,283,934,000
(University of Minnesota and
Foundation)
Public funding: $607,199,000 (+3.7%)

### Programs, Highlights, and Developments:

Minnesota offers undergraduate students more than 150 majors in 28 different schools, and they may design their own major with an advisor. Students may choose from the College of Architecture and Landscape Architecture, the College of Agriculture, Food, and Environmental Sciences, the College of Liberal Arts, the College of Biological Sciences, the College of Continuing Education, the College of Human Ecology, the College of Liberal Arts, the College of Natural Resources, the Carlson School of Management, the Institute of Technology, the College of Education and Human Development, and the General College. Many of Minnesota's colleges offer specific honors programs for their students. Honors programs for freshmen select students on the basis of a separate application in addition to the regular Minnesota application. Admitted students typically rank in the top 10 percent of their high school class and have an ACT score of 28 or higher or an SAT score of 1260 or higher. Some honors programs in the different colleges are more competitive than others, such as the Institute of Technology Honors Program, in which students had an average SAT score of 1400, an ACT Math score of 33, and an ACT English score of 29 (the program uses only these two sections of the ACT in its evaluation process). Other honors programs open to freshmen include those in the College of Agriculture, Food, and Environmental Sciences, the College of Biological Sciences, the College of Human Ecology, the College of Liberal Arts, the College of Natural Resources, and the Carlson School of Management. The honors programs provide students with research apprenticeships, small classes, internships, honors housing, study abroad, and honors advising.

# STATE UNIVERSITY OF NEW YORK AT BINGHAMTON

[
Box 6001
Binghamton, NY
13902-6001
(607) 777-2171
www.binghamton.edu
]

Total students: 12,091
Total undergraduates: 9,710
First-year retention rate: 92%
Graduation rate: 81% (six years); 72% in four years, 10% in five years, 1% in six years
Ratio of students to faculty: 18:1
Ratio of males to females: 47:53
In-state students: 95%

### Tuition and fees for 2000-01:

In-state: $4,463
Out-of-state: $9,363

### Admission statistics:

16,386 applied, 42% were accepted, 2,050 enrolled (30% yield)
Mid-50% SAT verbal: 540–640
Mid-50% SAT math: 570–660
SAT verbal scores over 700: 7%

SAT verbal scores over 600: 47%
SAT math scores over 700: 14%
SAT math scores over 600: 62%
Mid-50% ACT: 24–29
ACT scores over 30: n/a
ACT scores over 24: n/a
Average high school GPA: 3.6
GPA 3.0 or higher: 98%
GPA 2.0–2.9: 2%
Rank in top 10% of high school class: 50%
Rank in top 25% of high school class: 96%

Students living on campus: 96%
Students enrolled full-time: 98%
Total endowments: Over $35 million in 2000, according to the university
Public funding: n/a

## Programs, Highlights, and Developments:

The large majority of Binghamton's students are undergraduates, two-thirds of whom are enrolled in Harpur College. About 1,000 undergraduates are enrolled in the Watson School of Engineering and Applied Science, and another 1,200 are in the School of Management. Other undergraduate choices include the Decker School of Nursing and the School of Education and Human Development. Students apply to their choice of college, each of which has its own admissions requirements and standards, and the university has recently instituted an Early Action admissions plan. Binghamton maintains a comprehensive General Education requirement, a set of courses that must be fulfilled by all students across the different colleges, and offers a capstone General Education honors course. The Binghamton Scholars Program invites 80 freshmen each year to join its universitywide four-year honors program. These students may pursue collaborative and experiential learning programs and special courses in all four years. Students receive merit scholarships ranging from $2,000 to full tuition, mentoring, and research and teaching opportunities. The Campaign for Binghamton University has raised over $31 million toward a goal of $36 million. Work recently began on a $26.5 million field house, to be completed in 2004.

# UNIVERSITY OF NORTH CAROLINA AT CHAPEL HILL

Jackson Hall CB #2200
Chapel Hill, NC 27599-2200
(919) 966-3621
www.unc.edu

Total students: 23,321
Total undergraduates: 14,969
First-year retention rate: 94%
Graduation rate: 80% (six years); 62% in four years, 16% in five years, 3% in six years
Ratio of students to faculty: 14:1
Ratio of males to females: 39:61
In-state students: 79%

## Tuition and fees for 2000–01:

In-state: $2,768
Out-of-state: $11,934

## Admission statistics:

16,022 applied, 39% were accepted, 3,396 enrolled (55% yield)
Mid-50% SAT verbal: 570–680
Mid-50% SAT math: 570–670
SAT verbal scores over 700: 18%
SAT verbal scores over 600: 61%
SAT math scores over 700: 19%
SAT math scores over 600: 64%
Mid-50% ACT: 24–30
ACT scores over 30: n/a
ACT scores over 24: n/a

Average high school GPA: 4.00
GPA 3.0 or higher: 97%
GPA 2.0–2.9: 3%
Rank in top 10% of high school class: 66%
Rank in top 25% of high school class: 92%

## In-state admission statistics (fall 1999):

6,935 applied, 61% were accepted, 2,704 enrolled (64% yield)

## Out-of-state admission statistics (fall 1999):

9,451 applied, 18% were accepted, 589 enrolled (35% yield)

## Out-of-state children of alumni :

427 applied, 51% were accepted, 112 enrolled (52% yield)

Students living on campus: n/a
Students enrolled full-time: 97%
Total endowments: $925,746,000 (UNC at Chapel Hill and Foundations)
Public funding: $408,884,000 (+5.7%)

## Programs, Highlights, and Developments:

All first-year students enter UNC's General College Program in the College of Arts and Sciences. Students may then choose to major in the Kenan-Flagler Business School, the School of Education, the School of Journalism and Mass Communication, the Program in Clinical Laboratory Science, the School of Dentistry, the School of Nursing, the School of Pharmacy, the School of Public Health, or the Division of Radiologic Science. UNC offers more than 80 undergraduate degree programs. A set of general requirements must be completed in the first two years. The Honors Program at UNC offers more than 100 honors courses each year targeted toward first-, second-, and third-year students. These classes are small, usually under 20 students, and range across the curriculum. Also available are special honors sections of regular courses, interdisciplinary seminars, honors semester-abroad programs (in London, Prague, Rome, Madrid, and Australia), and research opportunities. The Honors Program is housed in the new Johnston Center for Undergraduate Excellence, along with the Office for Undergraduate Research and the Office for Burch Programs, which coordinates the Burch Fellows Program and Burch Field Research Seminars. UNC's Honors Program enrolls about 650 first-through third-year students, and some 300 seniors, who work on honors theses. About 200 students are selected for the Honors Program each fall without separate application. UNC's Morehead Scholars Program is an independent scholarship program that grants Morehead Awards to talented students from all high schools in North Carolina and selected schools in the United States, Canada, and the United Kingdom. Students are nominated by their high schools for these awards. Most Morehead recipients are also invited into UNC's Honors Program. Morehead scholars receive a full merit scholarship; summer internship, research, and study-abroad opportunities; and Morehead alumni mentor support. In 2000, UNC began requiring all incoming freshmen to own laptop computers. In 2001, UNC will select its first class of some 30 Robertson Scholars. Half of these merit scholars will enroll at UNC, and half will enroll at Duke University. The focus in the program will be on leadership, public service, and diversity.

# OHIO STATE UNIVERSITY (COLUMBUS)

3rd Floor, Lincoln Tower
1800 Cannon Drive
Columbus, OH 43210
(614) 292-3940
www.osu.edu

Total students: 47,992
Total undergraduates: 36,081
First-year retention rate: 83%
Graduation rate: 56% (six years); 19% in four years, 30% in five years, 7% in six years
Ratio of students to faculty: 14:1
Ratio of males to females: 52:48
In-state students: 87%

## Tuition and fees for 2000–01:

In-state: $4,383
Out-of-state: $12,732

## Admission statistics:

19,805 applied, 74% were accepted, 6,119 enrolled (42% yield)
Mid-50% SAT verbal: 500–620
Mid-50% SAT math: 520–640
SAT verbal scores over 700: 8%

SAT verbal scores over 600: 36%
SAT math scores over 700: 11%
SAT math scores over 600: 44%
Mid-50% ACT: 22–27
ACT scores over 30: 12%
ACT scores over 24: 59%
Average high school GPA: n/a
GPA 3.0 or higher: n/a
GPA 2.0–2.9: n/a
Rank in top 10% of high school class: 29%
Rank in top 25% of high school class: 61%

Students living on campus: 85%
Students enrolled full-time: 86%
Total endowments: $1,086,350,000 (Ohio State University and Foundation)
Public funding: $429,400,000 (+5.6%)

## Programs, Highlights, and Developments:

Undergraduates may choose from more than 170 degree programs at OSU. The university has 21 schools and colleges and more than 10,000 courses. Most incoming freshmen, especially those undecided about a major, enter OSU's University College, which prepares them with one or more semesters in a generalized curriculum for entry into one of the other programs. OSU's other colleges and schools are the School of Allied Medical Professions, the Knowlton School of Architecture, the College of the Arts, the College of Biological Sciences, the Fisher College of Business, the College of Dentistry, the College of Education, the College of Engineering, the College of Food, Agricultural, and Environmental Sciences, the College of Human Ecology, the College of Humanities, the School of Journalism and Communication, the College of Law, the College of Mathematical and Physical Sciences, the School of Music, the School of Natural Resources, the College of Nursing, the College of Pharmacy, the College of Social and Behavioral Sciences, and the College of Social Work. OSU has a number of honors and scholars programs. The honors programs offer over 240 honors courses each year, with most averaging under 25 students. Honors living is available, as is a Peer Mentor Program and an Honors Cultural Program Board. Honors enrollees usually have graduated in the top 10 percent of their high school class and have an ACT score of 29 or higher or an SAT score of 1300 or higher. Other students may submit with their OSU application an essay requesting admission to the honors programs. The scholars programs are residential learning experiences bringing together students with similar academic interests in special residence halls. These scholars usually have an ACT score of 25 or higher or an SAT score of 1140 or higher. Students may not participate in both the honors and scholars programs. OSU offers students research options across the curriculum, as well as many merit scholarships. OSU raised $153.4 million from 94,216 donors in 1998–99.

# PENNSYLVANIA STATE UNIVERSITY (UNIVERSITY PARK)

201 Shields Building
University Park, PA 16802
(814) 865-5471
www.psu.edu

Total students: 38,872
Total undergraduates: 33,209
First-year retention rate: 93%
Graduation rate: 80% (six years); 60% in four years, 18% in five years, 2% in six years
Ratio of students to faculty: 18:1
Ratio of males to females: 54:46
In-state students: 67%

### Tuition and fees for 2000-01:

In-state: $6,756
Out-of-state: $14,388

### Admission statistics:

26,079 applied, 49% were accepted, 5,069 enrolled (39% yield)
Mid-50% SAT verbal: 540–640
Mid-50% SAT math: 560–670
SAT verbal scores over 700: 10%

SAT verbal scores over 600: 46%
SAT math scores over 700: 16%
SAT math scores over 600: 62%
Mid-50% ACT: 26–30
ACT scores over 30: n/a
ACT scores over 24: n/a
Average high school GPA: 3.78
GPA 3.0 or higher: 95%
GPA 2.0–2.9: 5%
Rank in top 10% of high school class: 49%
Rank in top 25% of high school class: 88%

Students living on campus: 35% of total student body
Students enrolled full-time: 97%
Total endowments: $792,185,000 (Penn State University)
Public funding: $331,949,000 (+5.7%)

### Programs, Highlights, and Developments:

Undergraduates have their choice of some 225 bachelor's degree programs at Penn State. At the University Park campus, they may choose from the College of Agricultural Sciences, the College of Arts and Architecture, the Smeal College of Business Administration, the College of Communications, the College of Earth and Mineral Sciences, the College of Education, the College of Engineering, the College of Health and Human Development, the Eberly College of Science, the School of Information Sciences and Technology, and the College of the Liberal

Arts. Penn State's Schreyer Honors College is a universitywide honors program requiring a separate application. Average admitted candidates have an average SAT score of 1425 and an average high school GPA of 4.06 (with weighting for honors courses). All students admitted to the Honors College are awarded renewable Academic Excellence Scholarships of $2,000 to $3,000. They have access to honors courses and sections, independent study and research, and advisors. Some 1,700 students, including 300 freshmen, participate in the Honors College. Talented students in the visual arts, architecture, and design may be invited to pursue admission to the College of Arts and Architecture through the portfolio-based Special Talent Program.

# RUTGERS, THE STATE UNIVERSITY OF NEW JERSEY (NEW BRUNSWICK)

65 Davidson Road, Room 202
Piscataway, NJ 08854-8097
(732) 932-4636
www.rutgers.edu

Total students: 33,400 (total students, not necessarily pursuing degree)
Total undergraduates: 24,900 (total students, not necessarily pursuing degree)
First-year retention rate: 89%
Graduation rate: 73%
Ratio of students to faculty: n/a
Ratio of males to females: 47:53
In-state students: 91%

### Tuition and fees for 2000–01:

In-state: $5,220
Out-of-state: $10,398

### Admission statistics:

25,102 applied, 62% were accepted (% enrolled n/a)
Mid-50% SAT verbal: 1060–1280 combined
Mid-50% SAT math: 1060–1280 combined

SAT verbal scores over 700: n/a
SAT verbal scores over 600: n/a
SAT math scores over 700: n/a
SAT math scores over 600: n/a
Mid-50% ACT: n/a
ACT scores over 30: n/a
ACT scores over 24: n/a
Average high school GPA: n/a
GPA 3.0 or higher: n/a
GPA 2.0–2.9: n/a
Rank in top 10% of high school class: 33%
Rank in top 25% of high school class: 70%

Students living on campus: 49% of total student body
Students enrolled full-time: 89%
Total endowments: $389,712,000 (Rutgers University)
Public funding: $332,873,000 (+3.5%)

### Programs, Highlights, and Developments:

Rutgers University has three regional campuses, in Newark, Camden, and New Brunswick and Piscataway. The last is the largest and has the widest array of programs. Across the three campuses, Rutgers offers eight liberal arts schools and seven preprofessional schools. At New Brunswick, undergraduates can take advantage of programs in 12 colleges and schools. Several are co-ed liberal arts programs: Livingston College (which emphasizes diversity and service), Rutgers College (with more than 9,000 students, the largest residential college in the university system), and University College (for adult and part-time students). Douglass College is a liberal arts college for women. Cook College, allied with the New Jersey Agricultural Experiment Station, offers programs in life, environmental, food, marine, natural resource, and agricultural sciences. Other options are the College of Engineering, the Gross School of the Arts, the Bloustein School of Planning and Public Policy, the College of Nursing, the College of Pharmacy, the School of Business, and the School of Communication, Information, and Library Sciences. Applicants to Rutgers may apply to as many as three undergraduate colleges. The Rutgers Study Abroad program offers more than 35 choices in 14 countries and 28 locations. The university offers dozens of undergraduate research opportunities in academic disciplines across the spectrum. Rutgers also offers a variety of merit scholarships and honors programs across its colleges and campuses.

# UNIVERSITY OF TEXAS AT AUSTIN

Main 7
Austin, TX 78712-1157
(512) 475-7399
www.utexas.edu

Total students: 48,008
Total undergraduates: 36,164
First-year retention rate: 89%
Graduation rate: 66% (six years); 30% in four years, 28% in five years, 8% in six years
Ratio of students to faculty: 19:1
Ratio of males to females: 50:50
In-state students: 96%

## Tuition and fees for 2000–01:

In-state: $3,252
Out-of-state: $9,702

## Admission statistics:

18,919 applied, 63% were accepted, 7,040 enrolled (59% yield)
Mid-50% SAT verbal: 530–640
Mid-50% SAT math: 560–660
SAT verbal scores over 700: 6%
SAT verbal scores over 600: 27%

SAT math scores over 700: 6%
SAT math scores over 600: 30%
Mid-50% ACT: 22–27
ACT scores over 30: 9%
ACT scores over 24: 49%
Average high school GPA: 3.34
GPA 3.0 or higher: n/a
GPA 2.0–2.9: n/a
Rank in top 10% of high school class: 48%
Rank in top 25% of high school class: 83%

Students living on campus: 53%
Students enrolled full-time: 89%
Total endowments: $8,128,298,000 (University of Texas system)
Public funding: $1,355,483,000 (–0.3%) (UT system)

## Programs, Highlights, and Developments:

Freshmen enter UT in one of 10 colleges or schools: Architecture, Business, Communication, Education, Engineering, Fine Arts, Liberal Arts, Natural Sciences, Nursing, or Social Work. Those wishing to pursue pharmacy first enter into Natural Sciences. Business and Architecture tend to be more difficult to get into, with 88% and 69% of admitted freshmen, respectively, having ranked in the top 10% of their high school class, compared to 50% campuswide and 35% in the College of Liberal Arts, in 1999. The University Honors Center coordinates 50 honors programs at UT, foremost among which is the Plan II Honors Program in the College of Liberal Arts. This four-year program offers a broad-based curriculum in the arts and sciences. Students study in a generalized core curriculum but then specialize in a second major, which can be in one of UT's other colleges, such as Engineering, Business, or Architecture. Plan II was begun in 1935 and is highly selective. The average SAT scores of the entering freshmen are in the mid-1400s, and 80% graduated in the top fifth of their class. Students must complete an additional application for Plan II. Other major honors programs at UT include the Business Honors Program, the College of Pharmacy Undergraduate Honors Program, the Dean's Scholars Program for science and math students, the Engineering Honors Program, the Humanities Program, which offers opportunities for independent and interdisciplinary study, the Liberal Arts Honors Programs in particular disciplines, and the Senior Fellows Program in the College of Communication. With these various programs, students can find smaller and more challenging courses, freedom to design and choose among disciplines, interesting courses and combined majors, honors housing, faculty mentoring, and research opportunities.

# UNIVERSITY OF VIRGINIA

[
Office of Undergraduate Admission
Charlottesville, VA 22906
(804) 982-3200
www.virginia.edu
]

Total students: 18,046
Total undergraduates: 12,467
First-year retention rate: 96%
Graduation rate: 91% (six years); 83% in four years, 8% in five years, 1% in six years
Ratio of students to faculty: 14:1
Ratio of males to females: 45:55
In-state students: 70%

### Tuition and fees for 2000-01:

In-state: $4,335
Out-of-state: $17,584

### Admission statistics:

16,461 applied, 34% were accepted, 2,924 enrolled (52% yield)
Mid-50% SAT verbal: 600–700
Mid-50% SAT math: 610–710

SAT verbal scores over 700: 30%
SAT verbal scores over 600: 76%
SAT math scores over 700: 34%
SAT math scores over 600: 82%
Mid-50% ACT: 26–31
ACT scores over 30: 38%
ACT scores over 24: 87%
Average high school GPA: 3.78
GPA 3.0 or higher: 99%
GPA 2.0–2.9: 1%
Rank in top 10% of high school class: 82%
Rank in top 25% of high school class: 96%

Students living on campus: 100%
Students enrolled full-time: 99%
Total endowments: $1,398,068,000
Public funding: $157,507,000 (+5.9%)

### Programs, Highlights, and Developments:

Most students enter UVA in the College of Arts and Sciences, but they may matriculate into four-year programs in the School of Engineering and Applied Science, the School of Architecture, the Curry School of Education, or the School of Nursing. Some 300 students each year compete to enter the McIntire School of Commerce for their third year at the university. Virginia offers 61 majors in its 6 undergraduate schools and more than 1,000 courses each semester. Honors and merit-based programs are available throughout the university and include the Echols Scholars Program in the College of Arts and Sciences, which offers faculty advising, special housing, and academic flexibility. All UVA students are considered without additional application for the Echols program, although only a few hundred are invited to join. These students have average SAT scores in the high 1400s, but in general are sought for their commitment to academics and profile as "avid learners," as the university puts it. The Rodman Scholars Program offers students in engineering and applied science a first-year living and learning experience, as well as special courses in their discipline. Students across the university may also participate in the Distinguished Majors Program, which requires a senior thesis. UVA offers an Interdisciplinary Majors Program and a University Seminar Program, each providing more academic freedom, attention, and options. Fifteen percent of UVA's student body spends a full year, a semester, or a summer studying abroad during their tenure at UVA, and all students have access to the university's Overseas Study Resource Library to research programs overseas offered by UVA and other institutions.

# UNIVERSITY OF WASHINGTON

PO Box 355840
Seattle, WA 98195-5840
(206) 543-9686
www.washington.edu

Total students: 35,267
Total undergraduates: 25,346
First-year retention rate: 90%
Graduation rate: 72% (six years); 37% in four years, 27% in five years, 7% in six years
Ratio of students to faculty: 11:1
Ratio of males to females: 48:52
In-state students: 85%

## Tuition and fees for 2000–01:

In-state: $3,761
Out-of-state: $12,453

## Admission statistics:

12,785 applied, 77% were accepted, 4,353 enrolled (44% yield)
Mid-50% SAT verbal: 510–630
Mid-50% SAT math: 530–650
SAT verbal scores over 700: 8%

SAT verbal scores over 600: 38%
SAT math scores over 700: 10%
SAT math scores over 600: 49%
Mid-50% ACT: 22–27
ACT scores over 30: 12%
ACT scores over 24: 61%
Average high school GPA: 3.63
GPA 3.0 or higher: 97%
GPA 2.0–2.9: 3%
Rank in top 10% of high school class: 39%
Rank in top 25% of high school class: 76%

Students living on campus: 56%
Students enrolled full-time: 86%
Total endowments: $745,217,000 (University of Washington)
Public funding: $341,833,000 (+6.1%)

## Programs, Highlights, and Developments:

The University of Washington has three campuses, the primary one in Seattle. Two satellite campuses, smaller and with fewer offerings, are in Bothell and Tacoma. The University of Washington at Seattle offers over 130 majors and 1,800 courses every quarter. Students may enter the College of Architecture and Urban Planning, the College of Arts and Sciences, the competitive School of Business Administration, the College of Engineering, the College of Forest Resources, the School of Library and Information Science, the School of Medicine, the

School of Nursing, the College of Ocean and Fishery Sciences, the School of Social Work, or the School of Public Health and Community Medicine. During their first year, students have their choice of 100 freshmen interest groups, each enrolling 20 to 25 students with similar academic interests and course plans for the first quarter. Freshman seminars of 15 students are also available. Washington's University Honors Program is 40 years old and enrolls about 180 freshmen each year. Honors courses and advanced honors sections are offered across the curriculum and in students' majors. The Honors Program is not residential, and enrolls about 1,000 students overall in the university. Students must maintain a 3.3 overall GPA to stay in the program, and usually a 3.5 in their major. Students apply to the program during the university admissions process. Typically, admitted students have at least a 3.8 GPA and an SAT score of 1300 or higher. Through its International Programs and Exchanges office, Washington offers over 200 study-abroad choices, as well as exchanges at more than 100 U.S. universities. Undergraduate research opportunities are plentiful at Washington, during the academic year and the summer.

# COLLEGE OF WILLIAM AND MARY

PO Box 8795
Williamsburg, VA 23187-8795
(757) 221-4223
www.wm.edu

Total students: 7,281
Total undergraduates: 5,469
First-year retention rate: 95%
Graduation rate: 88% (six years); 78% in four years, 8% in five years, 2% in six years
Ratio of students to faculty: 12:1
Ratio of males to females: 42:58
In-state students: 66%

## Tuition and fees for 2000–01:

In-state: $4,687
Out-of-state: $16,904

## Admission statistics:

6,878 applied, 45% were accepted, 1,301 enrolled (42% yield)
Mid-50% SAT verbal: 620–710
Mid-50% SAT math: 610–700
SAT verbal scores over 700: 34%
SAT verbal scores over 600: 83%
SAT math scores over 700: 26%
SAT math scores over 600: 81%
Mid-50% ACT: 23–31
ACT scores over 30: 71%
ACT scores over 24: 100%
Average high school GPA: 3.90
GPA 3.0 or higher: 99%

GPA 2.0–2.9: 1%
Rank in top 10% of high school class: 74%
Rank in top 25% of high school class: 97%

## In-state admission statistics:

3,735 applied, 46% were accepted, 842 enrolled (49% yield)
Mid-50% SAT combined: 1220–1380
Rank in top 10% of high school class: 79%

## Out-of-state admissions statistics:

5,041 applied, 32% were accepted, 509 enrolled (32% yield)
Mid-50% SAT combined: 1300–1430
Rank in top 10% of high school class: 79%

Students living on campus: 99% of first-year students; 77% of total student body
Students enrolled full-time: 99%
Total endowments: $354,616,000 (College of William and Mary Endowment Association)
Public funding: $48,317,000 (+9.7%)

## Programs, Highlights, and Developments:

About 5,000 of William and Mary's undergraduates are enrolled in the Undergraduate Program in Arts and Sciences. The School of Business Administration Undergraduate BBA Program enrolls about 400 students. The School of Education offers teacher training at multiple levels. Two merit scholarship programs are available. Twenty to twenty-five William and Mary Scholars Awards are given to students who add diversity to the student body. The awards cover the equivalent of four years of in-state tuition and fees, and applicants are selected based on their admission application. About 10 percent of the freshman class are named Monroe Scholars. They, too, are selected through the regular admissions process. In addition to specific academic benefits, Monroe Scholars each receive a $2,000 research grant for the summer between their junior and senior years.

William and Mary is one of the few public ivies to offer an Early Decision (ED) application option. Of 1,712 Virginians accepted for the class entering in 2000, 338 (20%) had applied ED. Of 1,589 non-Virginians accepted, 122 (8%) had applied ED. Sixty-seven percent of Virginians who applied ED were accepted. Fifty-two percent of non-Virginians who applied ED were accepted. Overall, 62 percent of ED applicants were admitted.

# UNIVERSITY OF WISCONSIN—MADISON

716 Langdon Street
Madison, WI 53706-1400
(608) 262-3961
www.wisc.edu

Total students: 40,196 (total student body, not necessarily pursuing degree)
Total undergraduates: 29,974
First-year retention rate: 94%
Graduation rate: 75% (six years)
Ratio of students to faculty: 14:1
Ratio of males to females: 48:52
In-state students: 60%

### Tuition and fees for 2000–01:

In-state: $3,788
Out-of-state: $14,186

### Admission statistics:

16,456 applied, 73% were accepted, 5,880 enrolled (49% yield)
Mid-50% SAT verbal: 520–650
Mid-50% SAT math: 550–670
SAT verbal scores over 700: 17%
SAT verbal scores over 600: 62%
SAT math scores over 700: 19%

SAT math scores over 600: 71%
Mid-50% ACT: 25–29
ACT scores over 30: 31%
ACT scores over 24: 80%
Average high school GPA: 3.74
GPA 3.0 or higher: 95%
GPA 2.0–2.9: 5%
Rank in top 10% of high school class: 47%
Rank in top 25% of high school class: 90%

Students living on campus: 98%
Students enrolled full-time: 88%
Total endowments: $653,551,000 (University of Wisconsin Foundation); $269,772,000 (University of Wisconsin system)
Public funding: $954,584,000 (+9.4%) (UW system)

## Programs, Highlights, and Developments:

Wisconsin's College of Letters and Science (L&S) Honors Program, now 40 years old, is a highly selective program, whose students average a 3.87 GPA in high school and a score of 31.3 on the ACT or 1383 on the SAT. Honors students in L&S have three degrees available to them: Honors in the Liberal Arts, Honors in the Major, and Comprehensive Honors, each recognition being successively more difficult to earn. Honors in the Major, for example, requires students to apply with their department or program and conduct independent research during their senior year. Students apply to L&S Honors during the regular university admissions process. Students at Wisconsin are encouraged to engage in research with faculty through an Undergraduate Research Opportunities program across the disciplines. Wisconsin has nine undergraduate schools and colleges, which offer 4,500 courses and 150 majors. Students may apply to L&S, the School of Music, the College of Engineering, the College of Agricultural and Life Sciences, the School of Education, the Institute for Environmental Studies, the School of Human Ecology, the Medical School, and the School of Nursing. Students may enter the competitive School of Business in their junior year or enter the School of Pharmacy or School of Veterinary Medicine after completing certain requirements. The university's Office of International Studies and Programs offers students foreign-study options in 30 countries and at about 50 locations; 500 students participate in the programs each year. Wisconsin offers a comprehensive learning disabilities support program through the McBurney Disability Resource Center.

# Technical and Scientific Public Ivies

Below is a short list of institutions that are geared more toward the sciences and technology and are public ivies in their own right in these fields.

Colorado School of Mines
   Golden, Colorado
   www.mines.edu

Georgia Institute of Technology
   Atlanta, Georgia
   www.gatech.edu

Purdue University
   West Lafayette, Indiana
   www.purdue.edu

Texas A&M University
   College Station, Texas
   www.tamu.edu

Virginia Polytechnic Institute
and State University (Virginia Tech)
   Blacksburg, Virginia
   www.vt.edu

# Strong Contenders

Here are some other strong public institutions to keep an eye on as you evaluate going public.

University of California, Riverside
   Riverside, California
   www.ucr.edu

University of California, Santa Cruz
   Santa Cruz, California
   www.ucsc.edu

Clemson University
   Clemson, South Carolina
   www.clemson.edu

Florida State University
   Tallahassee, Florida
   www.fsu.edu

Iowa State University
   Ames, Iowa
   www.iastate.edu

University of Kansas
   Lawrence, Kansas
   www.ukans.edu

University of Massachusetts at Amherst
   Amherst, Massachusetts
   www.umass.edu

University of Missouri—Columbia
   Columbia, Missouri
   www.missouri.edu

Ohio University
   Athens, Ohio
   www.ohio.edu

University of Pittsburgh
   Pittsburgh, Pennsylvania
   www.pitt.edu

University of Vermont
   Burlington, Vermont
   www.uvm.edu

Washington State University
   Pullman, Washington
   www.wsu.edu

# [PART FOUR
# Advice If You Are Going Public

## A SUMMARY OF STRATEGIES FOR HOW TO GET IN

Your first task in understanding the public ivies will be a lot of legwork and research. Your ultimate question will be: How do I get in? Your goal will be to secure admission to one or more of the public universities that fit your needs and interests. Throughout this book, we have pointed out aspects of public university admissions that differ from admission to smaller, private liberal arts colleges. Preparing for admission to public universities is similar in many ways to preparing for admission to private universities.

1. A demanding college preparatory curriculum is essential for you to be well placed to apply to top public and private colleges and universities. Take a strong and balanced curriculum through high school. Challenge yourself in honors and advanced placement (AP) courses in your areas of strength and interest.

2. Do well consistently over time in that curriculum. Try to improve your performance as you progress through high school. A poor record in your first year or two will not prevent you from ultimately gaining admission to a selective school.

3. Be conscious of particular university requirements for admission. You must take the classes the institutions want to see.

4. Prepare for and succeed in the standardized tests (the SAT I and possibly SAT IIs, or the ACT) required for admission.

5. Try to commit to and show leadership in one or two key activities that you enjoy.

6. Write a strong application and secure recommendations from teachers who will support you well.

7. Match your interests and talents to particular colleges, and to colleges or schools within larger universities, that are looking for students like you to fill their special programs.

Here are some specific points regarding admission to the public ivies:

1. Numbers are important. Numerical factors that can strongly influence public university admission include class rank, overall academic GPA, and combined SAT or ACT composite score.

2. If your school does not rank students, this will be a nonfactor in admissions. If your school does rank, it will be important for you to be conscious of your standing in relation to the rest of your class. It is not a good idea to ignore the reality of your class rank in applying to the public universities. If you are ranked in the 40th or 50th percentile of your high school class, rather than in the top 10 percent, it is highly unlikely that you will be admitted to the more selective public universities. Many of the public ivies are very clear about how low they will be willing to dip into the class to admit students. If your school ranks students, ask your counselor or registrar for an unofficial transcript at the end of your junior year. Find out your rank and compare it to the admissions averages, standards, and requirements of the public universities you are considering. Be conscious of academic choices in high school. If taking a particularly challenging class will adversely affect your rank, you may want to rethink your choice. We are not thrilled about the educational consequences of this forced competition associated with class rank, or with the pressure to avoid challenging classes for fear of losing status. Nevertheless, these are the structures and incentives still in place in many high schools, especially larger public institutions.

3. Your overall academic GPA matters. Fluff classes and "nonacademic" courses will have little or no impact on your admissions chances, because most of the public ivies will try to recalculate a true academic GPA. Check the university requirements and admissions process information to see what classes count toward the calculation of your academic GPA, and focus on excelling in these. If your school weights your GPA (gives you extra grade points for honors or AP classes), that is to your benefit if you are taking the more demanding curriculum that the public ivies prefer. If your school does not weight GPA, however, you are in a bind. Some of the public ivies explicitly state that they will recalculate your GPA and add in their own "weight" factor for honors and advanced classes. Be conscious of your GPA after junior year ends. Will you qualify for admission to your state school or others you are considering? If so, will you qualify for honors programs or merit scholarships?

4. Think about what you can do to improve your GPA and your class rank. If you have a very poor grade in a class, consider retaking it in the summer. Work out with your school ahead of time what class you need to take, and whether the old, lower grade will be

replaced by your new, higher grade. Find out if the school will give you credit and recalculate your GPA accordingly. Substituting an A or a B for a D, C, or F grade can dramatically increase your GPA. Also consider taking new courses in the summer and seeing if your high school will add those to your GPA. This strategy can help you to overcome poor grades in your first year or two of high school.

5. Prepare early and seriously for standardized tests. The admissions process at public universities is much less nuanced than at private colleges, and you are unlikely to get the benefit of the doubt if your test scores are low. In fact, if your scores are very low, it is unlikely that a human being will ever review your transcript by hand. You will be eliminated in the first round. Start work on your own, with some of the books from the College Board (for the SATs) or ACT and with one of the many interactive test prep programs on CD. Regular work over a year and a half will no doubt improve your scores. Consider spending some time and money on coaching if you are not reaching the goals you have set for yourself. One-on-one sessions are more expensive and intensive, but a far better use of your time. This is something you can do from January to May of your junior year and/or during the late summer before your senior year.

6. Some public universities have specific high school course requirements for in-state applicants that are related to statewide standardized test and curriculum requirements. Make sure that you will more than fulfill these requirements prior to graduation.

7. In-state residents have a preferential status in admissions to public universities. If you are unsure of your residency, have moved during high school, attend boarding school, are an expatriate (an American living abroad), or have family residences in more than one state (through divorce or a second home, for example), talk with your parents about your residency status. Most likely, the state where they pay taxes and claim you as a dependent will be considered your state of residence. You may also call the public universities in question to ask for their advice and requirements for residency.

8. If one or both of your parents attended a public university in another state, talk with them and the admissions office at that university about how you will be grouped in the admissions process. It is likely that you will be treated in roughly equivalent fashion to a state resident.

9. Affirmative action is in flux, but if you are a member of an underrepresented minority group, do not be dismayed about your chances for admission to a selective public university, even if your grades and scores seem average or just below average. Talk with your guidance counselor or contact the admissions offices of public universities in which you are interested. Ask them about minority recruiting and affirmative action policies. If they are seeking to recruit students like you, you may still get some type of favorable treatment in the admissions process, as well as strong encouragement to visit campus and to apply.

10. Apply early in the year. The majority of the public ivies use a rolling admissions process, which means they review applications as they come in and fill spaces accordingly. Even if you are applying under an Early Decision plan with a binding commitment, get your application in well in advance of the deadline. Note also special deadlines for merit scholarships, financial aid, honors programs, and preferred housing opportunities. In many cases, if you submit an application to a public university in September of your senior year, you will get a response in 4 to 12 weeks. You normally do not need to commit to the university (unless you applied Early Decision) until May 1, but you will have applied with the first round of applicants and either learned some positive news, with great relief, or found out that you were not accepted early enough that you can plan to apply elsewhere.

11. Apply to multiple schools. Applications to the public universities are easy to complete and can be done online. The application to the University of California schools is, in fact, a common application. In general, you will need at most one personal essay and two teacher recommendations for the public universities—in some cases, not even that. It is easy for you to apply to more public universities, spreading out your applications and opening up more potential choices for the spring. You may also think about applying to multiple campuses within your state or another state. If you do well at a campus that's your second choice, your odds of transferring to the flagship campus are good.

12. Research the public university *system* in your state and perhaps a few others of interest. Find out about guaranteed transfer programs, specific programs of interest on different campuses, community and junior college options, and regional university agreements. Consider the whole range of options available to you. If your goal is a flagship public ivy campus, you can get there, but you may need to make one or two stops along the way.

13. Always consider adding your state's flagship public university to your college list. You just never know.

---

ADMISSIONS GUIDELINES FROM ONE HIGHLY SELECTIVE PUBLIC IVY
-----

Given all of the above, here is what the University of North Carolina has to say on its website about undergraduate admissions:

"Eight Myths about Admission to UNC–Chapel Hill
1. The Admissions Office sets quotas for class size, in-state, out-of-state, male, female, etc. UNTRUE! University Administration sets class size by considering overall budget and enrollment in various professional schools,

*(continued)*

the graduate school, summer school and continuing studies divisions. The quality of applicants from each gender who apply here will determine the male/female ratio. There has been no attempt by Admissions to skew this ratio in any direction. The Board of Trustees & General Administration of the University system set the in-state/out-of-state quota at 82% North Carolina residents and 18% out-of-state residents.

2. Only numbers count in the admission decision. UNTRUE! In addition to "the numbers" such as SAT or ACT scores and class rank, the single most important factor is in fact not a number: the difficulty of courses a student takes in high school is critical. We prefer Advanced Placement (AP) or International Baccalaureate (IB) courses if they're available in the high school. In addition, the level of competition within a particular high school and the extent & depth of leadership and extracurricular involvement all are considered in our decisions. Certainly, we will admit the top people from most classes. In each class, however, there should be a fairly wide band of rank and ACT/SAT scores where some people gain admission and some people do not gain admission.

3. The computer decides. UNTRUE! (See #2 above) There is no way a computer can be built to consider all the subjective factors which we evaluate when making individual admission decisions. The computer is useful for storing information such as how well people from particular schools have performed on their coursework at UNC. Admission staff members make the individual decision on an application.

4. ACT/SAT is the overriding factor. UNTRUE! The overall quality of the school record, including course selection, relative class standing and information we have about the level of competition within your high school class, is far more important than scores on the Scholastic Assessment Test (SAT) or the American College Test (ACT). One should take the most challenging courses the school offers especially in math and foreign language, attain a class rank near the top of the class and be involved in the life of the school and community in order to be a serious candidate for admission to UNC-Chapel Hill.

5. UNC–Chapel Hill is enrolling too many women. UNTRUE! We do not discriminate on the basis of sex in admitting. Today, nearly 55% of each graduating class and of North Carolina seniors for the last decade have been females. A larger number of women apply, a few more are accepted, and a few more enroll. Our class simply reflects these factors, there is no favoritism extended to women who apply.

*(continued)*

6. We have quotas for each school and county in North Carolina and will only admit up to a certain number from each one. UNTRUE! The only quotas we have are in-state and out-of-state. We can show interested parties "admitted" and "enrolled" figures from each high school or county which will often vary as much as 50%. When people are shown this, and then asked what our quota is, they cannot give us one. This myth is very prevalent, particularly in Chapel Hill, Raleigh, Greensboro, Winston-Salem and Charlotte. However, it is just that—a myth.

7. We favor: (pick one) rural vs. urban; urban vs. rural; private schools vs. public schools; public schools vs. private schools; large schools vs. small schools; small schools vs. large schools. UNTRUE! We hear all these complaints, and the fact that we hear complaints from all these sources simply demonstrates to us that we must be admitting in the fairest way possible. We will look at individual qualities in assessing one's chances for admission, and not any of these backgrounds by itself. We expect to admit and deny persons from each group, and no one from any of these groups has an undue advantage over any of the others when they are applying to UNC–Chapel Hill.

8. Alumnus connection is everything or doesn't count at all. UNTRUE! The alumnus connection for North Carolina residents is used as a tie-breaker among candidates who are very similarly qualified. The top students get in, regardless of the alumnus connection. The bottom students do not get in, regardless of the alumnus connection. However, in the areas where some make it and some do not, statistics will show that the alumnus connection does play a part in influencing the decisions. Again, the alumnus connection is down the list of qualifications, but it is a consideration."

# MAKING THE MOST OF CAMPUS VISITS AND RESEARCH

There is no substitute for a visit to a college campus. There is no other way to get a real feel for the atmosphere, geography, culture, architecture, size, location, student body, and movement of the place. Be sure to visit a school one or more times before you make a commitment to it, either through Early Decision or through a final decision in April. You may apply to some schools without visiting them, but you should try to see similar enough models of schools to know that you are barking up the right tree. If you are very excited about some out-of-state public universities but cannot see them all right away, visit your own state's flagship university for comparison's sake. What elements are the same? Which do you expect to be noticeably different? Was this public institution what you had in mind?

Before you visit any campus, you should conduct extensive research on the university by spending time with guidebooks, school publications, and the university website. There is such a wealth of information available online that you will have access to almost as much material as a currently enrolled student on campus. Read about programs, lifestyle, the different colleges and schools at the university, the campus layout. Plan your visit with your interests in mind. You will not be able to see everything on a first visit, nor need you try to do so. Focus on the areas of particular interest to you: the humanities or science or business library, the student recreation center, fraternity row, the biology labs, the music school and performing arts center, the student center, the art studio, or whichever facilities most interest you. Before your visit, make a list of those areas where you want to spend some time. Take a campus tour, which will start from the undergraduate admissions office. Ask your tour guide if you can see some of the particular places you want, and if he or she cannot take the tour in that direction, ask to be pointed that way once the tour is completed. Take some pictures and notes on your visit. What has impressed you? What worries you? What questions have been raised? Perhaps an admissions officer can answer some of them in a group information session, if one is available. As for interviews, it seems fairly safe to say they will not be available at all on these campuses.

If there is a registration book at the admissions office, sign in. Grab all the informational materials of relevance to you. Sometimes a full hard copy of the course bulletin is available, usually for a small fee. It will probably be worth your while to buy this, even though much of the information is available online. Also, take brochures for honors programs, research institutes, learning support services, or other areas that interest you. Your research into this and other universities will continue through the year, in an ongoing process. The more work you do to try to understand the schools you are considering, the more likely it is that you will make a good choice for college.

## CONTACTING UNIVERSITY PROGRAMS AND DEPARTMENTS

As you will discover in your research, the public ivies are multifaceted, with multiple admissions offices, academic programs, and requirements to be fulfilled. They offer hundreds of degree programs, majors, schools, departments, units, research centers, special scholarship and honors divisions, and study opportunities. Do not consider your work done when you have contacted the general undergraduate admissions office to ask for information and materials and to submit your application. Plan to make additional inquiries to the specific colleges, departments, and programs that interest you. Whether you are learning more about a creative writing project, an honors program, an undergraduate research division, or a study-abroad center, these contacts will help you to understand the university and its various components. More important, you will gain more perspective on the specific programs you would like to pursue. Although the connections you make may help you in admissions, that is not very likely and is really beside the point. What you are doing is investigating one part of a very large institution in order to discover the information you need to determine whether one or more parts of the institution are right for you. You are looking for your niche, and you must understand ahead of time that it is likely to exist, even if you change your mind more than once. Finally, your research may unearth special scholarship and program opportunities you might not have been aware of. For some of these, you may need to submit an additional application, to meet special program deadlines, or to fulfill specific requirements. Knowing about these opportunities early in the admissions process will help you meet these special requirements. Most programs have their own pages on the university website, with e-mail addresses and phone numbers for office directors and staff. Make use of this information.

## ATHLETIC RECRUITING

Athletic recruiting involves more than talent. It also requires timing, persistence, knowledge, and judgment. First, you must have the recognized ability to succeed in the almost entirely competitive Division I programs at the public ivies. You may develop your talent by continued participation in your school program, in summer and academic year premier leagues, tournaments, select teams, and traveling squads, and by personal training and coaching. In the summer before senior year and even before junior year, these camps and select teams will help you not only to build on your skills and talent, but also to begin to connect with college coaches and recruiters and to develop your own judgment about the viability of participating in your sport in college, and at what level.

Timing is crucial, especially at the Division I universities. They are governed by NCAA rules that specifically outline what you, the student athlete, and they, the coach and college, can do regarding contacts, recruiting, signing agreements, visiting campus, securing scholarships, and so forth. Spend time on the NCAA's website (www.ncaa.org) to learn about these procedures and requirements, and get yourself registered and qualified through the NCAA clearinghouse early during your junior year. Start preparing for college recruiting early, and plan to contact a large group of coaches at schools in which you are interested prior to some summer camps or tournaments. You may prepare an athletic résumé and a letter to the coaches (see our discussion of this in *Making It into a Top College* and *Presenting Yourself Successfully to Colleges* for guidelines and examples), as well as a video of some complete games or performances.

Persistence is another key quality. Follow up your meetings with coaches with a phone call or e-mail. Get cards from those you meet so you will remember their names and addresses and where you met them. Keep notes on the requirements and contacts at different schools, and record any words of encouragement or discouragement you may receive. If you receive unsolicited letters from coaches, respond to them, and research their school—it may be of interest to you even if it was not on your original list. Going into the summer before senior year, start narrowing your list of schools so you can concentrate on the most likely prospects through official school visits and continued marketing and promotion of your skills and your interest in these universities. This process will continue through senior year, although some of you may sign committal letters of intent in the winter. Others may continue contacting the schools throughout the spring to determine the outcome of the recruiting and admissions process. Coaches' recruiting lists change over time, as they learn who has been admitted to the university and who has committed to attending.

Scholarship money is another key issue for athletes at Division I public ivies. On this front, be persistent. Compare potential offers from schools, as well as any actual offer from a university. Be prepared to be assertive and to negotiate. What are you being offered, exactly? Is your award renewable after one year, or is it guaranteed through graduation? Is your scholarship based on continued participation in your sport, as many awards are today? What room is there to negotiate on these criteria or on the composition of the award—its proportion of loans versus grants?

It is important to ask questions about what academic support you as an athlete will receive on campus. Are there tutors assigned to help athletes through their courses? Where will you meet with them, and how much time are you guaranteed to have with them each week? Will they cover all subjects? Will they help you organize your schedule and assignments? What is considered academic warning or a probationary level of performance, and what happens if you get into academic trouble? To what extent do you feel that you are being treated as a student and member of the university community, as opposed to a professional athlete in residence?

Knowledge is key to the athletic recruiting process. The more you know about the process and about the individual schools you are considering, the better able you will be to protect yourself and your interests, make the right match, gain admission to the school of your choice, and ensure your success when you are there. Use your coaches at school and in your other selective programs as references for colleges and as resources to help you determine where you fit. Do not rely solely on college coaches' comments about university programs. Back up your admissions process by doing whatever is necessary to make sure you have choices, or at least one choice, in the fall. Make the contacts discussed here—with learning centers, academic departments, residential life offices, and so forth—to explore for yourself the university's resources outside the athletic department. Talk to athletes on campus, those on your potential future team, and those involved in other sports. Ask them about athletic and academic life on campus. Find out how many athletes are graduating and how many are staying with their sport through graduation. Think about your academic career as well as your athletic career, and think about them both in terms of getting through all four, five, or six years of college, not just surviving freshman fall.

## EVALUATING NEED- AND MERIT-BASED FINANCIAL AWARDS

All those receiving financial assistance, not just athletes, need to be conscious of the substance and form of their awards. The obvious distinctions are between need- and merit-based awards, and between loans that need to be repaid and grants and scholarships that do not. Clearly, grants and scholarships are preferable, and students should talk directly with the financial aid office at the university to see about structuring their aid package in the most desirable way possible. Sometimes a little honest, positive negotiation will lead a university to improve its aid package. Applying early in the admissions process, as we have mentioned, is also a good idea if you need aid. Merit-based awards do not need to be repaid, so do some research at the financial aid office to determine if you have been considered or can apply for any and all scholarships that might work for you. The universities will often suggest scholarships outside the institution that you can apply for, if not in your first year, then later in your career.

Be clear about the total size of your aid package, the amount that needs to be repaid, and the number of years you will be eligible to receive the aid. Is the aid guaranteed for four or more years? If not, is it renewable? If so, what are the criteria to determine whether you will receive the award again? If you have committed to a university through Early Decision admissions, you will have less flexibility in evaluating or negotiating your aid package in comparison to other schools, but you will still be able to communicate with the financial aid office to try to improve your offer. If you have not applied Early Decision, you should apply early in the year to multiple schools and then wait for all your decisions to come back from schools in which you are interested before you commit to one that has accepted you. Do not commit before you need to. No university should require a nonrefundable deposit prior to May 1, the Common Reply Date, although some are asking for small deposits earlier in the year, especially for honors and residential programs. You might put down a deposit at a university to which you have been accepted in order to secure such benefits as preferred housing and course selection, but you should wait to commit yourself fully until you hear from other schools and are able to evaluate other merit- or need-based financial awards, honors and special scholars program admissions, and so on.

Once you have entered a public ivy, the aid game is not over. Your situation and your offer can change every semester. If your family or personal circumstances change—through loss of a job, another family member in college, a move in or out of state, gaining state residency—your aid package can change significantly. Be sure to talk with the financial aid counselors about your situation, and continue to work to secure the best package for yourself. Be aware of how much debt you are accumulating. Take advantage of work-study opportunities when you can, and try to find such work-study jobs as doing research with a professor, staffing a hospital, teaching a daycare class on campus, or working on a campus farm, which may have some bearing on your academic and personal interests.

If you are doing well academically in college, almost anything is possible. If you did not make the honors program as a freshman, you might be eligible to apply for your second year, and this might bring you a merit-based award. Or you might apply to one or more of the special scholarships available to top students at the university. Keep your eyes and ears open, talk to your advisor and the financial aid office, and talk to the dean, chair, and secretary of the department where you are taking most of your classes.

# LOWERING COSTS

There are a number of ways to lower your costs of attending a public university. One is to enroll in a public institution in your state of residence. Alternatively, you may gain residency over time in the state in which you have decided to study at a public university. If you are a talented high school student with strong grades and good test scores, you may be eligible for one of the many merit-based awards offered by your state university or those in other states. Some of these scholarships will consider you automatically during the university admissions process. Others will require you to discover them on your own and complete a separate application. Transferring from an in-state public institution to an out-of-state public institution—one that fits your interests more appropriately and perhaps provides for greater academic challenge—is another way to keep costs down. Tuition, fees, and expenses are typically much lower at junior and community colleges, so you might consider beginning your education there and then transferring to your state's flagship institution or to an out-of-state public ivy. Of course, if you do well for that first year or two, your transfer admission chances will also be much higher than your freshman admission chances might have been.

The public ivies have more part-time students than the smaller private colleges do. If you cannot afford the cost of full-time tuition, you might consider enrolling part-time and working to help support yourself. This may be a less satisfying and more difficult "college experience," but it may be one way for you to take advantage of the resources of a public ivy. Taking a reduced course load may mean taking longer to graduate, but you can use your summers to study, too, and still probably make it through in six years. Your degree will be just as impressive, and you will have learned just as much!

If you live in the area, consider living with your family for a year or more to keep room and board costs down. If you want to save housing costs on or off campus, consider being a resident advisor in a college dorm during your junior and senior years. In most cases you will live for free and also receive a stipend for your work mentoring and counseling first- and second-year students.

# GAINING STATE RESIDENCY

Changing your status from nonresident (out-of-state) to resident (in-state) will probably have the most dramatic effect on the overall cost of your public university education. As we have discussed, most of the states and their public universities make it quite difficult for nonresident students to change their status. You will need to follow their requirements carefully, plan ahead, and convince the school that you are becoming a state resident for more than just tuition purposes. If your parents have a house in the state, are planning to move there, or want to set up a residence there, that can help, but most students will not find themselves in that situation. Some students may try to move to a state in the year before they apply in order to become state residents first. Others will be accepted to an out-of-state school, then defer admission for a year, move to the state, and work for the year while doing what it takes to get on the road toward residency. Even if they do not achieve this for the first or even the second year of college, persistence will generally pay off in the third or fourth year of school, with a significant savings in tuition costs in the long run. If you are trying to change your residency status, be aware of these key points:

- You will likely need to declare independence from your parents. In other words, you will have to file your own taxes, and they will not be able to claim you as a dependent on their taxes. This is usually not a problem for students age 18 or older, but you should talk with your parents about the ramifications of this for taxes, estate planning, and use of educational savings accounts or tuition prepayment plans they may have in place.

- You will most likely need to have several important pieces in place for a year or more before applying for and gaining residency through the university. Start early, as soon as you move to a state, and keep very good records. Do most of the following tasks immediately upon relocating to a state.

- Sign a lease (or, potentially, a mortgage). This establishes your residency in the state as of a specific date. Of course, if you will be living in college housing, this does not apply, but if you are living off campus during the summer, the year before you start college, or later in your college career, you can do this.

- Register to vote. You can do this at the Department of Motor Vehicles in the area.

- Apply for a driver's license. Yes, you will need to give up your home state's license, but you will not be planning to return there for some time, and you can always get it back.

- If you have a car, register the plates in your new state, and change your insurance accordingly.

- File tax returns in your new state of residence. If you plan to get a job, do so as soon as possible, even if it is part-time. Doing work study for the university counts because you will be earning income in the state. Open a local checking account.

- Contact the office on campus responsible for establishing in-state resident status, get their materials, and make sure you are fulfilling and documenting all their requirements. Apply for residency as soon as you are ready, well in advance of any approaching deadlines.

- This last should go without saying: Be forthright and act in good faith in this matter and in all dealings with the university.

# FOR STUDENTS WITH LEARNING DISABILITIES AND OTHER SPECIAL NEEDS

Avoid falling into the trap of feeling you need to hide a learning disability or other special need or handicap in your approach to the universities. Do you want to dwell on your difficulties in your communications to the schools? Of course not. But you should seriously consider the following:

1. Write at least part of your application about the challenges you have faced, how you have overcome or lived with them, what you have learned through this experience, and why you are confident about your chances for success at the university.

2. Explain to the university what accommodations, if any, you have received in high school, and what you expect to need in college.

3. Send at least a summary of a learning evaluation report or other medical documentation, either to the learning support center on campus, the admissions office, or both, depending on the university's requirements and guidelines. Before you share this report, make sure it reflects on you in a positive way overall.

4. Talk openly and honestly with your parents, your guidance counselor, a learning specialist, or others who know you and your situation well about what you will need in college to succeed, and what is appropriate for you to share during and after the application process.

5. Research and visit the learning support center and other sources of support services that you might need at the university in order to assess what is available, what you will need to do to secure that support, and how those services compare to those at other schools.

We have found that students tend to find the best fit for themselves by means of this more open approach to the admissions and school selection process. The public ivies have superior support services available to qualified students, as we have indicated through some of the school descriptions and case studies. These services are there so that you can take advantage of them, so you will only sell yourself short if you do not consider them as opportunities to help you do your best in college and beyond. Even if you have not used accommodations in high school, you may need to do so in a large university environment. As the SAT and other testing programs grapple with how to administer standardized tests to students in need of accommodations, and whether and how to indicate such accommodations in their official reports to colleges, you should focus on how to describe to the colleges what you need to do well. You will need to document the existence of your learning disability or other need within one to two years before entering college, so you might consider an updated evaluation during the summer before senior year. To get accommodations on the SAT or ACT, you will almost always need to secure those accommodations through your high school. If you have not done so, you should do this close to the beginning of your junior year, so that you are registered early enough to take extended time, for example, on an SAT in March of junior year. You may apply for accommodations directly through the SAT or ACT services, but this is very difficult to do and the success record is very low (according to estimates for the SAT, only about 15 percent of independent applicants for accommodations are successful in getting them).

Learning support or other assistance at a public university can help to make a big and demanding school more workable for you. If you have special needs, add this criterion to your research and admissions process.

## HOW TO GET THE MOST OUT OF YOUR PUBLIC EDUCATION

Many students look back during senior year or after graduation, and sigh. They say, "If only I had known . . . If only I had started that earlier . . . Why didn't I . . ." Typically, we need to learn many of life's lessons for ourselves, but if you listen to those seniors and graduates, and to your parents and counselors and advisors and professors, you might make the bumps in the road a little less rough, or even avoid some mistakes or trouble spots altogether. Here are some tips for not only surviving, but making the most of a public university education:

1.  Do everything early. Apply early. Make an enrollment deposit to the university as early as you are ready. Get into the housing pool early. Apply for scholarships and financial aid early. Arrive on campus early to set up your room, meet your roommate, and find your way around campus. Register for classes early. Meet with your advisor early in the first term. Meet with all your professors in the beginning of every term. Apply early for special programs, like study abroad, internships, or research situations. The public ivies are big systems. Getting through them takes a lot of negotiating and persistence, and you need to jump on things right away if you are to compete successfully against thousands of likeminded students for spaces and faculty attention.

2.  Be assertive. You must be self-motivated, independent, determined, and confident to take advantage of all these universities have to offer. No one will call you and ask, "Hey, where is your application for that internship?" or "Why didn't you come to class today?" You need to take control: Stand up for yourself, determine what you want, and then uncover the resources that are at your disposal.

3.  Make personal contacts. You will need to make the effort to meet with professors during their office hours or by appointment. Yes, you can use e-mail, but try also to meet with every instructor at least once per semester, if not once each month or even once a week. You should put your advisor in the once-a-week category. Even a brief "hello" visit will keep you in your advisor's mind, and he or she may have some information or advice for you. Becoming a leader in clubs and other organizations can help you carve out your

niche in a big school. These personal contacts and the support network you will be building will help you through tough times that might arise, and will also lead to a more satisfying and enjoyable college experience.

4. Go to every class. Yes, try to do at least that much. If you miss a class, get the notes from a friend, from the class website, or from the teacher. Think about it: How hard is it to make it to three fifty-minute class sessions per week, for four or five courses—approximately fifteen hours of class time, on average, each week. That is the least you can do to help yourself be successful in every course. Even if class notes are available on the web, or if you did all the reading and attendance is not required, lots of good and interesting information comes out in class, and the students who do best almost always are the ones who attend every class. Begin to learn where to focus your energies where they count the most. That means excelling on those midterms, finals, and papers. You cannot do that if you don't attend class regularly, go over your own notes, compare your notes with your classmates' notes, and talk with your instructors about their expectations for papers and exams.

5. Sit up front. Even if there are 400 students in a lecture, if you sit up front every day, you will be 5 to 15 feet away from the instructor, and you will begin to recognize each other, especially if you are following the previous advice. You can make it through these big classes by being there, being attentive, and being close to the instructor. You will be less likely to talk or be distracted by friends, and, in fact, you may not even notice the other 399 people sitting behind you.

6. Treat your week like a regular workweek. Think about your academic life as if it were a 40-hour-per-week job. If you have planned well, you should enjoy most of what this job entails, the course content, the lectures and discussions, the readings, the writing, the labs. Since you will be in class for probably only 15 hours each week, the majority of your time is free time. You are not required or expected to be in any particular place. The university has not scheduled this time for you, so you must schedule it for yourself. Plan into each day some time in the library, in a special place, where you go to do your reading, go over class notes, write up a lab, conduct research, work with classmates in a study group, or outline and write a paper. Find one or more regular spots where you go to be alone and get work done. Get out of your dorm room, apartment, or fraternity or sorority house, because there are too many distractions there. Perhaps find a friend or two to help motivate you and keep you honest, and go to the coffee house, student center, or library together. Study as a group with students in every one of your classes. Put in a few hours a day, regularly, on this academic work, and you will be prepared for papers and exams. College professors often grade their students on only a few pieces of work, for example a midterm, a paper, and a final exam. You cannot wait to begin studying or writing until just before things are due or the exam is being held. To be consistently successful and learn the material, you must work on a regular basis, right from the beginning of the term. Two or three hours a day, added to your class time, means about

30 hours of work a week. You can use the other 10 hours for activities, clubs, sports, navigating the bureaucracy, and reading the paper. And guess what, if you do all this during the "workweek," your evenings and weekends will be free. You will need to work at night and on the weekends sometimes, because there will be crunch times and deadlines, but these can be the exceptions rather than the rule. You may also try to schedule your classes to keep a day or two completely free each week. That will give you an open stretch of time that day to write a paper, conduct research, do an internship, meet with a professor, or, OK, head off early for the weekend to ski or fish. But you will have finished your work first, right?

7. Work on your work with your instructors. Go over outlines of papers with them during their office hours. Take advantage of opportunities to rewrite papers or exams for improved grades. Complete extra-credit assignments when offered. Don't be a grade-grubber with your instructors, though. Try to learn what it is they are looking for on each assignment and in the future, and try to meet their expectations. Better grades will follow. As you progress through college, take advantage of chances for independent study and research projects with faculty mentors. These will be some of your best learning experiences.

8. Attend special functions. Yes, you may go to the big football or basketball game, and even camp out for tickets, but also consider attending the film series, lectures by visiting faculty and VIPs, drama and music productions, and poetry readings. Find out what's happening on campus and broaden your horizons by doing things you have never done before and things you used to enjoy at home. You never know what you'll learn and whom you will meet.

9. Take classes for the teacher. Hear about that great professor in anthropology all the time? Take the course, even though you have never studied anthropology. That is what a liberal arts education is all about. Find the great teachers and classes, and take as many of them as you can, within the constraints of the university's general requirements and the strictures of your particular major and school.

10. Think about life after college. Planning for graduate school during senior spring is too late. You will have missed the opportunity to take courses you might need, for medical school, law school, an eventual business school application, or an academic graduate school (see our discussion of graduate admissions in *Making It into a Top Graduate School* for more on graduate and career planning). If you suspect early on that you might be headed in one or another direction, begin your discussions right away with the graduate and career planning office on campus, and find out what requirements you will need to keep in mind to be prepared for various tracks. You do not need to major in biology, for example, to go to medical school, but you will need to take six or seven classes to fulfill the premed requirements. Internships, service opportunities, and research pro-

grams are other ways for you to learn about and enhance your qualifications for various graduate and career options during your college years.

## REGISTERING FOR CLASSES

Gone are the days, for the most part, of waiting in long lines to register or even sleeping out on the lawn in front of the registrar's building to secure the classes you want. Today, almost all course registration is done by telephone and on the Internet. Often, students are assigned a registration date and time by lottery. Sometimes, they are given seniority and preferred registration based on their class or major, membership in an honors program, or status as a merit scholar. Some of these things you can control. A lottery you cannot.

What you can do is know ahead of time which classes you want most and register at the earliest time you can for those courses. You may register for one or more classes in addition to the four or five (for those on a semester system) you know you want or need. Before you call or log on to register, make sure you have gone through the course bulletin carefully and have backup choices ready. In a worst-case scenario, you will want to register for something that works for you. Secure your full-time registration as best you can, and then consider ways to change your course schedule.

Make sure not to be late when your time slot opens up, and try to balance your courses in the departments and distribution areas you need. See your course planning as a coherent whole, and try to structure each semester so that it is interesting and bearable. You will not want to take all sciences and maths in one semester. Nor will you want to "get all those humanities courses out of the way" and pile up on reading and writing all at once. Balance is key. Know that one class will always seem to take last place in your work and attention each semester. Try to take care of distribution and major requirements gradually, without leaving them all for senior year or grouping them all together right up front. Depending on the university, you will have more or less freedom in your first two years to determine your schedule, but you will always have some. Get to know the departmental or program secretaries and assistants in your areas of interest. They will help you plan your curriculum, advise you on good courses and professors, and tell you what a "normal" schedule looks like for majors in their fields. If you want to transfer from one college, school, or program in the university to another, or apply to one of the university's preprofessional programs, you need to make doubly sure that you meet that program's requirements in time and at a competitive level.

## AUDITING COURSES

Let's face it. At a big university, sometimes it's hard to get into the classes you want with the professor you want. Or you've got a tough schedule, but you really would like to experience that additional class. Auditing allows you to take advantage of more of what a university has to offer. Auditing means sitting in on a class without taking the course for credit or a grade. Consider auditing a class each semester in addition to your regular course load or if you initially are not accepted into the class for a grade. Usually, you are expected to attend most class sessions, and you may be expected to sit for exams and write papers. Auditing is governed by university and departmental rules and regulations and by the preference of the instructor teaching the course. You will often need to get the approval of the teacher to audit a class and to work with him or her to establish a satisfactory relationship for the term. Taking a class with a pass/fail option is another way to take that extra class or a class outside your normal area of interest or strength, but with a pass/fail class, you still get course credit (providing you pass the class) and the course appears on your transcript. Universities put limits on the number or percentage of courses you may take pass/fail. When you audit a class, you probably will not get course credit or a record of the class on your transcript. There are also fewer limits on the number of courses you may audit during your career. Auditing a class is another way to try to gain entry into a class that is listed as closed in the registration system. If the instructor agrees, you may begin to audit a class at the beginning of the semester while you wait to see whether an opening appears or whether the instructor is willing to use his or her discretion to add you directly to the regular class enrollment. If you are determined to gain entry to a course, this is a good strategy to pursue. You must be up front with the instructor about your intentions, however.

## "SHOPPING"

One of the reasons that spaces open up in supposedly closed course sections is that students are shopping around for the right courses for the semester. In fact, you may also be shopping. Having registered for five, six, or seven courses (if allowed), you spend the first two weeks or so of the semester attending all of them, getting the syllabus for each, and browsing the readings in the book store and the library. Universities have determined a time frame each semester for dropping and adding classes without penalty. This "drop/add" period, sometimes formalized as a "shopping" opportunity, lets you sample several courses that might be of interest and try to gain entry into some courses that are very full. Keep track of the drop/add deadline every semester. You do not want to go beyond it if at all possible, so that you do not run into the problem of having incompletes or withdrawals on your transcript or having to make formal appeals to the administration or faculty to make exceptions for you. Use the first couple of weeks of each term productively, and there should be no reason why you can't decide which courses to keep and which to drop. If a professor allows you later to add a class or even to drop one without penalty, so be it. But you will want to ensure that you secure enough appropriate courses, some of which may be second-best options for you, so that you maintain full-time enrollment. If you cannot get a class you really need or want during a particular semester, you may be able to take it in the summer, when course sections are often smaller and more available, or the next semester or year if that still works for you. Early contact with the instructor and the department will help you secure these important classes for the future. Typically, if you are an upper division student who needs a class for your major or for a university requirement, you are more likely to be added into it right away once you make an appeal.

Finally, you might view shopping as a way to explore some different academic areas to which you have not been exposed. Think about taking advantage of the wealth of opportunities at a public ivy. There are literally hundreds of majors and thousands of courses. Why not try some that sound intriguing or take a course just because you heard the professor was amazing? That is what a good liberal arts education is all about. Stretch yourself. Challenge your assumptions. Explore some different disciplines and ways of thinking about the world.

## MAKING THE MOST OF YOUR SUMMERS

We encourage you to see your summers not just as time out from a rigorous academic program during the year, but also as flexible time to pursue other areas of interest, build your nonacademic résumé, explore possible career paths, get involved in your community, or lighten your fall-winter-spring academic workload. Most of the public ivies have one to three summer sessions. These are short terms lasting four to eight weeks, during which you can take courses for full credit. Often, but not always, these courses are taught by graduate instructors. The course sections are usually smaller and more discussion based, and the graduate students doing the teaching are usually working in their particular areas of expertise. Course content is squeezed into a shorter time frame, but class periods are longer and you can focus on just one or two classes at a time. Trying to get that organic chemistry or foreign language requirement out of the way? Consider using your summer for just that purpose. You can also take classes at other universities, perhaps in a foreign country or at your home state university (or a university with which your university has a regional cooperative agreement) if you are an out-of-state student during the regular academic year. This can provide you with an exciting study-abroad opportunity or save you some money while you live at home and pay resident tuition.

You might also consider pursuing research, internship, or volunteer service opportunities. Or you might work to save up some money for the rest of the year. If you can afford to earn money in the summer, but not work full- or part-time during the rest of the year, that may help you to focus your attention on your studies and other extracurricular activities.

## QUALITY OVER QUANTITY, OR THE TORTOISE AND THE HARE

Remaining in good standing at your university and graduating from college with an impressive transcript and résumé is much more about building and maintaining the quality and consistency of your curriculum, academic performance, and special experiences than about the number of courses you take each semester, the number of hours you worked during the summer, or the number of years it took you to graduate. The tortoise, within reason, wins in this race, provided he or she earns strong and steadily improving grades over his or her college career and builds in interesting and valuable learning experiences and contributions to school and community over time. The hare, who overloads on classes, especially during the first two years, zips through every summer with no focus, avoids doing more than is absolutely necessary to get by, and somehow manages to graduate in four years, looks as rushed and unfocused as he or she may feel upon graduation.

It may be hard to accept that extra semester or two, or year or two, of college work for your future, but it may be absolutely essential for you to do your best and succeed. Some students may be so talented and focused that they are able to get it all in within that magical four-year window, including doing interesting things in the summer and getting involved on campus, but as the graduation statistics from the public ivies imply, these students don't necessarily set the rules these days. Taking a fifth year is not a sign of failure but potentially an opportunity to excel. Plan your college career as well in advance as possible, but approach each semester and summer individually. If you need to take the minimum course load acceptable for full-time enrollment to do well in some difficult but essential courses, then do so. If you need to take a time-out from school to recover, rest, or try something different, that is fine, but try to plan it so it does not look bad on your transcript. If you want to do part-time academic work for a while, that also is OK. If taking one more semester as a senior would allow you to secure a research internship or complete an honors thesis, then go for it. You will win in the long run.

There are so many options available at the public ivies, you will need to focus on quality over the long term to take advantage of everything you see around you, and even then you will miss some opportunities. Pace yourself, stay on track, and, who knows, you may still graduate in the four years you expected.

## USING FACULTY COURSE EVALUATIONS

Many universities have formalized the process of evaluating instructors to help students seek quality teachers and encourage faculty and graduate students to improve their performance in the classroom. This type of quality assurance also helps university departments judge how their faculty and graduate students are doing. A number of universities have implemented advanced teacher training programs for faculty and graduate students to help them continuously monitor themselves and improve their teaching, communications, and advising skills. These programs involve mentoring, videotaping of class performances, campus conferences, and departmental seminars. Well-developed teacher training programs for faculty and for graduate students are one sign that a university, even a large research university, is taking its teaching seriously and trying to improve it.

Posting faculty course evaluations online, where they are readily accessible to all students, is another way that universities are putting the emphasis on teaching and the pressure on instructors. At the end of each class, instructors hand out short questionnaires for all students to fill out. In our experience, students take these seriously, as a chance to rave, offer suggestions for improvement, punish poor teachers, or vent. Over several semesters and classes, each of which is always different in chemistry, substance, and class environment, these faculty course evaluations begin to indicate how instructors are faring in the classroom. Not all great teachers are popular, of course, but not all likable, easygoing, and entertaining teachers receive high marks for imparting knowledge or understanding. View the faculty course evaluations as one way to judge the relative ratings of various faculty, courses, departments, and even universities.

## GRADUATE STUDENTS VERSUS PROFESSORS

Guidebooks, students, parents, counselors, and the media often assume that having graduate student teachers and teaching assistants (TAs) teach undergraduate courses means poor-quality instruction and little concern on the part of the university for undergraduate learning. This conception is limited. As we have discussed, graduate students can add a great deal to an undergraduate's educational experience at a research university, and they perform essential academic functions as they progress toward their advanced degrees. Not all graduate students are bad teachers, just as not all full-time professors are good ones. Faculty course evaluations can help you sift through the excellent, good, bad, and terrible, and so can anecdotal recommendations from friends and other instructors. The knowledge base and experience of a professor who holds an endowed chair in your major department will be a lot deeper than that of a second-year TA. How great will his or her enthusiasm or accessibility be? How big is the class? Is it a lecture or a discussion-oriented course? What is the word on his or her teaching style and ability? There is almost no way around the fact that you will be seeing both graduate students and professors in your classes at the public ivies. Try to evaluate both fairly and consider the pros and cons of each course you are considering. Clearly, most of the weight of the evidence will fall squarely on the side of trying to take as many seminar-style classes as possible with senior faculty in your areas of interest. Even some of the great professors may give lectures to large classes that are outstanding and worth every minute of your time. Be prepared for both eventualities at a public university, and try to see the benefits of getting engaged in every class in which you are enrolled.

## ADVANCED STANDING

Advanced standing typically means you have accumulated college course credits before enrolling in a university. You may have taken a number of AP courses in high school and then scored well on the AP exams (usually you will need a 4 or a 5 on the 5-point AP exam scale). Or, you may have taken a few classes at local community colleges or at precollege university summer programs during high school. Perhaps you are a transfer student applying from a two- or four-year college or university.

Advanced standing allows you to do a number of things. First, you may be able to graduate early from the university, especially if you have enough credits to gain sophomore standing. This is highly unlikely, but we have seen it happen. Remembering our discussion of the tortoise and the hare, you may still decide to stay for four years and take a second major, study abroad, or do an honors thesis, making your record all the more impressive and your experience all the more valuable.

Second, you may be able to jump over some of the general requirements and introductory course sections during your first year of college. These classes are likely to be big lectures, so if you can avoid them, you will save yourself some of the trauma and hassle associated with the transition to a large university.

Third, with advanced standing, you may be able to enter a preprofessional or special program directly or at least more quickly. You will note in the university descriptions that many of the programs in business, architecture, pharmacy, veterinary sciences, or education, for example, require students to complete course requirements and course credits, sometimes in the college of liberal arts, before admission to their particular degree program. If you have some course credits under your belt before you enter the university, you will be able to advance more rapidly into your chosen school and field.

Finally, advanced standing may save you some money. The fewer course credits you need to take at the university, generally the less you will spend on your education. You can move through more quickly, keeping in mind Mr. Hare, and hold your overall costs down.

## UNDERSTANDING HOW COURSE SECTIONS ARE STRUCTURED

New students at the large universities are often bewildered by the array of courses available to them, in or out of any intended major or department. So many centers and units and programs and options. Interdisciplinary studies, freshmen seminars, research centers, honors programs, general requirements, major requirements, prerequisites . . . You need to seek the guidance of your current advisor, eventually secure an advisor in your area of interest, and sit at the desks of those departmental secretaries. You also need to know how course sections are structured. First, many sections of various classes are offered during one semester and during the academic year and the summer. You will have your choice of course sections, depending on their enrollment availability, the rest of your schedule, and what time you can stand getting up in the morning. Yes, those 8:00 A.M. classes are tough to bear for everyone concerned, so if you are not a morning person, then register for classes that you know you will realistically be able to attend and participate in regularly.

Among the course sections you see listed before you in the university bulletin or on the campus website, note that some are listed as being taught by one professor, with multiple course sections listed for the same class. These are the big lectures, and you will see their enrollment size listed as well. Maybe it is 500. The professor will lecture in these large classes two or three times per week. The sections, which may be listed with an enrollment of 30 to 50 students, are called recitations or discussion sections. They will be taught by graduate TAs once per week. These two aspects, the recitation and the lecture, are part of one class.

Now, what may confuse you is that there may be another course listed, taught by the same or a different professor, with the same title and university course number. The enrollment may be 75 or 125. This course will be taught solely by the professor or graduate student instructor listed, sometimes with the assistance of a TA for grading. Most likely, you will want to take this latter class. It will be taught by one person, and will be smaller overall. This is also the class that will tend to fill up first.

## CONNECTING WITH YOUR TEACHERS, DEANS, AND ADVISORS

It is essential that you make a consistent effort to connect with the people who will be teaching, advising, and assisting you throughout your educational career. You must be assertive in attending professors' office hours, meeting your academic dean, and scheduling regular meetings with your advisor. Believe us, you will not be perceived as a pain. You will be appreciated and rewarded for your efforts at communication. You will do better in your classes, will be alerted to potential pitfalls before you encounter them, and will have people who know you in that big university who can serve as references for internships, special programs, and graduate school admissions. Undergraduate departments often have social functions for their majors every year. Go to them. Meet with the departmental chair, the faculty you do not know yet, fellow students, and departmental staff and secretaries. Spend time in your department or school's building and offices outside of class time. Make the connections that will be extremely valuable to you during your college life.

## MAJOR AND DISTRIBUTION REQUIREMENTS

One of the things your advisor, professors, academic deans, and department staff can tell you about is the requirements you must fulfill for the university and for your major or particular program. As you may know by now, these two sets of requirements are complementary and overlapping, but they are not exactly the same. You have to fulfill additional requirements for your major and possibly for the college or school in which you are enrolled. Be sure you are making adequate progress on these parallel tracks right from the beginning. Don't lose time enrolling in classes that are inappropriate for you or above your level. The computerized registration system will probably not let you know that you have just signed up for a junior-level seminar, when you really wanted and were prepared for a freshman introductory survey class. By the time you find out what you have gotten yourself into, the class you wanted may be full, you might have missed the drop/add deadline, and you will be miserable. Talking with an advisor ahead of time about the right set of courses for you can help you to avoid such mistakes. In addition, if you are planning to apply to some of the preprofessional and other special programs at the university, make sure that you have covered the necessary prerequisites and gotten some university distribution courses out of the way before you begin to specialize.

## HONORS PROGRAMS AND COLLEGES

As you can see from our descriptions of the public ivies in Part Three, honors and other special scholars programs abound at these universities. They are available as collegewide programs, separate colleges within the university, departmental or college-specific programs, or scholarships and honors directed toward particular student groups. If you are at the top of an applicant class to a public ivy, and depending on the procedures of the university, you might be invited to join an honors program without any additional effort or application on your part. In many cases it will be up to you, the applicant, to find out about honors and scholars programs, their criteria and process for selection, and what you need to do to apply. The benefits of such programs in terms of honors classes, residential options, study-abroad programs, special advising, and other perks should be obvious to you. Honors and scholars programs are a major way of making a larger university smaller, more challenging, and more accessible. Apply for some of these programs and see what happens. If you don't make it on the first round, during first-year admissions, you may try again once you are enrolled, later in the first year, or beyond. If you are doing well at the university, you may become eligible for other honors opportunities through your career. Stay alert for these possibilities, and talk with your advisor, teachers, the career and graduate counseling staff, and the honors program coordinators about what you need to do to qualify and apply for them.

## UNDERGRADUATE RESEARCH OPPORTUNITIES

Undergraduate research and independent and interdisciplinary study options are there for the taking at the public ivies. In fact, these universities brag about the undergraduates engaged in research and creative study with the guidance of faculty. Will you be tracked down and asked to fly to South America for a semester, to interview local agricultural workers, and to write a paper as an independent study research project for your interdisciplinary environmental studies

---

APPLICATION ADVICE FROM A SELECTIVE PUBLIC UNIVERSITY:
THE UNIVERSITY OF VIRGINIA

On their website, the University of Virginia clarifies the admissions process to their highly selective Echols Scholars honors program, as well as to the univer-

*(continued)*

sity as a whole. UVA offers some pointers that should be helpful for applicants to any public ivy or honors program.

"How We Choose Participants

The Selection Process

All applicants to the College first-year class are automatically considered for the Echols Scholars Program. The UVA admission staff reads each file hoping to see the kind of "avid learner," with impressive accomplishment already, who needs Echols freedom and will use it well. Several hundred students in each year's applicant pool seem to fit that description . . .

What We Look For

We are not "numbers-driven," as some university honors programs are. Looking at scores and grade-point averages, we don't have cutoffs at one end or automatic entry on the other end. But scores on standardized tests do mean a great deal to us, as do high grades. We also don't assign points to certain intellectual achievements; Echols admission is not the reward for meeting certain predetermined criteria, since our students come from a diversity of schools, with different policies and differing opportunities. Some schools weight their grades for certain courses; others don't. Some offer an impressive array of AP courses; others have none or few. What's important to us is that the student take the strongest possible program and do well in it. The admission application asks the school to tell us whether the applicant has chosen the strongest program. If this achievement is absent, there's virtually no way to compensate. We want, for example, to see applicants go as far in sciences and foreign languages as their school allows. Then we look for evidence of intellectual liveliness. Examples often include summer Governor's School; magnet school enrollment; science fair projects beyond the routine; success beyond the school in forensics, Model UN, music performance, quiz bowl teams, and Olympics of the Mind; and other activities requiring substantial intellectual—and often creative—involvement. Please note that these examples are not requirements; they show what kinds of things catch our attention. Students in schools with few such opportunities should not be discouraged; we will look to see what they made of what was available. Finally, we pay attention to the quality and substance of all the essays in the application: vigor, clarity, imagination, development of the topic rather than merely mentioning things. We do disqualify people who seem otherwise qualified, if we see responses that are glib, formulaic, perfunctory, or otherwise discouraging. To sum up: UVA applicants are strongly urged to make all their intellectual strengths visible on the application. Show us how your mind works,

*(continued)*

and what's in it. We're able to judge applicants only on the basis of what's in the file, not on what's missing. Two quick examples: First, lots of UVA applicants are honor society members and even officers, so that alone doesn't distinguish prospective Echols Scholars. But if you as NHS vice-president personally arranged a half dozen programs during the year, inviting local government officials and journalists to speak, be sure to tell us that. Second, if you have an honor with a name and significance that we won't recognize, explain it ("I was one of fifteen students nationwide awarded a scholarship to Socorro Summer, an eight-week archaeological dig in New Mexico"). When it comes to teacher recommendations, we can't use those that merely give adjectives, or list the activities you've already supplied. They need to tell us something we won't find elsewhere, and anecdotes and details help. **99**

major? Will the research opportunities office call you out of the blue and beg you to apply for the $2,000 of summer research grant money available for just such a trip? Will the school newspaper or alumni magazine find you to suggest that you write up your experience for a publishable article? Will those graduate programs in environmental studies you're considering write you a letter to suggest you show some initiative and scholarly curiosity by engaging in independent and original field research? We doubt it. You must again take the reins and direct yourself to these wonderful programs. You may not believe it, but there is a great deal of money and support for such endeavors in every field at the university, just waiting for you to apply and make the argument for why you should be able to make that trip, structure that class with your professor, join that archaeological dig, or spend the summer in the biogenetics lab. These are the programs that will make your college experience much more enlightening, interesting, and impressive.

## FOREIGN STUDY

Education-abroad opportunities are other great experiences to build into your university years. Again, the public ivies are thrilled with the numbers of their students who travel abroad. They expand their horizons, bring their university name and foundation around the world, and come back renewed and excited. They interact with other cultures, go outside their boundaries and expectations, and return with new perspectives and ideas. If you can, you should try to study abroad during the academic year or the summer. Financial assistance may be available to help you. You may be able to engage in a work or community service trip abroad, if that is easier to manage or preferable to a study experience. Head to your university's study-abroad office and take a look through the many possibilities there are for going near or far afield. If you are not highly proficient in a foreign language, you may find programs in countries that speak English or your native language. Or you may choose a program that is taught in your language but in another country. This may be a great way for you to fulfill your foreign language requirement, and there is no better way to learn than to immerse yourself in a foreign culture and language environment.

## INTERNSHIPS

Internships are available in law firms, investment banks, schools, social work agencies, hotels and restaurants, advertising agencies, television studios, newspaper offices—you name it—and are excellent ways for you to gain exposure to potential career paths, make some connections, and develop your interests. You may be paid, or you may not. You may find an internship opportunity outside the university that you bring to a faculty advisor or career office or service learning program on campus to set up a mentoring or advising situation. Or you might go to these people and offices to research possible internships of interest. Volunteer service is limitless, and service learning programs allow you to gain academic credit and maintain advising while you are working in community or public service. An internship at a law firm is an excellent way to see if you like the work and build a foundation for a strong law school application. The universities also maintain extensive alumni networks. Many alumni put themselves on a contact list to indicate they are willing to serve as references or networkers for students. Often, these alumni can link students with internship and job openings. Be confident and call some of these alumni if you find some who are working in your area of interest. Internships are available in any area and in many forms. You can certainly find one that works for you or create one that has never been tried.

## EXCHANGE PROGRAMS

In addition to studying abroad, you may decide to study at another U.S. university for a semester or a year. University exchange programs set up networks, usually with complementary institutions, to let a small number of students study at one another's campuses for specified lengths of time and with particular qualifications for student participation. Sometimes, these exchange programs are linked to specific academic areas. Other times, students may study anything within the liberal arts college at either university. In any case, you will want to look for a university switch that will be exciting, different, and stimulating and will allow you to pursue the academic and extracurricular programs you care about. Tired of the Midwest? Head to California or the South for a term. Tired of the heat? Go north! Try a bigger school, a smaller school, a

---

### ADVICE FOR GETTING THE MOST OUT OF A PUBLIC IVY, FROM A PUBLIC IVY: THE UNIVERSITY OF WASHINGTON

Here are some tips from the University of Washington's website on how to take advantage of what a large university has to offer.

"Making the Most of the Big U

Trying to connect what you learn in the classroom to the world you live in? Eager to gain experience that gives you insight into a possible career? The UW offers a wealth of opportunities for experiential learning.

Do at least one internship every year of college, beginning with your freshman year. We'll show you how.

Take a Service Learning course or volunteer at a neighborhood school or agency to connect your course work to the bigger picture.

Get involved in research. There's no better way to get to know faculty, prepare for graduate school or a career, and feel connected to the exciting advances in knowledge that occur every day at the UW. Research here takes place in all fields of study (not just science!).

Looking for a job can be challenging, but the process itself and the end result can be very rewarding. The staff of the Center for Career Services is available to assist you with your journey into the world of work—and they'd like to see you as early as your freshman year!"

---

public school, a private school. You may find something you like a lot better. Such an exchange may be a prelude to an eventual transfer. Being accepted for an exchange program is not the same as being accepted as a transfer student, and you should not consider it as such.

## HOUSING

Where you live in college matters, especially in your first year. If you are new to the area, the first people you will meet and befriend will be your roommate(s), the people who live on your floor, and the people who live in your dorm. Provided you live in college dormitories, that is. We generally recommend that first-year full-time students try to live on campus in college-provided housing if at all possible. Most of the public ivies require this or guarantee freshmen housing availability. Again, start early to get the most preferential situation. A visit to campus and some contact with the office of residential life will help you find out which are the most desirable dorms. You may also want to consider applying for some of the special living–learning residential communities that are available. Here, you will live in a dorm or on a floor with others who share your academic interests and find faculty advising, common course schedules, and so on to help your transition from smaller high school to bigger university. Other housing options include off-campus apartments, fraternity and sorority houses, honors dorms and floors, and family housing.

---

### CHOOSING TO GO SUBSTANCE FREE

If you are concerned about being pressured to drink or use other drugs or cigarettes, you might consider applying for what's called "substance-free" or "chemical-free" housing on campus. This will keep you somewhat removed from peer pressure where you live and will help you avoid secondary effects of substance abuse—messed-up dorm rooms, hallways, and bathrooms, excessive noise, assaults, vandalism, partying roommates, and so forth. In a recent study, Henry Wechsler of the Harvard University School of Public Health compared drinking among 2,555 students in various residences at 52 colleges that had substance-free residential options. He found that students living in substance-free dorms were less likely to experience these secondary effects and were less likely to drink heavily. There is no doubt some self-selection is going on: students who choose to live in substance-free housing are less likely to abuse substances anyway. The findings are nevertheless compelling, especially when combined with anecdotal and other survey evidence from students on campus. Wechsler found that in his sample, only 32 percent of students in substance-free housing reported drinking heavily (five or more drinks in a row for men; four or more for women) at least once in the prior two weeks, compared with 53 percent of those living in regular housing. More colleges and universities are beginning to offer substance-free living, and you should ask the admissions and residential offices about these options at the universities you are considering. If they do not currently have such dorms or floors available, ask them to consider making them available.

*Source:* Alex P. Kellogg, "Study Documents Success of Substance-Free Dorms in Curbing Residents' Drinking," *Chronicle of Higher Education,* February 7, 2000, www.chronicle.com/daily/2001/02/2001020705.n.htm.

## JOINING A FRATERNITY OR SORORITY

Making the choice to join the Greek system is a personal decision. You must decide what is right for you. Frats and sororities have a negligible to modest presence at the public ivies. Since these campuses are so big, even if a third of the students are involved in the Greek system, there are a million other things to do and people to meet. Some students join Greek houses because they are just that, houses. You may be able to assure yourself of housing by joining a frat or sorority and thereby create your own smaller residential community. You may then live off campus with some of your brothers or sisters during your upper division years. We tend to feel that joining a fraternity or sorority in your freshman year, particularly in the fall, is making a choice too early. You may be limiting yourself too much in terms of the social interactions you will have, and you may group yourself with people with whom you do not connect well in the long run. Adding the pressures of Greek life to your schedule—and these vary from school to school and house to house—may be too much to bear just when you are starting college. Greeks perform many positive functions on university campuses, from offering a niche and community, to performing community service, to establishing strong friendship bonds and a social network. They can also divide students and campuses, pressure students to party too much, reinforce high levels of drinking and negative attitudes toward the opposite sex or different groups of students on campus, or present too many social distractions each week. Carefully consider whether to join a Greek house, and, if so, which one and when. It might be good to wait a semester or a year before rushing, to give yourself time to meet a variety of people on campus and acclimate to university life.

---

ADVICE FOR NEW STUDENTS FROM RUTGERS UNIVERSITY,
THE STATE UNIVERSITY OF NEW JERSEY

---

These words of advice from Rutgers University's website should help students heading off to any public ivy.

"Get familiar with the Rutgers campuses! You can get a great map from any campus center. New Brunswick students especially need to be familiar with the different campuses in New Brunswick and Piscataway so that they can take advantage of the resources available on those campuses, regardless of what college or school they are affiliated with.

For those who will be living on campus, don't bring a lot of things. Only bring the stuff you'll need! You can get more things later. Contact your new roommate to discuss beforehand who will bring which appliances. You might wind up with

*(continued)*

two TVs and no alarm clock. Things to bring with you to the residence halls: extra long bed sheets, pillows, laundry baskets, extension cords, storage boxes, shower buckets, flip-flops for shower, toilet paper, towels, alarm clock, and reminders of home.

If you are planning to move in later than expected, contact your respective housing office promptly. You do not want to incur unnecessary penalties.

Commuting students should take advantage of the commuter and/or off-campus student services offered through their school; they'll be able to help you with parking, getting involved with activities, and other concerns of commuters.

Rub shoulders with your professors . . . If you take the time to talk with them, you'll better understand what they expect from you.

When planning your schedule, you do not want to overwhelm yourself during your first semester. Talk to an academic advisor about how many credits you should take. Always be sure to leave yourself plenty of time to get to classes, especially those that require a bus ride . . . It is wise to find your class before you head for the first meeting; wander around the campuses a bit and find all the buildings where you will be attending classes.

Transfer students should wait to buy their textbooks for a class until they have attended the first meeting. Sometimes, the professor will announce a different text than what the bookstore had on display. First-year students should go to the bookstores early, since the introductory classes usually don't switch or add texts at the last minute, and since by going early you'll avoid lines. Visit the bookstores.

Check your campus mailbox often for academic information and read the official announcements in our campus newspapers . . .

If you are interested in joining clubs and student organizations (a great way to meet people), contact your college's student activities office . . . Commuting students should especially look into getting involved with these activities since they can help you become part of the Rutgers community when you're not actually living on campus.

If you are ever having difficulties with your classes or need academic assistance, your options include the Learning Resource Centers, Writing Centers, Math Science Learning Centers, and your school's office of Academic Services or Academic Affairs.

If you ever happen to experience a non-academic problem or situation that is affecting your academic performance, the best resource for you is a helpful Information Assistant . . . He or she will be glad to direct you to the appropriate

*(continued)*

resources. Since there are so many different offices and programs at Rutgers, each Information Assistant is trained to differentiate and provide the caller with the best possible referral to match their needs.

For any situations dealing with your health, contact any of our health centers. Every campus has a health center, and full-time students can use any of them.

You will not be able to cash a check around Rutgers unless you have an account with a bank in the area. There is a website available which compares banks and fees in the New Brunswick area. The information contained here is generally transferable to branches of the bank in other parts of the state.

Always know your deadlines, whether it be for registration, library book expirations, that parking ticket you've neglected, or the term paper you've been dreading. Keeping ahead of due dates will help keep you from getting buried under piles of papers and thereby reduce unnecessary stress and aggravation later.

Start planning your future early. If you intend to find an internship, plan for your career, or move on to graduate school in the near future, visit with a counselor at Career Services early in your academic career to discuss the steps that you'll need to take. There are offices in New Brunswick, Camden, and Newark.

Become familiar with all of the reference facilities at the libraries, especially IRIS, and use them! No better place to study than a room filled with information!

If you are interested in an on-campus job, meet with someone at the Student Employment Office to discuss the opportunities.

Rutgers University also provides the Lesbian/Gay/Bisexual Hotline, as well as the Office of Diverse Community Affairs, to answer questions or just listen to gay, lesbian, and bisexual students' concerns.

Volunteer. Exchange a few hours of your time for the joy of being looked up to by a little kid who thinks you're tops. Being involved in community service projects also helps you hone those important leadership skills.

Stay in touch with your family. A letter, a call, whatever; they can be incredibly supportive, especially when you're not around and they realize how much they miss you.

Sleep! With all you're going to be involved with, getting enough sleep at Rutgers is a challenge, but well worth it. Students report that after eight hours of sleep, they're more alert in class and can study longer and more efficiently."

# FINDING YOUR NICHE

Join something. It's that simple. It may be a fraternity or sorority, a club sport, a service organization, a class, or school leadership council. You need to create your niche at a large university, and there are many available to you. If what you are interested in does not exist, start a new club, a new magazine, a new band. You are sure to find others who share your interest. Check the bulletin boards at the student center and online, and you will discover people looking for connections, just as you are. Go to student activity fairs at the beginning of each semester. See what catches your eye. What are people in your dorm up to? Maybe you can go along with them and try something new. Get involved volunteering with a local community service organization or project. Go to the student recreation center and sign up for an exercise or skills class in something. That is a great way to stay in shape, relieve stress, and meet new people. The gyms of old have given way to multimillion-dollar, multipurpose recreation, health, and wellness centers, with climbing walls, bicycle spinning classes, kick-boxing, saunas, and scuba diving. You don't have to join every club, but you should try some new things and form some bonds through one or two activities while you are in college. You will be building your support network, making lasting friendships, and discovering new interests.

# ASSERTIVENESS TRAINING

**as-ser-tive** *adj.* persistently positive or confident
**as-sert** *vt.* 1) to declare; affirm 2) to maintain or defend (rights, etc.)
**assert oneself** to insist on one's rights, or in being recognized

—*Webster's New World Desk Dictionary*

If you haven't gotten the message yet, let us be perfectly clear: *If you plan to attend one of the public ivies or any larger university, you will need to become assertive.* As the above definitions suggest, you will need to learn to assert yourself, defending your rights, declaring your intentions, affirming your choices, calling for recognition of your needs and interests, and, most important, remaining positive and confident. Being assertive is not the same as being *aggressive.* You will not get far, in life or in academia, by being tough, annoying, aggressive, obnoxious, negative, or pushy. Neither will you have much success by being shy, withdrawing, passive, silent, disinterested, or a pushover. You will need to strike a balance, and know when to stand up for yourself, which questions to ask, and which people to ask them of. Stand up for yourself, because no one else will be there to do it for you, and politely demand to be noticed.

# SPECIAL ADVICE FOR PARENTS

Much of this book has been directed to students, but we expect and hope that many parents are readers as well. In this section we want to address you parents. Many parents are nervous to start with when they send their sons and daughters off to college. Combine that transition with the fact that the "college" to which John or Jane is going contains 25,000 undergraduates on an 800-acre campus 2,000 miles away from home, and panic may start to set in.

Do you have reason to be concerned? Frankly, yes, you do. Fewer than half of all freshmen entering college in this country will return to their college as sophomores. We know that the rates of freshmen retention are higher than the national average at the public ivies, as their statistics indicate, but we can also see that in some cases 10 percent or more of first-year students will not return, even at these strong institutions.

What can you do to help make sure your child is successful during his or her first year and beyond? Just as first-year students must be assertive and fend for themselves once they begin college life, you, too, must be assertive with your child and the university and stay involved in his or her life. Of course, you do not want to smother your freshman. Calling every day, visiting every other weekend, constantly asking invasive or personal questions—that's too much. There is a happy medium between being the overly aggressive, protective, or concerned parent and being the absent, disconnected, or naive parent, and you must try to find it. Every son's or daughter's situation is unique. As a family, you will have to communicate to establish the proper and acceptable relationship boundaries for this next stage in your child's life, stepping out of the nest, probably for good. You had better stock up on tissues now. Here are some bits of advice, particularly for parents of students headed off to the public ivies and similar universities:

1. Take an active interest in your children's education. Just because they are no longer at home does not mean you should stop asking them about their academic interests, their good and bad teachers, papers and projects, and goals. Of course, you will be less directly involved even than you were by the time they were a senior in high school. But parents remain one of the most important voices of influence in a college student's life. If they know you are interested in their progress, that you care and remain hopeful about their success, that you really want to know about their plans each semester and year, they will try to rise to your expectations and keep you involved in their thought process.

2. Try not to be overly demanding or to set unrealistic expectations. Express your hope that they will do consistently good work and attend to their studies amid all the other amazing new things they will find in college life. Demanding all As and a chance to review every paper is a recipe for disaster and a major break with your child. Be there to be helpful, but you should be encouraging independence, not dependence, at this stage of life. Help your son or daughter to set realistic goals and cheer from the sidelines when they are achieved.

3. Encourage your college student to take advantage of all the opportunities available at the university, and to find his or her niche. This is an essential aspect of being happy and successful at these universities. Ask about available programs. E-mail a suggestion for an internship or project or volunteer opportunity.

4. While we're on the subject, if you haven't already, you had better get used to e-mail. That will be your primary means of communication with your child for the next four or more years. It will be the easiest and least expensive means of connecting, as well as the most reliable.

5. Go to parents' weekend and a couple other events. When these occasions arise, take advantage of them to make some personal connections with your son or daughter and his or her friends. Go shopping for food and clothes. Go out to dinner. Go to the football game. Embarrass your child a little. Why not? It's your job, you know. Even if it does not seem like it, these trips mean a lot and go a long way toward staying in touch. You will be able to see your son or daughter in his or her environment and pick up any signals of unhappiness or crisis.

6. Ask to see grade reports. You will not receive them automatically in the mail, as you did when your child was in high school, so don't expect them to arrive. And don't wait for a crisis to occur before checking in on this front. It is not too much to ask your child, especially if you are paying the tuition and room and board, to see end-of-semester grades. Talk about the good and the bad, what is working and what is not. Do so without bias or criticism. Try to let your son or daughter tell you what it is really like, and what is going well or poorly.

7. Set some goals for each semester. Again, don't wait for a crisis to help your son or daughter stay on course. It is not too much to set reachable goals for course credits earned, a major declared, a GPA reached, an internship set up, and so forth. Keep in mind our advice about the tortoise and the hare, and reassure your student about the importance of quality over quantity.

8. College students, most of whom are over 18, have achieved majority status and are for all intents and purposes independent adults. The university will treat them as such and protect their rights and privacy. Communications should primarily be between you and your son or daughter, and you should respect your child's space and wishes. If you sense that something is wrong, do call an advisor, an academic dean, or a counselor to see if there is any way you can help or if there is anything they can tell you positively or negatively about your son or daughter. You cannot rely on the school to pick up warning signs of academic failure or personal troubles before they blow up. If you sense problems, make some calls, including ones to your son or daughter.

9. Offer to be available to work through such key decision points in your child's academic life as registering for courses, deciding on summer plans, selecting where to live, choosing a major or college or school within the university, or making plans for graduate school. You should in general defer to his or her wishes and preferences. Ask questions to get at what your child is most interested in, and what he or she will be most successful at. Remember, this is not about you; it's about your child. It is her life, and she is in college. Encourage his dreams and aspirations, and try to present him with ideas and options in line with what he wants.

10. Be open to questions or concerns that your child raises. Is he or she unhappy and thinking about transferring or dropping out? Why? What can be done to improve the situation? Be forewarned that the transition to college is not always an easy one, and you may be presented with the "I want to transfer, this place is terrible" dilemma from the first week of the fall semester all the way through the term. Listen, reassure, encourage, don't prejudge one way or the other. Unless you sense that there is something seriously wrong, our advice is generally to suggest sticking it out through the fall, focusing on academics, joining something to start finding that niche, and meeting people to start making some friends. Usually, by the end of the fall or at latest the middle of the spring, these first-year jitters have subsided and students are happily ensconced in their new environment. If not, it's time to think about taking some time out or transferring.

## A FINAL WORD

College is different now. Parents, what you may have experienced 20 or more years ago has radically changed. Students, what you heard your parents talk about from 20 years back likely no longer applies to your experience. Co-ed dorms, drinking and drug use, political correctness, race relations and diversity awareness, AIDS and other sexually transmitted diseases, date rape, professional level athletics, interdisciplinary studies, high levels of academic challenge and competition—things have evolved, in some cases for the better, in some cases not. Students today encounter new people, new lifestyles, and new challenges to their worldviews and personal values in college more rapidly and in different ways than they did in the fifties, sixties, and seventies. Although the latter two eras in particular were times of upheaval and change, the Internet generation of today will still experience university life in a different fashion, at a faster pace, and under such an overwhelming amount of information and demands on their time and attention that by the time they graduate from college, the academic world likely will have already reinvented itself. As you communicate with one another and go through this university experience, remember to listen to one another, to be open to the many new perspectives and lessons to learn, to protect your own values, and to take everything you can out of these amazing public research universities.

# Index

costs, 7, 37. *See also* financial aid
  evaluating, 89–90
  how to lower, 55, 185
Council for Aid to Education, 85–86
course requirements, 177

deans, access to, 197
debt, educational, 7, 37, 89
dependent status, 51
distance education, 56–57
diversity
  affirmative action and, 66–68, 177
  demographics of at U.S. universities,
    16–17
  evaluating, 99–101
  fit at public universities and, 12

Early Decision programs, 11, 26, 178
  vs. rolling safety, 46–48
education. *See also* public education
  costs of, 7, 37
  demographics in, 4–6
  distance, 56–57
  reasons for increasing, 6–9
  staging, 55
  statistics on graduating seniors, 81
  time taken to complete, 20–21, 193–194
  trends in, 4–6
endowments, 7, 9
  evaluating, 85–88
evaluation of universities, 71–114
  athletes, academic support for, 112–113
  class size, 84–85
  costs of, 89–90
  diversity at, 99–101
  endowments, 85–88
  facilities of, 90
  faculty, 80–84
  financial aid programs, 101–102
  flagship campuses of, 109–110
  graduation rates of, 103–109
  honors programs, 92–99

interstate agreements and, 113
learning disabilities/special needs programs,
  110–112
program specifics, 78–80
ranking guides, 71–77
retention rates of, 102–103
social and residential life at, 91–92
state ranking in, 97–98
use of statistics in, 113–114
exchange programs, 201–202

facilities, 64–65
  evaluating, 90
faculty
  access to, 19, 60, 61–64, 197
  course evaluations, 194–195
  evaluating, 80–84
  graduate students as, 65–66, 195
  research orientation of, 3–4, 61–64
  salaries, 82, 83–84
  tenure and, 61–64
  turnover, 78
  working with, 190
financial aid. *See also individual colleges and
    universities*
  availability of, 36–37
  evaluating, 101–102, 183–184
  merit scholarships, 7, 26, 90
  need- vs. merit-based, 183–184
  rise in, 90
  work-study programs, 55, 184
flagship campuses, 109–110
foreign study, 95, 200–201
fraternities, 91, 204

Georgia Institute of Technology, 174
Gillilan, Sandra H., 116
goals of public universities, 3–4
governing boards, 20
government funding, 88
  of public education, 20
  research grants and awards, 9, 20

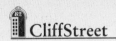

# CliffStreet

GREENES GUIDES
TO EDUCATIONAL PLANNING

## Making It Into a Top College
ISBN 0-06-095363-2
This definitive step-by-step plan for organizing the admission campaign reveals an inside look at how the admissions process works at the most competitive colleges, what the top colleges are looking for, how to choose the best college for you and much more.

## Making It Into a Top Graduate School
ISBN 0-06-093458-1 (Available December 2001)
A ten-step strategy for finding and getting into the right graduate schools, complete with time-tested worksheets, executive task checklists, sample essays and résumés, inspirational case histories, interviewing techniques, and program categories and rankings.

## Presenting Yourself Successfully to Colleges
ISBN 0-06-093460-3 (Available October 2001)
A step-by-step guide to help students market their strengths and uniqueness in outstanding college applications, including essays that will be noticed, targeted interest résumés, portfolios, and letters to coaches and instructors. Complete with actual samples from the files of thousands of Greenes' clients.

## The Hidden Ivies
ISBN 0-06-095362-4
An in-depth survey of thirty colleges and universities of exceptional merit that will not only challenge gifted students but also provide them with the competitive edge needed upon graduation. This book distinguishes each college's personality as described by students and campus educational leaders, as well as its unique academic strengths.

## The Public Ivies
ISBN 0-06-093459-X (Available August 2001)
An excellent resource providing a better understanding of the differences between various public universities, the contrasts between public and private higher education, the admissions process for public schools, and what it takes to succeed in the larger public university environment.

## Inside the Top Colleges
ISBN 0-06-092994-4
The quality of education and quality of life at the country's 20 most elite universities are explored, based on a survey of 4,000 undergraduates using advanced polling techniques, extensive focus groups, and one-on-one in-depth interviews with students.

**Available wherever books are sold, or call 1-800-331-3761 to order.**